Charles A Jackson D.C.

Charles.

In appreciation

of professionalism &

fellowship.

Bob Thompson

June 25/88

Liberation - The First To Be Freed

by Robert N. Thompson

BATTLELINE BOOKS
1987

© 1987 by Robert N. Thompson

Copyright No. 363775
ISBN-0-920849-03-2

First Printing 1987

Canadians At War Series
Printed in Canada by
Trinity Western University Press

Published by
BATTLELINE BOOKS
Box 48448 Bentall Centre
595 Burrard Street,
Vancouver, British Columbia, Canada V7X 1A2

(1935)

O'er the bloody fields of Tigre!
And the mountains of Harar,
'Midst the clash of arms and battle
Shone again the Natal Star.
Wearied Coptics dropped their weapons.
Sons of Rome looked to the Sky;
For an instant ceased the clamour,
Still'd awhile the harsh war-cry.

Mars the war-god was forgotten,
Men turned to the God of Love;
'Peace on Earth' their souls were saying,
As they saw the sign above.
But they stifled inward passions,
Sentiment is not for men!
Stuttered once again machine-guns,
Mars they worshipped once again.

Col. A. Strom Galloway,
from The Yew Tree Ballad

ACKNOWLEDGMENTS

I would like to thank the many people who assisted in the production of this book. Particular thanks go to my many Ethiopian and expatriot friends who were a part of the East African campaigns, who shared their experiences, and added their comments. Also, I am grateful to Murray Mitchell, our Publisher, to Hazel Campbell, and Elaine McLeod for their typing, to Mayson and Kamalini Abraham, David Cunningham, and Doug Makaroff for their editorial input, and to Pat Kohut who drew the maps, Wayne Piper who typeset the copy, and the other Trinity Press staff.

If, however, it had not been for the assistance and support of my wife, Hazel, both now and during those early difficult years in Ethiopia, this project would never have been accomplished.

TABLE OF CONTENTS

DEDICATION

Dedicated to the Ethiopians who gave their lives in the cause of freedom that the land of their forefathers might be free and that their children, in turn, might know the truth that makes them free.

Amharic Translation

የሕዝት፡ የቀይ፡ አያቻች፡ አገር፡ ነፃ፡
እንጹት ህንና፡፡ ልጃቻተው፡ የዚህ፡
ነፃነት፡ ተካፋይ፡ የማያጻ ር ጋቸውን፡
አመነት፡ ያውቁ፡ ዘንድ፡ ሕያወታቸውን፡
መሥዋዕት፡ ካደረጉ፡ኢትዮጵያውያን፡፡

ሩብርት፡አን፡ፉጋበን፡፡

INTRODUCTION

Many of us young Canadians who landed in Sicily with the 1st Canadian Division and who took part in the subsequent drive north through Italy were only vaguely aware of the importance of the earlier victory in East Africa, preceding the victories of North Africa which at that time claimed greater public attention.

After the war, it was realized that this was the first victory against the Axis powers. If Fascist Italy had not been so completely defeated and demoralized in East Africa, the North African and Italian campaigns could have been entirely different.

I am grateful to Lt. Col. Robert Thompson for this intriguing story of the battles that liberated Ethiopia and destroyed Mussolini's East African Empire. It has been my privilege in the post war years to come to know the author as an acquaintance and friend. His experience in Ethiopia and in all of Africa in the post war years provide him with the insight to comment on both the military campaign and post war liberation with the demise of colonialism.

I recommend these pages not only to military historians, but to all readers, in the way they show how the East African Campaign contributed to the final victory in World War II.

Major General E. Deighton Danby,
DSO, OBE, CD, KCLJ, KSJ

PREFACE

This book is the story of how the ancient land of Ethiopia was freed from the tyranny of Benito Mussolini and his rule of force in what he proclaimed as his Italian East African Empire. The military strategies that were employed by the Allied forces to route the Fascists are documented by region, but the story revolves much more around the pathos of the struggle toward national identity and rehabilitation.

The name Abyssinia is the French corruption of a profane name given to the Ethiopians by their Islamic enemies. The Arabic original of this name is 'Habash' or 'Abash' which carries the connotation of a mixed or mongrel peoples or a people without a legitimate father. Ethiopia had been slow in emerging from the medieval centuries. The Portuguese in the fifteenth and sixteenth centuries were the first Europeans to really encounter the Ethiopian culture. The French followed, but because their first contact was with the Egyptians and the Arabs on the east side of the Red Sea they picked up the Arabic pejorative for Ethiopia. From this Arabic word, the French coined the name Abyssinia. The rest of Europe followed this precedent and Abyssinia became the popular name for the country — with the exception of the Ethiopian people themselves. Throughout the Italian-Ethiopian war and the liberation campaigns of World War II, the country was known as 'Abyssinia.' Even the records of the League of Nations referred to the country as Abyssinia.

The historical and Biblical name of the country is, however, Ethiopia, and so the text of this book uses the proper name. As well, a number of other countries which were British Colonies at the time have, since independence, adopted names with local meaning. For the purpose of easy understanding, the current Anglicized names of such countries and regions are used rather than the previous colonial names, e.g. Gold Coast is now Ghana, Northern Rhodesia is Zambia, Tanganyika is now Tanzania, Southern Rhodesia is now Zimbabwe. There were, in the course of events, several simultaneous battlefronts. It was, therefore, impossible for any single individual to be involved in all fronts and to construct a complete historical record from personal experience. For this reason much of the literature on this campaign is incomplete, or tends to emphasize those aspects or regions in which the authors were themselves involved. However, in the years immediately following these events, I was able to personally inspect each major battlefield and interview many of those directly involved. From the many sources available to me I have recorded an overall historical perspective of the East African Campaign, including those areas in which I was directly involved.

Flight Lieutenant Robert N. Thompson at 37 S.F.T.S., RCAF, Calgary, Alberta, Canada.

Robert Thompson: The early days — Imperial Ethiopian Air Force at Bale Airport.

1 ETHIOPIA ON CENTER STAGE

ACT I

ADVANCE NOTICE —May 10, 1936, from Jerusalem to The
League of Nations at Geneva.

SENDER —Haile Selassie, King of Kings, Lion of
the Tribe of Judah, Emperor of
Ethiopia.

MESSAGE —*We now demand that the League of
Nations should continue its efforts in
order to ensure respect for the Covenant, and that it should decide not to
recognize territorial extensions, or the
exercise of an assumed sovereignty,
resulting from an illegal recourse to
armed force and from numerous other
violations of international agreements.*[1]

DATE —June 30, 1936.

LOCATION —Geneva, the beautiful Swiss city of international diplomacy.

SETTING —In the vast Assembly Hall of the
League of Nations, the predecessor of
the United Nations.

AUDIENCE —Delegates of the 52 member nations.
With the exception of the United States
of America, every major country of the
world was represented.

GALLERY —Filled with reporters representing every
major newspaper and radio in the
world.

DEMONSTRATORS —a loud and boisterous demonstration of Italian journalists protested the presence of the Ethiopian monarch. They were quickly and forcibly removed by the Swiss guards.

ON STAGE —Emperor Haile Selassie I

THE SPEECH —*I, Haile Selassie I, Emperor of Ethiopia, am here today to claim that justice that is due to my people and the assistance promised to it eight months ago by fifty-two nations who assented that an act of aggression had been committed in violation of international treaties. None other than the Emperor can address the appeal of the Ethiopian people to these fifty-two nations.*

There is perhaps no precedent for the head of a state himself speaking in this Assembly. But there is certainly no precedent for a people being the victim of such wrongs, and being threatened with abandonment to its aggressor.

In order to kill off systematically all living creatures, in order the more surely to poison waters and pastures, the Italian Command made its aircraft pass over and over again. This was its chief method of warfare. The very refinement of barbarism consisted in carrying devastation and terror into the most densely populated parts of the territory — the points farthest removed from the scene of hostilities. The object was to scatter horror and death over a great part of the Ethiopian territory.

These fearful tactics succeeded. Men and animals succumbed. The deadly rain that fell from the aircraft made all those whom it touched fly, shrieking with pain. All who drank the poisoned water or ate the infected food succumbed too, in dreadful suffering. In tens of thousands the victims of the Italian mustard gas died. It was to denounce to the Civilized World the tortures inflicted upon the Ethiopian people that I resolved to come to Geneva.

The Italian provocation was obvious. I did not hesitate to appeal to the League of Nations. . . . Unhappily for Ethiopia this was the time when a certain Government considered that the European situation made it imperative at any price to obtain the friendship of Italy. The price paid was the abandonment of Ethiopian independence to the greed of the Italian Government. This secret agreement, contrary to the obligations of the Covenant, has exerted a great influence over the course of events. It was constantly repeated that there was not merely a conflict between the Italian Government and Ethiopia, but also a conflict between the Italian Government and the League of Nations. That is why I refused all proposals to my personal advantage made to me by the Italian Government if only I would betray my people and the Covenant of the League of Nations. I was defending the cause of all small peoples who are threatened with aggression. What have become of the promises that were made to me? . . . I assert that the issue before the Assembly today is a much wider one (than that of the situation created by Italy's aggression). It is not merely the question of a settlement in the matter of the Italian aggression. It is a question of collective security; of the very existence of the League; of the trust placed by states in international treaties; of the value of promises made to small states that their integrity and their independence shall be respected and assured. It is a choice between the principle of the equality of states and the imposition upon small Powers of the bonds of vassalage. In a word, it is international morality that is at stake. . . . No subtle reasoning can change the nature of the problem or shift the grounds of the discussion. It is in all sincerity that I submit these considerations to the Assembly. At a time when my people is threatened with extermination, when the support of the League may avert the final blow, I may be allowed to speak with complete frankness, without reticence, in all directness, such as is demanded by the rule of equality between all states members of the League. Apart from the Kingdom of God, there is not on this earth any nation that is higher than the other. If a strong Government finds that it can, with impunity, destroy a weak people, then the hour has struck for that weak people. I appeal to the League of Nations to give its judgment in all freedom. God and History will remember your judgment.²

A solemn silence followed the speech, but as the frail, slight figure withdrew from the platform, a thunderous applause broke out from the audience, joined in by all but the delegation from Italy and Germany. Comments voiced by Eamon de Valera from Ireland were typical of those made that day by the delegates when he said, "Does any delegate deny that, in so far as it relates to what has happened, there is truth in every word of it?"[3]

However, even after a strenuous debate, the League of Nations only moved to approve the sanctions already imposed on Italy. Italy had been critcized for its aggressive and violent takeover of the nation of Ethiopia, a full member of the League of Nations. Not surprisingly the imposition of sanctions did not work, as has tended to be the pattern of history to the present day. Signatories simply did not fulfill the agreements they had pledged to keep. In all but three instances (New Zealand, Canada and Sweden), the members of the League of Nations, one after another, either lifted or ignored their sanctions against Italy giving de facto recognition to Italy's East African Empire.

In another similar, fateful move, Britain's Prime Minister Neville Chamberlain commented on his meeting with Adolph Hitler by pronouncing "Peace in our time." The fallacy of this presumption was to reveal itself a few months later as Hitler took over Czechoslovakia and Poland and moved with Mussolini to form the Axis which was intended to rule the world — but at a cost of more than ten million lives!

His historic appeal made, Haile Selassie returned to England where refuge had been given only two weeks before. He lived in a private house at Bath, just north of London, where he led a quiet and unassuming life. He was impressive in his unfailing faith in the ultimate triumph of right and in the sure protection and destiny of Almighty God. His speech and actions were reassuring and convincing in those dark and difficult days.

In this refuge, he did not go into seclusion but continued as a member of the League of Nations to pursue his country's rights. The conscience of the leaders of the world's democratic nations did not rest comfortably during the troublesome months to follow. Emperor Haile Selassie's plight had won for him and his people the sympathy and friendship of kings, prime ministers, presidents and the general public of the world, as his quiet dignity welcomed visitors from many lands. No one was more understanding of his plight than King George VI, whose friendship was shared by the monarchs of Sweden, Norway, Denmark and Holland. Each of these royal families gave recognition to him as sovereign of his country, as did the representatives of most countries at the League of Nations. The Ethiopian delegation at Geneva retained its credentials, even to the point of having the question of sovereignty referred to the International Court of Justice at the Hague — however, even this legal action was to no avail!

With gracious and wise persistence, the Emperor watched, waited and worked to perpetuate international interests in the plight of his country and to provide a living memory of the tragic injustice and suffering of his people. History has not adequately portrayed the tragedies that the Emperor sought to publicize at that time.

As recorded evidence of this suffering, Vittorio, the aviator son of Benito Mussolini, authored a book entitled *Flying Over Ethiopian Mountain Ranges*, describing the results of bombing raids on the crowded country markets of Ethiopia. He boasted that the bodies cascading into the air as the bombs from his aircraft fell in the market place reminded him of the opening of rose petals in his garden at home![4]

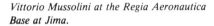

Vittorio Mussolini at the Regia Aeronautica
Base at Jima.

The horrors of the bombing of defenceless people, including Red Cross Hospitals, was only exceeded by the stories of the effects of mustard gas upon an innocent enemy endeavoring to fight for its very life. Added to that was the absurdity of Ethiopians fighting with only spears and outdated rifles against machine guns and modern aircraft. The hurt came closest to home when the Emperor's own son-in-law, Ras Desta, was murdered at Butajira as a prisoner before the eyes of military officers and government officials. The anti-climax came in July 1938, when Britain and most other nations recognized the status quo in Ethiopia, as Il Duce's legions endeavored to enforce servitude at the point of bayonet.

The world at large had not rejected Emperor Haile Selassie in his cause, but the development of a greater tragedy caused many to forget him. Almost simultaneously to the recognition that the sanctions were not working, was the increasing sense of the inevitability of the European crisis. Hitler and Mussolini conspired to subdue the world under the axism of Nazism and Facism.

We now come to the ACT II. This time the stage setting is far away in Africa. It takes place, following the occupation of most of Europe by the Nazi war machine, when Europe was in a state of confusion and near despair concerning the inevitable invasion of Britain. Yet, in Haile Selassie's homeland, victory had been gained. The tide of tyranny had its first setback. It was Liberation for the First to be Freed!

Emperor Haile Selassie I

ACT II

DATE	— May 5, 1941
LOCATION	— The capital city of Ethiopia, Addis Ababa
SETTING	— The street leading to the palace of Ethiopia's first modern monarch, Menelik II.
AUDIENCE	— Thousands of cheering people, waving the flags of both Ethiopia and of Britain. The street side galleries were occupied by the journalists of the Allied world, who also cheered. In addition, the uniformed soldiers from India, Britian and many African nations gathered after victory to watch this important ceremony.
STAGE PROCESSION	— British Colonel, Orde Wingate, astride a white horse, led the 2nd Ethiopian Battalion of troops drawn from Ethiopian exiles and trained in Kenya and the Sudan. They were followed by the Emperor and his faithful Rases and officers who had fought for the freedom which was now theirs. Close beside Haile Selassie was another British officer, Brigadier Sandford, a gentleman farmer turned soldier, leading the 101 Mission. Sandford had inspired the Patriots, including Ras Ababa Aregai and so many others as they had watched and fought and waited for their Emperor's return.
ON STAGE	— To receive the Emperor was Lieut. General Sir Alan Cunningham, the General Officer Commander of the East African Campaign, with a Guard of Honour of the King's African Rifles of Kenya who had fought so valiantly

SPEECH

to defeat Benito Mussolini.

— On this day which men of earth and angels of Heaven could neither have foreseen or known, I owe thanks unutterable by the mouth of man to the Loving God who has enabled me to be present among you. Today, I must first tell you, is the beginning of a new era in the history of Ethiopia. In this new era new work for all of us begins.

Let us go briefly over the history of those evil days through which Ethiopia has had to pass. When Italy committed her first aggression on our independence which we had maintained for thousands of years, our warriors won the victory of Adowa and saved our independence. The origins of that campaign are not only to be found in the clauses of the Treaty of Uccialli. Italy believed that the moment had arrived for her to crown her old unceasing intrigues and to rule Ethiopia. After her defeat she pretended to be Ethiopia's friend, but she secretly prepared another aggression which, delayed by the Great War, came into the open in the last few years.

Though Italy when she invaded our country was clearly our superior in modern arms, it was our duty to defend our country to the best of our ability. When she used poison gas against our people and defeated them, we were compelled to go to the League of Nations to appeal for justice. This aggression that Italy had begun was sure to spread through the entire world. Responsible statesmen in the world did their best to bring peace to the world and to prevent the fire from spreading. Great Britain, our greatest friend, received us at this time separated in the spirit from the people of our country whose blood was cruelly shed by the Italians; from the churches and those who suffered in the mountains and wildernesses of their own.

During those years how many young men and women, priests and monks, were cruelly murdered by the Italians! In Yekatit, in the Year of Grace 1929, on the feast of St. Mikhail (17th February 1937), you know that thousands of people were massacred. The blood of those has cried aloud, whose bodies were split with spades and shovels, axes and hammers, who were stabbed to death with bayonets and stoned and killed with clubs, who were burned alive with their children in their houses and died of hunger and thirst in the prisons! Everybody among you knows that this cruelty was practised not only in Addis Ababa but in almost every corner of Ethiopia. No single person has not suffered, been trampled down and humiliated.

Five years ago exactly to this day the Fascist military entered our capital. Mussolini then announced to the world that he had established a Roman Empire in Ethiopia. The nations who recognized his conquest of Ethiopia believed that he would hold the country for ever. The martial qualities of the Ethiopian are universally known, but we had been unable to import the arms necessary for our defence because we had no seaport. Mussolini had been pronounced the aggressor by fifty-two nations, but that was nothing to him; he boasted the more! So the past five years were an age of night for you, my people, but you grazed like sheep upon the mountains of Ethiopia and you did not surrender your hope! In those five years your patriots (arbegnoch) endured all hardships and maintained your liberty, and the Italians did not dare approach the mountains where you grazed.

Though the enemy did not control the country, yet he spent many thousands of millions of lire to exploit that part which was under his control. This money was not spent to raise the standard of living of the oppressed Ethiopians nor to compensate them for Italian aggression; but to establish a Fascist colony and a brutal rule in our sacred land. The enemy did not offer Ethiopia a mandate or a protectorate, which in themselves are a harsh yoke upon the independence of a nation; all that he wanted was the annihiliation of the races of Ethiopia.

But the end of the thousands of millions of lire spent here was not what Mussolini thought that it would be.

When Italy declared war in order to snatch the booty of conquered France she had a mass of men, guns, and money in Ethiopia. Her troops numbered not less than 150,000 and she had foodstuffs for many years. She thought that she was so prepared as to be impregnable. But what has happened is not in accordance with Fascist aspirations. The 'spirit' and 'morale' that are so important a weapon in modern war were revealed in you. Because you co-operated and knew the enemy's methods, because you understood one another and were the warriors of 'one nation', you were able to defeat an enemy superior to you in arms and men.

The English were fighting on many other fronts for the liberation of the world, and they needed time to prepare the liberation of Ethiopia. You patriots meanwhile obliged the enemy to remain hidden in his fortifications, you cut his communications and made his life a burden to him. He had powerful defences; but you taught him that his tenure was short and that he could not long remain among people who disliked him and his ways of government. He learned that the people around him were stronger than he, and he abandoned the hope of meeting his other strong opponent with his remaining forces.

When the time came that our ally the Government of Great Britain was ready to attack the enemy in full force, I came with my soldiers from the far Sudan on our western boundary, and entered the heart of Gojjam. The enemy in Gojjam had powerful forts and a powerful army, aircraft, and guns. He was twenty times as strong as us in every respect. Besides this, we had no aircraft or guns at our command when we needed them. But my presence alone among my brave people gathered thousands of men, and the enemy's panic was ever increasing. While my troops were cutting his communications and pursuing him beyond the Blue Nile in Shoa and Begemder, I heard the happy news that the formidable armies of Great Britain had occupied our capital and were pushing northward to Dessie and southward to Jimma. The army of the Sudan had smashed the enemy's strong positions at Keren.

I therefore gathered my men who were scattered everywhere in pursuit of the enemy, and I am in my capital today. My happiness is boundless: I have been granted the opportunity to lead my own soldiers, crush our common enemy, and reach Addis Ababa. I owe thanks without limit to Almighty God, who has enabled me to be with you today in my Royal Palace from which the Fascist Government has been forced to flee!

People of my country Ethiopia!

On this day Ethiopia indeed stretches out her hands to God, shouting and telling out her joy to her own sons!

This day also is the day when Ethiopia will yearly celebrate her national feast, for it is the day of the liberation of the sons of Ethiopia from the heavy yoke and the chains of the stranger's government, and the day when we are reunited with our dear and loving people, severed from us for five

*years. On this day we will remember
the heroes who loved their country and
gave themselves for her, who shed their
blood and crushed their bones to
defend that independence which they
had inherited from their ancestors,
who honoured their King and their
Flag.*

*Those sufferings which we have
sustained in the last five years and of
which we forbear to speak shall be a
lesson to us. It is for you to aid us in
the work of progress which we will
undertake on behalf of Ethiopia. You
shall be united, honouring and loving
one another. In the new Ethiopia we
want you to be an indivisible people,
equal before the law, free men all.*

*You are to collaborate with us in our
endeavours to develop the country, to
enrich the people, to increase
agriculture, commerce, and education
throughout the land, to protect the life
and wealth of the nation, and to
complete those changes in our
administration necessary to our new
condition.*

*Since today is a day of happiness for
us all, for on this day we defeated the
enemy; therefore you should rejoice
heartily in the spirit of Christ. Do not
reward evil for evil. Do not commit
any act of cruelty like those which the
enemy committed against us up to this
present time. Do not allow the enemy
any occasion to foul the good name of
Ethiopia. We shall take his weapons
from the enemy and make him return
by the way that he came. St. George*

> *who slew the dragon is the patron both*
> *of us and of our allies. We should*
> *therefore fasten our friendship for ever*
> *in an indissoluble bond, to defeat this*
> *ungodly and newly spawned dragon*
> *that vexes mankind. Our allies are our*
> *friends and our own blood. Take them*
> *to your hearts!*[5]

Review of Events

Five years to the day had elapsed between Act I and Act II. It was high drama throughout; in defeat, in patience, in the perserverance of exile and suffering, and finally, in courageous armed struggle that ended in victory.

The pace of drama had been accelerated in Munich in 1938 with the initial Nazi mobilizations. On September 3, 1939, following the brutal invasion and conquest of Poland, Britain declared war on Hitler's Germany, the third Reich. In quick succession, the iron heel of Nazism ground resistance into submission in Holland, Belgium, France and Norway, not to mention the earlier conquests of Czechoslovakia and Austria.

On June 10, 1940, Italy declared war on Britain, aligning herself with Germany to cement the Axis concept, later to be joined by Japan. Italy, at the time, ruled Tripolitania and Cyrenaica, the territory of modern Lybia. Only French Algeria and its Protectorate of Tunisia and the narrow waist of the Mediterranean Sea separated the Axis line of supply between Germany and Egypt. This supply line was crucial to the defence of the continent.

France capitulated on the 17th of June, and the way to Cairo now opened to the ambitions of Mussolini and Hitler. To the south of Egypt were the armies of the Italian East African Empire, numbering some 300,000 well equipped troops. Thus, Britain's line of communications to the Far East via the Suez canal was threatened from two directions, the north and the south. British forces in the Middle East and in East Africa were few and scattered. There was the additional threat of a German attack through Turkey.

General, Sir Archibald Wavell had been appointed General

Officer Commander of the Middle East and the Africa theatre. He faced a grim situation. European France was disintegrating. Holland and the low countries had fallen, as had Norway. Great Britain was preparing for the inevitable onslaught which everyone knew must come. She was unable to provide arms or men which the Middle East demanded so urgently.

On the 4th of July, Kassala and Gallat, in the Anglo- Egyptian Sudan, were attacked and occupied by overwhelming forces from Eritrea. On the 8th of July, Kurmuk, to the south, fell. A few days later, an Italian brigade attacked and took Moyale on the Ethiopian/Kenyan frontier and then moved on towards Lake Rudolph. On the 4th of August, three major Italian columns attacked British Somaliland. Within two weeks, it was occupied. Marshall Graziani, the butcher of Ethiopia, moved his Italian army across the Libyian/Egyptian border some 90 kilometers into Egypt on the 12th of September. Mussolini's objective was to gain access to the outside oceans. His plan was to push Britain out of Egypt, taking over complete control of the Suez Canal. The British had not expected an attack from Libya, and Graziani took Sidi Barrani without resistance.

If Mussolini's generals had moved to take Kenya and the Sudan, and Marshall Graziani had moved to occupy Egypt — all of which they could easily have done — the outcome of World War II could well have been much different. In hindsight, had the Italians immediately employed an aggressive strategy in Africa, the war in Europe could have been concluded prior to Pearl Harbour and the involvement of the Americans. This was obvious to many observers at the time. Axis control over the continent of Africa and the supply routes via the Suez, not to mention subsequent Italian mobilization, was a staggering possibility. The ramifications of the early faltering phases of the Italian campaign were highly significant.

In spite of the bleak picture facing the Allied forces, a counter offensive was being planned against seemingly insuperable odds. This book is about this offensive and the first victory which it brought for the Allies in World War II.

END NOTES

1 **Arnold Toynbee, ed., Survey of International Affairs 1935,**
Vol. II (London, Oxford University Press, 1935), p. 483.

2 Ibid., p. 490.

3 Christine Sandford, **The Lion of Judah Hath Prevailed**
(London, J. M. Dent and Sons, 1955), p. 82.

4 Laura Fermi, **Mussolini** (Chicago, University of Chicago
Press, 1961), p. 325.

5 Sandford, **The Lion of Judah Hath Prevailed,** pp. 100-4.

2 THE BACKGROUND TO LIBERATION

The least known of the regional wars of World War II is the East African Campaign. For too long, it has been neglected or ignored. It was the first major victory of World War II, as it tore to shreds the best of Il Duce's armies and abruptly stopped the ambitions of the Axis to move into and conquer the east. If the forces of Hitler and Mussolini had been able to conquer the Middle East, ultimately to join India with the forces of Japan, the outcome of World War II could well have been entirely different. The victory in Ethiopia was the beginning of the end for the Axis cause.

As a military operation, the Ethiopian Campaign was in many respects a rag-tag affair, with a poorly equipped and diverse military force and a strategy that lacked design and coordination. Hitler showed little concern and Mussolini scoffed at it. Yet the initiative of individual units, the audacity and the skills of the Commanders, and the bravery of individual soldiers and airmen, brought the Ethiopian Patriot guerilla forces, the South Africans, the Rhodesians, the Nigerians, the Ghanaians, the King's African Rifles from Kenya, the Sudan Defence Force, the Indian regiments, the British Imperial Army Units and the renegade British Units of the RAF into a heterogeneous but formidable military force. As fighting progressed, the Fascist bravado wilted on every front as a plucked flower in the desert sun.

It is a story that deserves to be known, both for its historical fact and for its incredible feats, which gave courage and inspiration to the Allied cause at a time when the Nazis had overrun most of Europe, in such disastrous battles as Dunkirk and the Battle of Britain. The initial North African battles caused many to lose hope. Still they fought on in desperation for the victory which, to everyone, seemed out of reach. Even more important, the Ethiopian Campaign restored an Emperor to his throne, easing the guilt of the shameful betrayal by the League of Nations in 1936.

Truly, the Ethiopian Campaign is noteworthy because an army 300,000 strong was outgeneralled, outfought and destroyed. Thus, a promise of Great Britain was redeemed and an Empire was freed.

Italy's Move Into Africa — 1869-1896

The presence of Italy in East Africa goes back to 1869 when the Italian based Rubattino Steamship Company purchased the territory of the Bay of Assab from the Sultan of Raheita. In 1882, this territory was ceded to the Government of Italy and an Italian colony was established. In 1885 Italy annexed the second Red Sea port of Massawa, a short distance up the Red Sea Coast, following the defeat of an Egyptian force which had occupied this major port area in 1872. The British gave approval to this second Italian colony as they found themselves involved with the Mahdist Rebels in the Sudan and found the Italian presence on the Red Sea Coast of some comfort to them in their problems with Egypt and the Sudan.

The Ethiopians, under Emperor John, resented this and resisted militarily. The Italian military force was defeated by the Ethiopians at Dogali in January 1887. However, Emperor John, two years later, was killed in battle against the invading Dervishes of the Sudan. Menelik II, King of Shoa, to the south, became Emperor following John's death. His friendship with the Italians helped him consolidate his power as Emperor. In return, Emperor Menelik, on May 2, 1889, signed the Treaty of Ucciali, giving Italy further territorial land including the city of Asmara. This established a delicate, friendly relationship between the two countries. On January 1, 1890, Italy proclaimed the territory as a full Italian colony, adopting the name Eritrea, meaning, in Greek, Red Sea.

The traditional tribal name of the main body of the Eritrean people had for centuries been Hammassein, a name which the European world took no notice of, although it was and still is in use for identifying the culture and language of the Eritreans. For many centuries prior to this, Eritrea had been an integral part of Ethiopia, closely related by culture and religion to its neighbour, Tigray, to the south.

The relationship with Emperor Menelik soon cooled and in 1893, Menelik renounced the Treaty of Ucciali because the Amharic and the Italian scripts of the Treaty varied. The Italian government insisted that their version of the Treaty was correct, causing Menelik to accuse the Italians of a deliberate betrayal, which was likely the case.

Italy, in comparison to Britain and the European powers, including Belguim, Germany, Portugal and Spain, had been slow to gain a colonial foothold in Africa. It was, therefore, determined to enlarge its new colonial foothold in Eritrea. Through an accord with Britain in 1891, Ethiopia was recognized as lying within Italy's sphere of influence in exchange for a similar recognition of Britain's interests in Egypt and the Sudan. This accord encouraged Italy to extend its control by forcibly moving its Eritrean boundaries southward. Emperor Menelik resisted and on the March 1, 1896, he met the invading Italian army at the ancient city of Adwa in Tigray province. He inflicted a crushing defeat, decimating the Italian army. Ten thousand Italians lay dead and any hope of an Italian expansion into Ethiopia was destroyed.

Later that year, on the 26th of October, a new treaty with Italy was concluded in Addis Ababa, confining the Italian Colony to Eritrea. Its boundaries reached from the Sudan on the west and the north to the Red Sea on the east, including the ports of Massawa and Aseb. This treaty, while losing Ethiopia the Eritrean territory, firmly established her as an independent nation with full diplomatic recognition from most of the European nations.

The Battle of Adwa was the first time in history that the armies of a European nation, fully equipped with modern tools of war, had been defeated by the primitive military force of an African nation. This humiliating disgrace and decimation had not been forgotten by Italy. The memory of Adwa still lived, and the vanity and ambitions of Benito Mussolini saw the conquest of Ethiopia as a means of restoring Roman grandeur. This strengthened Mussolini's determination to avenge the ignominious memories of 1896. Thus in 1934, 1935 and 1936, he carefully planned his own invasion of Ethiopia which resulted in the conquest of that country. On May 9, 1936, Italy annexed Ethiopia and Marshall Bagdolio was appointed the first Governor General with the title of Viceroy. On the 1st of June, the King of Italy, Victor Emmanuel, was proclaimed Emperor, as Eritrea, Ethiopia and Italian Somaliland were united as Italian East Africa.

The Rape of Ethiopia in 1936

The revengeful conquest of Ethiopia by Fascist Italy began with a frontier clash on December 5, 1934, at Wel Wel, a watering place in the southeast desert, near the poorly defined border with Italian Somaliland. The dispute was referred to the League of Nations, of which both countries were members. The decision, given nine months later, held that neither nation was to blame. Finally, Britain and France joined to call a Conference with Italy and Ethiopia. It was decided that formal negotiations between the two countries should seek a settlement of the border problem. Ethiopia agreed; Italy refused. In the meantime, Italy had assembled large military forces of more than 200,000 men, 400 guns, in Eritrea and Somaliland, and an Air Force of some 200 aircraft.

On October 3, 1935, without a formal declaration of war, Italy invaded Ethiopia simultaneously from the north and the southeast. On the 18th of November, the League of Nations invoked economic and financial sanctions against Italy. Appeals to the League of Nations went unheeded as the invasion progressed with modern tanks and a ruthless Air Force. Indiscriminate bombing of civilian markets and the use of mustard gas on Ethiopian soldiers and civilians amounted to wholesale massacres.

After seven months of brutal warfare, Mussolini had achieved his objective and Emperor Haile Selassie was in exile. Italy, for the first time as a nation, had won a war and Adwa was avenged. General Il Duce's African adventure was a success — a Roman triumph! Mussolini now proclaimed the resurrection of the Roman Empire. "At last Italy has her empire!" Il Duce proclaimed from the balcony of the Palazzo Venezia,

"Legionaires, in this supreme certitude raise high your insignia, your weapons and your hearts to salute, after fifteen centuries, the reappearance of the empire on the fated hills of Rome."[1]

Though a great success at home, Mussolini's invasion of Ethiopia isolated Italy from the democratic countries of Europe, as Hitler was to experience in his European campaign. However, the lethargic response of the League of Nations and the sanctions imposed on Italy were a total failure. The only result of this alienation was that Mussolini turned to Hitler and Germany for an ally. On October 25, 1936, only five months after the victory in Ethiopia, the "Berlin-Rome Axis" was formed. Mussolini sent his son-in-law, Count Galeazzo Ciano, who was also his foreign minister, to Berlin to work out the details of the collaboration between the two countries. It was at this time that Hitler declared Mussolini to be "the leading statesman in the world, to whom none may even remotely compare himself".[2]

It is an interesting footnote of history that Hitler, as an ambitious young politician in Germany, had taken the Italian dictator, Benito Mussolini, as his political model. In 1922, Mussolini had brought down the government of Italy and proclaimed himself as the defender of law and order. This also was Hitler's secret pattern for Germany. On January 30, 1933, Hitler attained the German Chancellorship and the Third Reich was born.

It was in September 1937 that Il Duce went to Berlin to approve the agreement which coordinated their foreign policies. It bound Mussolini's Italy and Hitler's Germany into an 'indissoluble' friendship. It was a repeat of the days of Otto the Great, when Germany tied its destiny to Italy. In that same year, the two dictators entered the Spanish Civil War on the side of General Fransisco Franco, using that situation to test their new weapons, in preparation for a much greater conflict to come.

The Axis Agreement takes Shape

As Italy attempted to establish and stabilize itself in its newly won African colonies, Hitler's Germany started the planned conquest of Europe. On March 7, 1936, German armies occupied the demilitarized zone of the Rhineland, suffering nothing more than weak protests from France. In March 1938, Hitler occupied Austria, thereby incorporating that country into the Third Reich. In September of the same year, he took over the Sudetenland of Czechoslovakia.

On May 22, 1939, Hitler and Mussolini again strengthened their alliance through a formal ten-year military and political agreement known as the Pact of Steel (see Appendix I). The Italian newspapers boasted that "the two strongest powers of Europe have now bound themselves together for peace and war."[3] In August 1939, just three months after the Pact of Steel was negotiated, Germany and Russia signed a non-aggression pact which guaranteed Soviet nonintervention in Hitler's ventures in Europe and beyond (see Appendix II). This stabilized eastern boundaries. The scene was set for Hitler's greater ambitions as he attacked Poland the next month.

World War II was now about to start — a struggle towards the goal of the mastery of the world. In a matter of a few months, the seemingly invincible military force of Nazi Germany would take over all of democratic Europe, with the exception of neutral Sweden and Switzerland. The outcome of the Battle of Britain would threaten the very home of democracy.

Into this tragic milieu, Mussolini's Italy had become allied with Hitler's Nazi Germany. The die was cast. Mussolini had stated at the September meeting with Hitler that the two countries would 'march together to the very end.' However, in less than six years, both Hitler and Mussolini would be dead, suffering ignominious deaths within days of each other — their grandiose visions of a world empire completely shattered.

The declaration of war by Italy against Great Britain and France was made by Signor Mussolini, President of Fascist Italy, on June 10, 1940. Mussolini's speech to the cheers of an enthusiastic audience at the Palazzo Venezia, in the heart of Rome, on that fateful afternoon included the following paragraph:

"Fighters of the land, the seas and the air, Blackshirts of the Revolution and of the Legions, men and women of Italy, of the Empire, of the other Kingdom of Albania — listen. The hour marked out by destiny is sounding in the sky of our country. This is the hour of irrevocable decisions. The declaration of war has already been handed to the ambassadors of Britain and France. (Loud cheers.) . . . We have only one watchword, which is clear-cut and binds everyone. This word is abroad in the air and is living in Italian hearts from the Alps to the Indian Ocean — to conquer. And we shall conquer — to give at last a long period of peace with justice to Italy, to Europe and the world. People of Italy, to arms! Show your spirit, your courage, your worth!''

History was to reveal the fallacy of those boastful, ill fated words. On April 28, 1945, Mussolini was executed and hung by his feet by a vengeful crowd of Italian patriots in the northern village of Jiulino de Messenegra, near Dogo, on Como Lake. His attempt to restore the Roman Empire ended in disastrous ruin and his country was devastated.

Ethiopian Resistance

The formal annexation of Ethiopia into Mussolini's Italian Empire did not mean that the conquest was over or that the entire country had been occupied, although the Italian population thought differently. The President of the Fascist Confederation of Industrialists, in a public statement, declared that:

"In the Highland of 'Ethiopia', Italy has now some eight to ten million new subjects who are now pacified. A new stage in her existence; and in the life of Fascism is dawning now, one which requires resolution and enterprise, qualities of which our recent glorious past gives sure promise. We already know the existing economic resources of Ethiopia; the large production of coffee, the best in the world, can be greatly increased; the cotton already grown in the north and south, and which grows wild in many parts of the country, appears to be of excellent quality and susceptible of great development. The vast verdant plains we hear of from those who return from that country, can support a vast current of emigration and allow the development of a well-organised ranching industry. Hardwoods of the most prized varieties are assured us; and day by day we are receiving news, which does not yet amount to a technical certainty, but which justifies well-grounded hopes of the mining resources of the country. In fact, a new and unexplored world awaits the Balilla, the Avanguardisti, and the young Fascist of today, one which they must develop with the same daring and in the same spirit in which the sons of Italy have enriched immense territories in North Africa and in the two Americas. But now and henceforth Italians are no longer obscure emigrants, but soldiers, blackshirts, and workers under the flag of a great King-Emperor and led by a great leader.''

To Italian ears, these goals were noble sounding and it was not long before many physical accomplishments were evidenced such as the building of roads, airports, and small industries. Modern cities such as Harer, Dire Dawa, Jima, and Dese were built and inhabited mainly by Italians. Asmara became a beautiful showplace, a well planned city, but to the Ethiopians it was only an economic white elephant, for there was a very different sentiment among the Ethiopian population. Patriot forces carried on a never ending guerilla warfare. Even Addis Ababa became a fortified city, ringed with barbed wire, sentry stations and military road blocks. In fact, many outlying areas were never occupied, and even main roads were subjected to ambush attacks.

Against this inability to placate or win over the population, the Italians used extreme cruelty and sheer armed force to subjugate them. People were arrested, imprisoned, tortured and more often than not, summarily executed. Also, Marshall Graziani expropriated the most valuable Amara property. He trained a strong supplementary army of dissident tribal units, mainly from the Eritrean and Galla areas, who willingly donned the Fascist uniform to take revenge against the Amara patriots.

To these were added thousands of Libyan 'Askari's', the name given to native Blackshirt troops — a word derived from the Amharic word 'ashkara', meaning 'servants.'

The Graziani Massacre

On February 19, 1937, Marshall Graziani, Viceroy and Commander in Chief of Ethiopia, summoned the populace of Addis Ababa to the old palace of Haile Selassie, to celebrate the birth of the Prince of Naples. Part of the celebrations included the distribution of Maria Teresa coins to the poor of the city. As the crowds gathered, Ethiopian and Italian dignitaries, including Graziani's senior officials also assembled. Then out from the crowd a hand grenade was hurled at Marshall Graziani and the other officials. Several additional grenades followed the first and Graziani fell, wounded in the back. Several officials were instantly killed. Some 30 others were wounded, including the Mayor of Addis Ababa. The soldiers standing on guard immediately opened fire and most of the Ethiopians who could not quickly escape were killed on the spot.

Later that afternoon orders were issued from the Viceroy's Military headquarters to kill all Ethiopians on sight. Most of the Ethiopian intelligentsia were liquidated as these reprisal orders went out to all of the main towns and cities. Grass roofed 'Tukul' houses were drenched with petrol and the inhabitants burned within, or shot as they emerged. The Colonial police stayed out of sight as the hate massacre, led by the Blackshirts, continued for three days.

The foreign embassies present in Addis Ababa delivered protests in the strongest possible language. Finally, orders were given on the 22nd of February, that all reprisals were to cease. No calculation of the numbers murdered in those grim blood baths was possible, although estimates vary from 30,000 to 50,000.

Typical of the savage tactics used by Viceroy Graziani in the so-called rebel areas were those employed in the mountains of Menz, some 100 kilometers north of Addis Ababa. This area was never subdued or occupied by Italian officials. Instead, raiding parties of Rya Galla 'Askaris' troops were used to plunder and kill. Bounty rewards were offered to these native troops for the number of male sexual organs or female breasts delivered to Italian Commanders following such forays. It was customary of these northern Ryan Galla tribes to collect such trophies as evidence of a warrior's success in battle. In the post war gathering of evidence for the expected war crimes trials against Graziani, some 600 male young men without sexual organs and 300 young women without breasts were counted, all who had managed to survive these atrocities and were living in the various Menz villages. (Post-war politics in Italy resulted in the allies not carrying through on the War Crimes trials of Italian senior officers and officials. Graziani was never charged for the Ethiopian atrocities, for which he was responsible. The author was responsible for the gathering of evidence in Menz and personally supervised the count of surviving victims).

Following the February massacre, Graziani rarely emerged from his heavily guarded Viceroy's palace. Gradually, criticism built up against him, from Italians and Ethiopians alike. As a result, and to the relief of all, he was replaced in 1938.

Eton's Duke d'Aosta

The Duke d'Aosta, graduate of Britain's elitist Eton School, who took Graziani's place as Viceroy and Commander in Chief of Mussolini's East African Empire was a different type of person, humane and cultured. Standing well over six feet tall, this able and respected Italian nobleman adopted a much more conciliatory policy towards the Ethiopian population. His orders, before leaving Rome, were to pacify Ethiopia. His goal was to persuade the Ethiopians to accept and cooperate with their Italian rulers. However, the scars and terrorizing wounds of Graziani's iron fist made his task nearly impossible. The distrust of Italian authority ran so deep that the general population, quite separate from the militant resistance of the Patriot guerilla fighters, became part of a new resistance movement. So widespread was this resistance that in 1938 Britain adopted a policy of cooperation with the Ethiopian resistance group by supplying it with money and arms. Khartoum became the headquarters for both French and British help to the Ethiopians.

Had the Duke d'Aosta had his way, Ethiopia might have

remained an Italian colony well past the war. However, any hope of this was aborted by Mussolini's alliance with Hitler. The Duke d'Aosta faced an impossible task. In spite of the new Viceroy's personal attitudes and desired policy, his forces maintained firm control of security, keeping the conquering Italians quite separate from the subjected Ethiopians.

The Italian administration in Ethiopia was hampered in that they had had no colonial experience or established administration as did the French, the British, the Belgians and the Portuguese in their respective colonies. Beyond this, they tended to be poor administrators. Finally, the dominant control of the Fascist party made the Italian presence in Ethiopia a hopeless existence. Corruption and inefficient, monopolistic, governmental policies added confusion on top of confusion. Italy spent in excess of $80,000,000 (U.S.) a year on the East

Viceroy Duke d'Aosta with his senior Generals — 1939.

African Empire, but it was badly spent. It is estimated that at least one third of Italy's colonial budget went into the pockets of corrupt officials. Bribery and bullying were rampant as the bureaucracy pyramided.

There were three levels of controlling powers in Addis Ababa. The first was the Military, the second was the Italian Civil Service administration and, finally, the Fascist Party itself. The latter dominated the first two and was the most corrupt of the three. No one could retain his position or authority unless he belonged to the Party and the Party was ever present in the military and the administration alike. An example of the overlapping of authority was the fact that there were five different police forces: the Carabinieri, the Colonial Police, the Police of the Army, the Police of the Blackshirts (the Party) and the Secret Police (The OVRH, also of the Party).

The Italian colonizers made mistakes in every direction. Instead of treating the Ethiopian chiefs well and winning them to their side, many of them were summarily executed. Many conscientious Ethiopians and potential friends of a peaceful Italian government were simply eliminated. In fact, opposition was invited through inefficient policies and poor administration.

END NOTES

1 Laura Fermi, **Mussolini** (Chicago, University of Chicago Press, 1961), p. 327.

2 Ibid., p. 349.

3 see Keith W. Stump, **The History of Europe and the Church,** "The Third Reich", forthcoming.

THE ITALIAN EAST AFRICAN EMPIRE

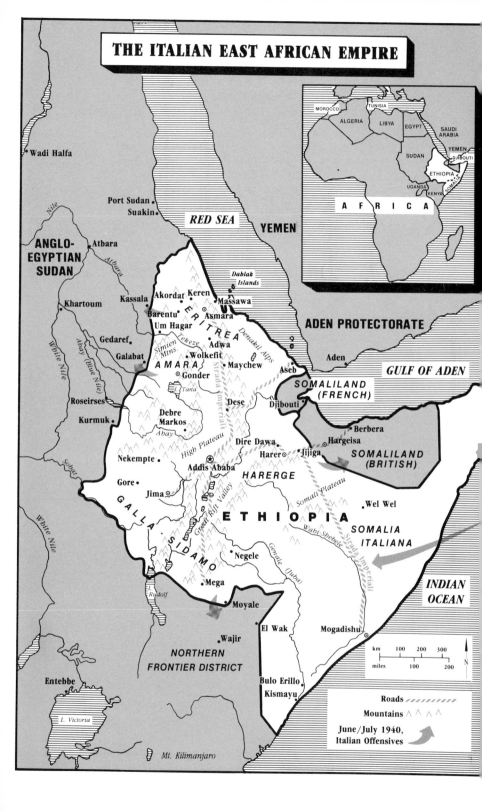

AFRICA

MOROCCO · TUNISIA · ALGERIA · LIBYA · EGYPT · SAUDI ARABIA · SUDAN · YEMEN · DJIBOUTI · ETHIOPIA · UGANDA · KENYA · SOMALIA

Wadi Halfa

Port Sudan
Suakin

RED SEA

YEMEN

ANGLO-EGYPTIAN SUDAN

Atbara

Nile

Atbara

Khartoum

Kassala

Akordat · Keren
Barentu · Asmara
Um Hagar
Massawa

Dablak Islands

ERITREA

ADEN PROTECTORATE

Gedaref
Galabat

Simien Mtns.
Tekeze
Adwa
Wolkefit
Maychew

Denakil Alps

White Nile
Abay (Blue Nile)

AMARA
Gonder
L. Tana

Dese

Aseb

Aden

GULF OF ADEN

SOMALILAND (FRENCH)

Roseirses
Kurmuk

Debre Markos
Abay

Djibouti

Berbera
Hargeisa

Sobat

High Plateau
Strada Imperiale

Dire Dawa
Harer
Jijiga

SOMALILAND (BRITISH)

Nekempte

Addis Ababa

HARERGE

Gore
Jima

GALLA

SIDAMO

Great Rift Valley

ETHIOPIA

Somali Plateau
Wabi-Shebele

Wel Wel

SOMALIA ITALIANA

Strada Imperiale

INDIAN OCEAN

White Nile

Negele

Genale (Juba)

L. Rudolf
Mega

Moyale

El Wak

Mogadishu

km   100   200   300
miles   100   200

N

Wajir

NORTHERN FRONTIER DISTRICT

Entebbe

L. Victoria

Bulo Erillo
Kismayu

Roads ///////
Mountains ∧ ∧ ∧ ∧
June/July 1940, Italian Offensives

Mt. Kilimanjaro

3

THE ITALIAN OFFENSIVE

Mussolini declared war on Britain and France on June 10, 1940. For Mussolini, this was the greatest moment of his life. His confidence in the future was unbounded — this was the crest of his climb to success. He had successfully defied the League of Nations. Now he had teamed up with Europe's greatest leader, Hitler! It was this alliance which was to prove catastrophic. The Ethiopian war and the vast sums he invested in it brought the Italian economy to virtual bankruptcy and extreme imbalance. Yet, he had been able to convince his Generals that Italy had become a great military power. Indeed, he himself was convinced of this — thus, his boastful statement as he announced the declaration of war to the cheers of his Blackshirts of the Revolution. His call to conquer quickly became merely a boastful echo, scoffed at by the Allied leaders and even by Hitler himself. The more accurate prophecy came in the response of Duff Cooper, the British Foreign Minister, who said on the same day: "The foolish crowd of young Fascists, who were cheering this afternoon in Rome, little know the fearful fate that awaits them. Whatever temporary successes they may achieve in the early days of warfare, they will certainly be defeated in the end."[1]

The Italian army had no alternative but to move to attack. Its Generals knew they had to break out to live. Mussolini did too. Thus, they quickly planned their first attack strategy on three fronts. The Italian military was as prepared as an Italian Army could be. Mussolini was well aware that the British in East Africa were practically non-existent. Therefore, he knew it was to his advantage to attack immediately — which he did. His plans were to advance on three fronts, to capture Nairobi, Khartoum and British Somaliland. He almost succeeded!

Italy now had, in Ethiopia, 400 guns and an army of 300,000 men equipped with a full complement of artillery. This military ground force strength was backed by at least 200 aeroplanes and 9,000 to 10,000 military vehicles, including personnel carriers and tanks. A string of aerodromes had been built from Keren and Asmara in the north, through Addis Ababa to Jima in the southwest, and on to Mogadishu in the southeast.

The great distances and mountainous and desert terrain had been bridged by the construction of highways from Asmara, through Keren, to the border of the Anglo-Egyptian Sudan; from Asmara through Addis Ababa, Jima, Shashemene, Dila and through Moyale, on to the Kenyan border; and from Addis Ababa through Dire Dawa and Harer to Italian Somaliland. Also, a number of secondary roads had been built connecting outposts such as Gonder, Gojam, Gambela, Asosa, Maji, Bale, and Asela, all the scenes of battles yet to come.

It was a different story for the British and French in the territories which surrounded Ethiopia. There were probably 7,000 men under arms in the Sudan, consisting of not more than 2,500 British soldiers amongst an untried and inadequately equipped Sudan Defence Force of 4,500 men. The British troops consisted of three Battalions. Their duty was to defend Khartoum, the Port of Sudan and Atbara, the rail junction. The Sudan Defence Force role was to defend 1,800 kilometers of frontier border. Together they had seven armoured cars, and twelve unarmed vans and trucks. There was not a single tank, no mobile artillery and no guns, except for some obsolete howitzers at the Governor's palace used for salutes. There were seven obsolete aircraft at Khartoum and two bomber squadrons at Port Sudan assigned to keep the Red Sea open to naval convoys.

For the defence of Kenya, there were not more than five battalions of native troops, one of which was the King's African Rifles numbering 3,000 assigned, for the most part, to control the 3,000 German settlers in Tanzania (Tanganyika). For the defence of Djibouti, British Somaliland and the Aden Protectorate, there were not more than 5,500 troops — all native under British or French officers. Artillery and motorized vehicles or tanks provided nothing more than transportation. Air strength did not exceed 80 airplanes, with the exception of a squadron of Vickers Wellesleys, which were antiquated and virtually useless in warfare. The aerodromes were found only in the main centres and anti-aircraft batteries were virtually non-existent.

The comparative statistics gave odds of nine to one in manpower, three to one in aircraft and ten to one in artillery. In any warfare with Britain, Italy not only had the means to attack, but the ability to achieve a quick victory. It was inevitable that Italy would attempt a takeover of these adjacent areas for her own security. If Kenya, the Nile Valley and British Somaliland were not taken, Mussolini's Commanders knew that any external sea blockade of Mogadishu and Mombassa would be disastrous. Any acceleration in the rebellion of the partial forces internally would cut off staple foodstuffs and the Italian troops would starve to death.

The military situation was simply that Khartoum could be taken in a week and Kenya could be bombed from Mombassa to Nairobi, as the few British planes were without accompanying ground defences. An attack from Dire Dawa and Harer through Hargeisa to the Port of Berbera would give the Italians victory within a week. The French Somaliland at Djibouti could be expected to capitulate in a matter of a few days, following the fall of Dire Dawa and British Somaliland. The attacks on all three fronts were inevitable and Mussolini moved immediately.

The Kenyan Attack

The Kenyan and Ethiopian borders met at the remote frontier post of Moyale. At this point a British fort housing a force of 200, plus some 30 cooks and employed servants, faced an Italian village, barely a mile away. It was here that Italy launched its attack on June 10, 1940 within hours of her declaration of war.

The first attack came in the form of an artillery barrage and a week long siege of the fort. The Italians tried to destroy the Fort by shellfire, aerial bombing and infantry attacks which were repulsed with heavy casualites. A force of the King's African Rifles attempted to relieve the fort but could not get there in time. With the water supply depleted, the attacking Italian forces having been reinforced to full brigade strength, the fall of the Fort was inevitable: the garrison decided to withdraw. A dramatic escape followed on the Sunday night, a full week after the first attack.

The Italians did not shell on Sunday. In knowledge of this the garrison force prepared for a Sunday night withdrawal. There had been comparatively few casualities and the Sunday passed with very little visible activity. The besieging Italian force interpreted this quiet inactivity as a sign that the defendants were resigned to their fate. Instead, they were planning the escape strategy. Captain Harrison commanded the Fort. He knew the Italians had their evening meal at exactly 8:00 p.m. and rarely sent out patrols until 9:00 p.m. A full moon promised a moonlit night. The actual breakout was in the charge of a South African 2nd Lieutenant, Du Toit, who knew the bush intimately. In the afternoon, they destroyed the food supply by soaking it in kerosene. They sliced up and destroyed all equipment and stores, including their own boots. They buried the survey instruments and the locks of the machine guns, burned the documents and smashed the lorry engines and the radio equipment.

At 7:00 p.m. they entered the trench surrounding the fort with each man carrying his rifle, with bayonet fixed, and 50 rounds of ammunition. Everyone of the 230 souls wore dark clothing and moved out without shoes — only socks so as to make no noise. At 7:30 p.m., the barbed wire had been cut. Lieut. Du Toit led the way with two local Somali herdsmen. They were followed by two machine gun and mortar platoons and behind them followed the cooks, signallers, medics and more soldiers. Captain Henderson, the Commander, brought up the rear. Crawling through the cut wire entanglements, they silently crossed a gorge and slipped into the surrounding bush country. The sounds of the Italian Brigade finishing their supper hour were the only noises to be heard. Four hours later, without firing a shot, or without a single casualty, the evacuation party met a Reconaissance Squadron that was looking out for them. Five more hours of foot travel took them out of reach of the Italian patrols. Not until daylight, after a few hours of rest, did anyone realize how cut and bruised their feet were, and how their muscles ached.

Moyale had fallen — the first victory of the Italians in the new

Liberation War. However, their aggression in Kenya, as they dreamed of capturing Nairobi, soon petered out. Except for patrolling KAR units, there were no fixed battles in the vast Northern Frontier District which, in its harsh climate and terrain, threatened and repulsed any forward march of the Italian forces. There were several skirmishes between Italian patrols and the East African Reconnaissance Squadron between Moyale and Buna, but none of military significance. The East African Reconnaissance Squadron was a unit composed of British settlers using commercial, open Ford trucks, along with the King's African Rifles, who patrolled the vast Frontier District so successfully during the summer months that the Italians couldn't reach any farther south, not even to Buna. The KAR, combining with elements of the Ethiopian Patriot forces, repulsed Italian patrols to the west of Lake Rudolf, up as far as the territory where the Omo River empties into Lake Rudolf. Kenya had been just as concerned as was the Sudan, with equal reason. However, other than occupying a single border outpost and a few isolated waterholes, the Italians had been prevented from making any substantial penetration into Kenya.

During the intervening five months, the dominating factor of the southern front was the heat and the vastness of both the North Frontier District between Kenya and Ethiopia and the Italian Somaliland. While the terrain and vegetation of these areas differ greatly from what is usually considered desert, there is one common factor: desolation. For the most part, the terrain is flat and featureless, particularly in the coastal plains north to the hills of the Ethiopian Sidamo and Bale and northeast to the hills of British Somaliland. It is covered by thick bush which impedes travel by foot or armoured cars. The scrub thorn tree growth makes navigation difficult, as visibility is often limited to 100 meters. Westward the bush thins and the country east of Lake Rudolf is all but treeless, becoming a fantastic lava landscape in the immediate vicinity of the lake. In the dry season, it is a blistering, hot, arid wasteland. In the rainy season, covering hundreds of thousands of square miles, the desert becomes a quagmire across which no human or animal can travel. It was this latter condition which prevailed through the rainy summer months, making the possibility of an Italian takeover of Kenya a fanciful dream; a dream made impossible by a natural barrier defeating any fullscale invasion before it had begun. From September to December, both the Italian and British Armies seemed lost in the vast desert wilderness area. There was no actual front — rather it was a series of patrols, scouting raids and manoeuvers across a vast no-man's-land, 1200 kilometers wide. Gradually the British forces were strengthened by the addition of two full Divisions, the 11th and 12th, each consisting of one East and one West African Brigade. In August, a South African Brigade joined the 12th Division. Until mid December, these units were responsible for the defence of Kenya against the Italian forces: several Brigades of Native Banda troops and specially formed colonial troops, led by European officers. These included two Somali Irregular Companies chosen for their knowledge of the country and several units made up of Ethiopian refugees who had been caught in the desert as they fled from Ethiopia, headed for refuge in Kenya.

Gradually the British forces grew. The addition of the 2nd and 5th South African Brigades made up a full South African Division under the command of Major General A.E. Brink. The addition of several units from Rhodesia also strengthened the British build-up. Many Rhodesian officers served in other units. Within a few days after the fall of the Moyale Fort, a Rhodesian RAF squadron, the 237th, reached Kenya. It gave valuable assistance to the patrols operating through July and August, keeping the Regia Aeronautica (the Italian Air Force) behind the Ethiopian border frontier.

On the 1st of November, General Cunningham arrived in Kenya to assume overall command of the southern front. The offensive had petered out — indeed, the offensive was reversing itself!

The Sudan Attack

On the 4th of July, the Italian Army launched a two pronged attack on the Sudan, with Khartoum and the Nile Valley as their objective. If this goal of taking over the Anglo Egyptian Sudan could have been achieved, the East African campaign would have turned out quite differently. The supply lines to the Middle East, up the Red Sea and across North Africa, would have been gone. Egypt would have been untenable. There could have been no front in the Middle East, and the wasp-waist of the British Empire would have been severed by the Italian forces moving eastward from Libya and the East African forces moving northward from the Sudan.

The delay in the Italian offensive towards Khartoum, from the 10th of June to the 4th of July, will never be fully understood. It was as disastrous to the Italians as Hitler's march into Russia was a few years later for the Germans. The only apparent reason why the attack was delayed was that the strength of the British was greatly overestimated. In reality the odds were ten to one in favor of the Italians — a fact which they somehow were not able to comprehend.

The only force facing the Italians on the eastern desert was two Motor Machine Gun Companies based at Kassala, made up of Sudanese soldiers, with two British officers in each. Their only capability was to harass any enemy column marching towards Khartoum, Atbara and Port Sudan. The only backup support was a few Sudanese infantrymen belonging to the Camel Corps of the Western and Eastern Arab Corps. The only other available forces were six infantry companies of the Equatorial Corps, to the South of Kassala, and the Provincial Police Force who served in default of troops patrolling the frontier between Galabat and the Boma Plateau.

The Italian forces facing the Sudan Frontier and poised to attack, included two colonial Brigades, 6,000 strong, four cavalry regiments, 2,000 strong, a camel regiment, 18 tanks, a strong artillery backup and an Air Force of Caproni bombers based in Asmara and Keren.

The British forces, while few in number, were excellent soldiers. Major General Platt, Supreme Commander, was innovative, cool and competent. He and his men succeeded in bluffing the Italians into thinking that the British forces were far stronger then they actually were. The Italians were well trained and included regular troops as well as loyal colonial troops (for the most part Eritrean), although they also had some Banda companies, who from the beginning, were prone to defect rather than fight.

The Italian initiative was blunted by the quick action of General Platt. On the 11th of June, the day after Mussolini's declaration of war, Italian aerodromes and fuel tanks were bombed by seven vintage RAF planes stationed in Khartoum. The Motorized Machine Gun Companies, rattling about the frontier opposite Kassala on offensive patrols, were fast and fearless, making hit and run attacks on every Italian outpost in sight. On one occasion, two of their "unarmoured cars", which were four wheel trucks, scattered in panic 1,200 native Italian cavalry. The official Imperial Army record states that, "they deserve in the Battle of Africa the same tribute as the Prime Minister paid to the fighter pilots of the RAF in the Battle of Britain, for rarely has 'so much been owed by so many to so few'."[2] These patrols delayed the Italians for three weeks, which prevented the attack expected on the 4th of July.

The attacking forces, upon crossing the border into the Sudan, circled around the base of Kassala Mountain, as a follow-up to a 12 hour continuous bombing raid by the Italian Air Force on Kassala, as well as an artillery barrage. They were able to destroy six enemy tanks, inflicting at least 500 casualties. Their own casualties were limited to one killed, three wounded and 16 missing. All material was evacuated from Kassala except for one truck, one spiked machine gun and some small arms ammunition. The Motor Machine Gun Companies took up new positions north and west of the Kassala town, continuing their original assignment of harassing any enemy advance towards Khartoum, Atbara and Port Sudan. The Italians dug in at Kassala, consolidated their position but did not attempt to make further progress towards their objective.

Simultaneous to the attack on Kassala, the Italians attacked the Kenyan Fort Galabat to the south, with a force of 2,000 men, using artillery bombardment and Air Force bombing. The garrison force of one company retired according to plan, after a stiff fire fight which inflicted heavy casualties on the attackers. On the 8th of July, the Italians crossed the Sudan border at Kurmuk, taking the garrison which was defended by the District Commissioner and 70 Sudanese Police.

In their cautious way, the Italians amplified their border

defences at their newly acquired territory but failed to continue their attack into the Sudan. Without question, because of their superior strength, they could have taken Khartoum and Port Sudan had they chosen to continue their advance. There would have been heavy casualties but with their heavy artillery, their Air Force, tanks and superior manpower, the results seemed inevitable. With a permanent garrison of five or more batallions at Kassala, the miniscule strength of the British forces could not do much more than harass. The Italians may have felt secure, but they were nervous about the British strategy. It is assumed that the Italian command was waiting for word that Marshall Graziani was moving eastward from Libya to take Cairo.

At the end of July, the RAF left its base at Port Sudan where it kept a vigil surveillance of the Red Sea, and carried out a two day heavy bombing raid on Kassala, to remind the Italians that their hold on that Sudan territory was tenuous. A month later, two contingents of the Worchestershire and Essex Regiments, which had been added to the Sudan forces, joined the Motorized Machine Gun Companies and attacked, briefly occupying the Italian outpost at Adardeb (north of Kassala, but inside of Eritrea). This served to remind the Italians that any further advance into the Sudan would face heavy resistance, a risk which the Italians never dared to take. Thus ended the intended Italian invasion and takeover of the Anglo Egyptian Sudan.

The only other action against the British on the Sudan frontier was taken through propaganda via the Press and Radio. The Italian newspapers reported that in taking Kassala they had killed or wounded more British troops than the toal number of their own troops. At Bumbodi, north of Keermuk, where no action ever took place, they were said to have defeated a British division. At the same time, the Press reported a plan to continue their takeover of the Sudan in September, as soon as the rainy season was over. The propaganda war had a respite through the more successful advance into British Somaliland. Here, too, the reports were greatly exaggerated. However, the propaganda war soon reversed itself as full scale operations by the British drove the Italians back into Eritrea and Ethiopia on all fronts.

The Takeover of British Somaliland

On August 4, 1940, an Italian army of 25,000 troops launched a full scale attack against British Somaliland, planning on an easy and quick takeover of this isolated, desolate, sparsely populated, yet strategic British Colony. The invasion took form in three separate columns, intended to converge in the takeover of the seaport town of Berbera on the Gulf of Aden. The largest of these columns was from Jijiga in Ethiopia, which moved directly to Hargeisa and on to the sea.

Before the war, the European population of British Somaliland was less than 100, of which practically all were administrative officials. Hargeisa, in a nest of hills which rise from the coastal plain, was the capital. The area was small, only 120 miles in width and 400 miles long. Locked between Djibouti, the small French Somaliland, and the much larger Italian Somaliland, all but 60 miles of its 600 mile inland frontier was with Italian East Africa. The small and basically unimportant piece of territory had now become a grave threat to the Italians. Djibouti, in French Somaliland, was the eastern terminus of the Addis Ababa railroad which was the easiest access to the Ethiopian capital. The German takeover of France had moved French Somaliland away from the British insofar as friendly relations were concerned. There was at this time no help or collaboration from the French.

There were three courses open to the British in Somaliland. One was to reinforce Somaliland at the expense of the scanty and widespread Kenyan forces; another was to evacuate the colony without a fight, which was the easiest alternative; the third was to offer the greatest resistance possible, with the small forces available, inflicting as much damage as possible and then to deliberately withdraw. The latter was the strategy adopted.

The defending forces were outnumbered by fifteen to one, and consisted of one Northern Rhodesian regiment, the 2nd KAR regiment, the Black Watch, two companies of Punjabis, the Somaliland Camel Corps and the African Light Battery.

At first, there was no serious attempt to stop the invading columns, apart from an occasional road block, demolition or a bombing. Hargeisa fell on the 6th of August. Some 20 miles down the Berbera Road, the defending forces took their stand at the Tug Argan Gap in the hills, which rises steeply from the plains and through which flows the Tugargan River during the rainy season. For six days, the troops, African, Asian and European alike, most of whom had not had previous battle experience, demonstrated a lesson in bravery and determination in the face of vastly numerically superior forces, as they were part of the desperate fighting which followed.

The official British Army record of the Battle of the Argan Gap vividly relates what took place:

A Rhodesian officer, who was in the thick of the fighting, wrote of this grim battle:

"From 11th to 15th August, every day and once or twice at night as well, they used all they had got to try and break through the gap and get their mechanised column along the road to Berbera. There were at least ten thousand Italians, and they seldom attacked a company position with less than a brigade of three battalions, complete with tanks and artillery, while we were not more than 700 or 800 strong in the actual gap. It seems incredible, when I think of it now, that in spite of the number of things that were shot at us and dropped on us, our casualties were so light, and certainly negligible in comparison with the Italian casualties. We must have killed thousands."

Inevitably the numbers told. Positions which the Italian waves could not carry away were slowly encircled. As day followed day, our men were compelled to withdraw, first from one hill and then from another.

These days were packed with excitement and marked by many deeds of individual gallantry. There was 2nd Lieut. McCalman of the King's African Rifles, the son of a Kenya farmer, who led a party by nightfall through the Italian lines to rescue his mortars which had been buried during the day. There was 2nd Lieut. Peter Smith, son of another Kenya farmer who was twice cut off with his platoon, but each time broke through the enemy and brought his men to safety. On the second occasion, by personally manning a Bren gun, he silenced two enemy machine-gun posts and prevented the Italians from flooding down the pass. There was 2nd Lieut. Palmer, whose Lewis gun broke down, when he and Captain Watson were covering a withdrawal. Undaunted, though the advancing enemy were only 100 yards away, he squatted down and repaired it in the text-book manner. It was here, too, that Captain E. T. C. Wilson, of the Somaliland Camel Corps, earned the twelfth Victoria Cross of the war. Though badly wounded in both arms, he carried on for three days at his machine-gun posts until they were finally overrun by the enemy. There were occasional humorous incidents. A private, after continuous shelling, rummaged in his haversack for something to eat and pulled out a tin of meat. "Picnic Ham, indeed," he read in an injured tone; "Do they call this a ruddy picnic?"

One Askari dispensed with sleep for the five nights of the battle, and would not stop firing his rifle by day or night. Nothing rattled him, till a burst of machine-gun fire cut off the side of his gas cape, which he had folded up as an elbow pad. Unconcerned at his escape from death, but furiously indignant, he picked up his tattered cape and took it to his officer. "Look Bwana," he said, "look what they have done to my coat."

The spirit of the native troops was magnificent. An eye-witness writes:

"The African soldier was fighting during these five days and five nights under the most unfavourable conditions for him. He is in his natural element when fighting out in the bush, but here he was given a position to hold and, however much stuff the Italians showered on him, he had no opportunity of using his bush tactics. He just had to stay put and take it, and he certainly did this well."

One of the guns of the light battery was in a desperate position. It had been moved right round till it was facing the rear, firing downhill over open sights at less than 900 yards, while all the spare men were blazing away with rifle fire as hard as they could go. "The African ranks,", an officer says, "had

The Duke d'Aosta inspecting his field officers on parade — 1940

reached their peak."

Meanwhile at Berbera the Navy had rigged up an all-tide jetty, and the evacuation was going on. Hundreds of Ethiopians, Arabs, Indians, even many Somalis themselves, with their wives and families, preferred to leave for unknown lands rather than change their rules. The civilians and administrative officials left first, then the base personnel, in order to make room for the troops arriving from the interior. The troop embarkation began at 1 p.m. on 16th August. It continued through the night into the following afternoon, unhindered by the Italians, who were licking their wounds and failed utterly to take advantage of the opportunity to harass our forces at the last. They had been dealt with especially roughly at the fight at Barkasan, where the Black Watch, left behind to cover the final stages of our withdrawal, had charged with the bayonet to chase for at least a mile first the native levies and then their Blackshirt masters. Everything was carried out in an orderly manner, and those Somalis who remained behind amid the smoke of burning equipment in Berbera watched the convoys sail away and remembered the promise that the British would soon return.

Seven months later to a day that promise was redeemed.''[3]

END NOTES
[1] British War Office, **The Abyssinia Campaigns** (London, His Majesty's Stationery Office, 1942), p.22.
[2] Ibid., p. 12.
[3] Ibid., p. 18.

A PLAN TAKES SHAPE AND AN ARMY ASSEMBLES

Emperor Haile Selassie, along with his two sons, Asfau, the Crown Prince, and Prince Makonnen (later to become the Duke of Harer), returned from exile to the African Continent landing at Khartoum on July 3, 1940, just three weeks after Mussolini's declaration of war on Britain. The Emperor's departure from England had been a closely guarded secret, as was his arrival at Alexandria and then his trip on to Khartoum via Wadi Halfa. It was a mysterious Mr. Strong who took off from Poole Harbor on the 25th of June in a Sunderland flying boat. Haile Selassie, alias Mr. Strong, was on his journey home! Arriving in Alexandria his party remained on board until after dark and then disembarked for only a few hours rest. They left before dawn for Wadi Halfa, this time his alias being Mr. Smith. He remained incognito until he reached Khartoum, living in the home of one of the Holy men of the Sudan, Sherif Yossef. There, with the Commander of the British Forces, General Sir William Platt, and his senior officers and Patriot confidants of the Emperor, a campaign strategy was gradually planned to free Ethiopia from the Italian imposter.

Upon the declaration of war by Mussolini against Britain and France on June 10, 1940, the ratio of the Italian military strength in East Africa as compared to that of Britain in Africa was at least fifteen to one. This applied to manpower, artillery, armored vehicles, tanks, cavalry and aircraft. Yet, the only real victory for the Italians during the summer months had been on the south eastern front where they had been able to take over British Somaliland. The southern front against Kenya, and likewise the northwest front against the Sudan, had quickly become bogged down in lethargic and defensive action. Even up until the end of August, 1940, the Italians were still in a very strong position. At this time, they controlled the southern access to the Red Sea. There was virtually nothing to stop them from a complete take over of the Sudan. Likewise, there was no valid reason why they could not have duplicated their success in Somaliland into Kenya, through the desert frontier to Nairobi. Why the Italian forces did not move to complete their takeover of all of East Africa, and then to join up with Marshall Graziani in Egypt for the further takeover of the Middle East, is a sad commentary on the Italian Generals and on Mussolini himself. The waste of the precious weeks through June, July and August, when the British army was literally non-existent, was to loose their East African Empire. If Mussolini and his generals had only known it, they could have moved in a quick coordinated attack to wipe out British resistance, in both the south and the northwest. In this event, Italy could have contributed Africa to the Axis cause, even as Germany was contributing Europe to the Axis goals of world domination.

The strategy of the Italian Forces upon the declaration of war against Britain was based on their military strength in the East African Empire. Their strategy was to attack the British on three fronts. This failed to materialize. As one British commentator so well expressed it:

"The wave of Italian opportunities swelled, rose, hung and sank back again with a whisper like 'Italy' instead of bursting with a roar like 'Rome' as well."[1]

The Armies Assemble

In Kenya to the south, the British Colonial Army had two basic Battalians of the local Kenyans, the King's African Rifles, known better as the KAR's. A quick recruiting campaign enlarged these permanent regiments. These JUMBO troops were to prove themselves as a powerful front line troop, not only in Ethiopia, but later in the Burma Campaign as well.

From South Africa

The largest and most formidable outside forces to reach Kenya were the South African First, Second and Fifth Brigades, composed equally of African and English troops. These

Brigades included the Transvaal Scottish and the Cape Coloured Mechanical Transport Companies. In their components were several battalions of engineers who, in the construction of replacement bridges and blown up highways, were to prove themselves the key to many battle victories making possible the continued advance of their own liberating troops. Without heavy artillery, armoured carriers or tanks, the South Africans were mobile in Canadian built three ton commercial trucks which had been fitted locally with steel-plated boxes and were driven and maintained by the Cape Coloured Mechanical Transport Companies. These trucks functioned as troop carriers and light armoured vehicles, and along with a limited number of armoured cars, they were a key factor in both the advance from the southeast to Addis Ababa, and the final collapse of the central Italian forces north of Dese where they joined up with General Platt's forces coming south from Eritrea.

South Africa also supplied two Air Force Squadrons which joined a Rhodesian R.A.F. Squadron, No. 235, to make up the Air Arm of the planned advance. (It is a footnote to history that Ian Smith, later to be Prime Minister of Rhodesia, was a lead Hurricane pilot in the Rhodesian RAF Squadron. He later fought in North Africa and in Italy where he was shot down, parachuting into Italian patriots territory. He joined the patriots in ground action for a period of five months up to the capitulation of Italy.)

From West Africa

The other Empire units which gathered in Kenya deserve special note, as later they often carried the brunt of the attack. There were two Battalions of Nigerian troops and a full Brigade from the Gold Coast (Ghana) which stopped at Durban and later disembarked at Mombassa. For the Nigerians, as well as those from the Gold Coast, the long voyage around the Cape of Good Hope was a memorable experience. They were well trained, commanded by British officers, and soon made themselves at home in Kenya with the King's African Rifles. They already knew what freedom meant and were more than willing to fight for those who had lost it.

The Gold Coast/Ghanaian Brigade assembled at the Accra

Railway Station on the 30th of May, headed for East Africa which was a very far and unknown place. Thousands of friends and relatives saw them off amongst a crescendo of wailing, as many feared they would never see their men folk again. Most of these soldiers suffered from sea sickness in their long voyage around the Cape, broken by a stop at Simonstown Bay, the location of the South African Naval Base. Of greater interest was Durban City, and as they marched through a well planned parade, receiving a tumultous welcome, they were showered with gifts and hospitality. After a week's visit and training, the Gold Coast/Ghanaian Battalion continued its voyage on to Mombassa where they boarded a train for Nairobi, joining the Nigerian Battalions which had preceeded them to meet the King's African Rifles. There was also a regiment from Zambia (formerly Northern Rhodesia) and two companies of Punjabis which had come from India. These units complimented the forces already there. In addition to the KAR, there were the East African Reconnaisance Squadrons, manned by Kenyan settlers and the Somali Camel Corps.

From the Ethiopian Refugees

Within Kenya's borders, thousands of exiled refugee Ethiopians were being trained into a special force known as the 'Ethiopian Irregulars' with a built up strength equal to two divisions. The senior officers were British, as they were in the other Colonial units from Nigeria and Ghana. The exception was the South African unit which was self contained, commanded by Major General G. E. Brink, C. B., D.S.O. The Ethiopian Irregulars, performing as full military units, made and carried the brunt of the attack in the central southern areas of Ethiopia, the Borena, Sidamo and Arsi. In support of these overall forces gathered in Kenya, there was also within the Ethiopian boundaries, both in the south and the north, Ethiopian patriot guerilla forces which were to add to the fighting strength of the assembling armies in Kenya, preparing to open the Southern Front.

From the Sudan

In the north, it was a different situation in that there were no colonial forces to draw from except those already in the Sudan and, in the latter stages, several companies from the Belgian Congo (Zaire) and a battalion of Ethiopia Irregulars from Kenya. It is here that credit must go to the decision of the British Government, supported by the Dominions and Colonies, to assign troops to East Africa from North Africa, despite an hourly threat of invasion by Germany of Britain. The fall of France and the seemingly impossible odds in Europe made this strategy even more difficult. Yet, in spite of this precarious situation, Churchill and the War Office, with the senior Generals, decided to release several military units from North Africa to take part in the East African campaign. This decision was made with the consent of Field Marshall Wavell, Commander in Chief of the British forces in the Mediterranean Theatre, in the face of the extremely critical situation then developing in North Africa. In North Africa, the main forces involved the armoured formations from Britain and the Fourth and Fifth Indian Divisions, as well as the Australian Division, which held and finally broke the North African Pincers formed by the Italian forces in Libya, and the assembling German forces in Tunis and Algeria. The decision to strengthen the planned assault on the Italian East African Empire resulted in the diversion of the Fifth Indian Division to Khartoum. This full division was to complement the forces already at hand that did not total more than 7,000 troops. It included the Sudanese Motorized Machine Gun Companies, the Sudanese Camel Corps and the Equitorial Corps, consisting of six Infantry Companies, the Sudan Defense Force, the Worchester and West Yorkshire Regiments and the Provincial Police of the Sudan. In addition, there were two squadrons of the RAF based at Port Sudan and a few outdated aircraft based at Khartoum. These forces had already performed valiantly and well against heavy odds at stopping the Italian advance in June at Kassala on the Sudanese side of the Ethiopian frontier.

From India
The Infantry of the Indian Fifth Division, including its artillery and armoured vehicle units, had no experience or training in mountain combat. It was to attack from the

Sudan into Eritrea and the Tigray province of Ethiopia, through very high mountainous terrain. The Division command of Major General Heath was divided into three Brigades for a three pronged attack from the North and the Northwest. The three Brigade Commanders of this Division were Marriott, Mayne and Slim. The performance of the Colonial Indian troops of the 5th Division was far beyond expectation as they penetrated the Eritrean and Ethiopian ramparts to confirm the victories on the interior plateaus.

Again, the planned strategy of the attack was to stimulate the Ethiopian rebellion against the Italians. The close coordination with these Patriot forces made victory possible for the British. For the most part, there was no need to ask the Ethiopians why they were fighting — they fought for the freedom of their own country.

The Italians had recruited a number of Eritrean troops who, at the beginning, were loyal to their Italian Commanders, although in the final stages of the battles many of them deserted to the British. In the fall months, the Italians had moved two Eritrean Brigades from Somaliland, where they had performed well, to Asmara to act as reserve units. Even the 11th Brigade of Colonials had been moved to Eritrea from the Shewa district surrounding Addis Ababa. There were, in addition, a number of Colonial Banda Brigades, all of which were integrated into the defending Italian armies on the Northern front as they reinforced their overall strength in the expectation of the British attacks. The story of these Italian Ethiopian units could not compare to the battle expertise of the Ethiopian Patriots who had carried on their continuous guerilla attacks in the mountainous terrain. Throughout the rural areas, they had scoffed at the Italian call to surrender, beginning in 1936, carrying their attacks to the very perimeter of Addis Ababa, forcing it to become a fortified city behind barbed wire entanglements.

In the months ahead, the Italian military power in East Africa was to be broken by a strong Pincer movement in the north, beginning with the attack on Kassala, up the escarpments on to Asmara and Massawa, and then south to the heart of the country, finally joining up with the rapid advance of the southern forces from the Kenyan frontier. These two forces were to meet on the top of Mount Ambalage where the Viceroy, the Duke d'Aosta, had dug in for a final defence. Those from the north were under the overall command of General Platt and the southern forces based in Kenya were under General Cunningham. It was planned that the northern forces would conquer Eritrea and in so doing break the core of all Italian resistance. On the southern front, the plan was to take Italian Somaliland, recapture British Somaliland and then move on in a rapid advance to Addis Ababa before the beginning of the heavy rains, paving the way for the return of the Emperor. Here the plan was to infiltrate the western province of Gojam with a force, called the 101 Mission, under the command of a Colonel Sandford. It was later to join with the "Gideon" forces, which the Emperor himself was to lead under the command of Colonel Orde Wingate (later promoted to Brigadier General) with the capital city of Addis Ababa as their goal.

The Plan in Summary

In the north, the attack began on the 10th of September with the first shells fired into Kassala. The attack of 101 Mission from the west, operating under the code name of "Scheme Planex", advanced across the Ethiopian frontier on the 12th of August. The attack from Kenya in the south did not begin until some five months later. General Cunningham, the Commander of the southern front, arrived in Kenya on the 1st of November. His forces crossed the Italian Somali border on the 24th of January. The speed at which the southern forces advanced became the most spectacular part of the East African campaign, as the forward elements entered Addis Ababa on the 6th of April. The 101 Mission, now joined with the "Gideon" units, reached Addis Ababa on the 5th of May, the date of the formal capitulation of the central Italian East African Government. The odds had been fifteen to one in June when the Italians took the initiative, attacking the British on three fronts. Four months later, the British had assembled an army equal to four divisions, made up for the most part of Colonial troops from Africa and India, three Brigades from South Africa and two divisions of British trained Ethiopian Irregulars. The next move was to implement a four pronged strategy, attacking from the southwest, from the south, from the northwest and the west. By October, the odds had now dropped to approximately three to one.

It was to become a brilliant attack of loosely coordinated troops, heterogeneous in their make up, but united in their determination to drive the forces of Mussolini out of East Africa, and bring liberation to the Somalilands and Ethiopia — the first countries to be freed in World War II. Thus, the plan for the liberation of Ethiopia and British Somaliland from Mussolini's Fascist rule gave the first victory of World War II for the Allied cause.

At the planning stage, it seemed that the ultimate victory would require many months of bitter fighting with heavy casualties. The Italian East African Empire covered a vast area larger than all of Europe, its perimeter a hot, rough, desert terrain, which blended into rougher foothills, without roads or navigable rivers. These foothills quickly became rugged and mountainous, leading to high plateaus of up to 3,000 metres altitude. It was on these plateaus and in the valleys, where the bulk of Ethiopia's population lived, and where some 500,000 Italians now resided, more than half of whom were military. A web of new highways, beautifully engineered, radiated out in five directions from Addis Ababa including one to each of the cities designated by the ruling Fascists to be the regional capitals of their East African Empire's four provinces.

One of the great unknown obstacles facing the attacking forces was transportation. The mountainous terrain of Eritrea could only be penetrated on existing roads through river valleys and mountain passes. The engineering expertise of the Italians in building roads would be matched only by their equal ability to destroy them, particularly the passes and the tunnels, in the face of retreat. There were roads in neither the foothill areas, nor the mountains in the middle western area traversed by the 101 Mission and the "Gideon" attacking force. Mules and horses were not available in sufficient numbers, so the planners schemed to use a one way camel train. Facing well planned gun emplacements and small arms fire from the defenders in these areas, the prospect of advancement was most precarious. In the south, the vast stretches of desert looked less formidable, although the long distances against superior guns and aircraft caused the planners to have heavy doubts about a quick, successful advance. The problem of inadequate supplies of ammunition, water and food was also a heavy hurdle to be overcome if the attackers were to reach their objectives. In addition to these land transport and supply problems, the British military strategists knew that the Italians had a strong Air Force, with the Italian Navy controlling all sea accesses, in the Red Sea, the Gulf of Aden and the Indian Ocean. They also knew, all too well, that they were facing tremendous odds both in manpower and firepower, at times as high as ten to one.

The question of weather compounded the planners' apprehensions. The heavy monsoon rains covered the highland areas of Ethiopia from mid June to September, making it almost impossible for trucks, armoured cars and all motorized transport during these months except on completed highways. The lesser rains in February and March and again in November and December were also cause for concern for most motorized transport. General Platt, in the north, knew he had to reach Asmara not later than June if his campaign was to be successful.

The Plan Moves into Action

The beginning of the offensive began on January 19, 1941, when the British moved to retake Kassala. In the west, the 101 Mission crossed the Ethiopian frontier on the 20th of January through terrain which would be impassable during the summer rains. Asmara and Massawa, in the north, were taken on the 5th and 7th of May, and the "Gideon" force marched into Addis Ababa on the 5th of May with the sourthern forces already in control. It all had taken less than four months. General Platt was well aware that a quick victory would have been impossible if it had not been for the support of the RAF based in Port Sudan and Khartoum. He also was to find that the morale and fighting courage of his colonial troops were superb, far superior to the defending Italians' and their Eritrean and Banda compatriots'.

In the south, General Cunningham took over command in early November. His forces crossed the Somaliland border on the 24th of January. On the 6th of April, his troops entered Addis Ababa. It had taken just over two months to cover the 3,000 kilometers offensive — less than half of the time that he had originally anticipated. In fact, he had not expected to reach Addis Ababa until after the heavy rains. Again, it was the fighting ability of his troops, the agility and ability of the South African Engineers and their supporting Colonial troops and the effective advance cover of a miniscule, but a most impressive Air Force, which was spear-headed by ten well used Hurricane fighters and a few light vintage bombers, which made this possible.

In both the north and south campaigns, the British forces had the advantage of being met by a friendly population who saw the British and colonial forces as Liberators. In each area, there were also supportive guerilla forces which had resisted the occupying Italians for five full years. The two full Divisions of Ethiopian Irregulars from Kenya also served most effectively in the central southern attack and later in the clean up operation in the south and southwest following the capitulation of the Italian forces at Addis Ababa and at Ambalage.

Another factor in the successful campaigns was the desertion of the Italian Eritrean and Banda Brigades when the going was rough for the defenders. While there were many instances of Italian bravery and stiff resistance, the general attitude of the Italian troops was one of half-heartedness and unwillingness to obey their officers' call to fight to the end. It was easier to raise the white flag of surrender.

The strategy of the British and Ethiopian planners was most commendable. The officers in the field were willing to take the initiative, with the complete support of their troops who so often faced overwhelming odds in both manpower and the terrain. The Indian and various African Brigades, shoulder to shoulder with their British Officers and the South African Brigades, were to prove that they were a solidly united integrated military force.

It is now time to turn to the actual campaigns — in the north, the southeast, the south, and lastly, the west, with the final victory and clean up in the centre and southwestern areas. It was to be the first victory for the Allied cause in World War II: the liberation of Eritrea, Ethiopia and the Somalilands.

END NOTES

[1] British War Office, **The Abysssinian Campaigns** (London, His Majesty's Stationery Office, 1942), p.22.

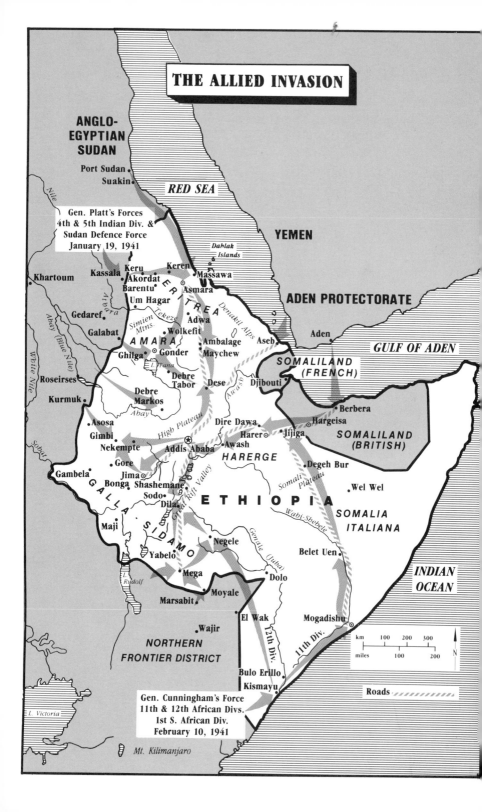

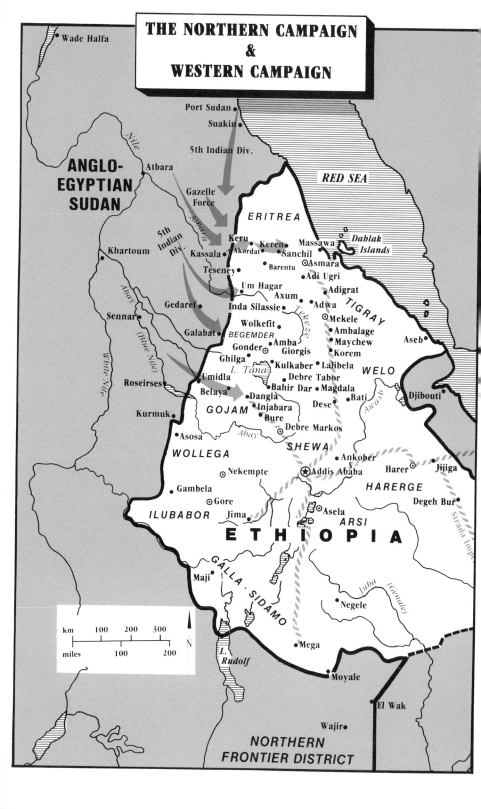

THE NORTHERN CAMPAIGN
&
WESTERN CAMPAIGN

Wade Halfa

Port Sudan
Suakin
5th Indian Div.

RED SEA

ANGLO-
EGYPTIAN
SUDAN

Atbara

Nile

Gazelle
Force

ERITREA

Khartoum

5th
Indian
Div.

Kassala

Keru • Keren
Akordat
Teseney

Massawa
Sanchil
Barentu
Asmara
Adi Ugri

Dahlak
Islands

Um Hagar
Axum
Inda Silassie

Adigrat
Adwa

TIGRAY

Aseb

Abay (Blue Nile)

Sennar

Gedaref

Galabat

Wolkefit
BEGEMDER
Gonder
Ghilga
Umidla
Belaya

Amba
Giorgis

Tekeze

Mekele
Ambalage
Maychew
Korem

Lalibela

WELO

Roseirses

White Nile

Kurmuk

Asosa

Belaya

GOJAM

L. Tana

Kulkaber
Debre Tabor
Bahir Dar
Dangla
Injabara
Bure

Magdala

Bati

Dese

Awash

Djibouti

Abay

Debre Markos

SHEWA

WOLLEGA

Gambela

Nekempte

Ankober

Addis Ababa

Harer

Jijiga

HARERGE

Gore

Maji

ILUBABOR

Jima

Asela

ARSI

Degeh Bur

E T H I O P I A

GALLA - SIDAMO

Juba (Gende)

Negele

Strada Imp.

km   100   200   300

miles   100   200

N

L.
Rudolf

Mega

Moyale

El Wak

Wajir

NORTHERN
FRONTIER DISTRICT

5 THE NORTHERN CAMPAIGN

The strategy of the planners in Khartoum had three main objectives. The first was to stabilize the frontier areas which formed the Ethiopian borders with the Sudan and Kenya, making sure that there could be no further incursion of Italian forces into the Sudan, thereby safe guarding Khartoum and the Nile River Valley. The same held for the southern border of Ethiopia, making sure that any major attack leading to the takeover of Nairobi would be stopped before it started in the Northern Frontier District, which stretched from the Indian Ocean to Lake Rudolf and on to the White Nile.

The second objective was to give all possible help to the Gojam Patriot forces in the area between Lake Tana, the valleys of the Blue Nile River, and the Sudan border. The Patriot forces had been discouraged and divided by tribal and leadership divisions, but it was understood, particularly from the advice given by the Emperor and by Colonel Sandford, who was to later lead the 101 Mission into the area, that the cooperation and support of the Patriots was essential to a successful campaign. The regional province of Amara, as established by the Italian Administration stretched from the southern province of Galla Sidamo, northward through what was known as the Ethiopian province of Gojam, across Lake Tana, and on up to the Sudan border on the west and the Tigray border on the east. The ancient city of Gonder, Amara's capital, was the major military base for the western part of Ethiopia. It included a major base of the Regia Aeronautica — the Italian Air Force. The plan was to have this area infiltrated by the 101 Mission to form the southern flank of the northern area. Infiltration of this area would have been necessary in the event of any incidents in the Eritrean — Tigray border areas. Successful

Patriot guerilla activity would also be most troublesome to the defending Italian military and government.

The third objective was to move forward in a frontal attack, through Kassala on the Sudan side of the border, across the frontier to Teseney, Keren, Asmara and, finally, the Red Sea Coast at Massawa. This would involve the occupation of the Galabat area, which would strengthen the central attacking force moving eastward from Teseney and Akordat toward Keren.

To accomplish these objectives, the British forces gathering in the Sudan were assembled for a three-pronged attack formation under command of Major General Heath. The approximately 21,000 troops now available to General Heath were composed basically of the Fifth Indian Division, supported by several British regiments based in the Sudan and by other elements of the Sudan Defense Force. The first Brigade was to operate from Port Sudan under command of Brigadier Marriott. It intended to move directly south towards Kassala along the frontier. The central Brigade would carry the frontal attack through Kassala across the border to Teseney and on to Keren under the command of Brigadier Mayne. It was to include the Gazelle Force, commanded by Colonel Messerey. It was a fast reconnaissance force of light tanks, mobile artillery, armoured cars and Skinner's Horse, a motorized cavalry unit better to be known as the 'tin cavalry.' There was also three units of the Sudanese Motor Machine Gun Group which had, in early July, so effectively blunted the offensive of the Fascist forces at Kassala as they moved in planned attack to take Khartoum but then failed to get farther than Kassala.

The third Brigade group, under the command of Brigadier Slim, was given the task of protecting the flanks in the vast area between Port Sudan on the Red Sea Coast and Sennar on the Blue Nile, south east of Khartoum. The component units of this Brigade included the 10th Indian Infantry Brigade, the 1st Essex Regiment, the 4/10 Baluchi Regiment and the 3/8 Garhwal Rifles with an attached Squadron of the Royal Tank Regiment. The vast distances involved more than 1000 kilometers of desert area from Port Sudan to Sennar on the Blue Nile. The protection of the vital communication lines were the responsibility of the 6/13 Frontier Rifles and the 2/5 Mahratta Light Infrantry. General Platt established the headquarters of the 5th Indian Division at Gedaref, midpoint between Kassala and Sennar.

In September 1940 General Wavell struck at Cyrenaica on the Mediterranean Coast in Lybia. His first major victory was at Sidi Barrani in October, followed by a westward thrust that virtually neutralized Italian resistance in Lybia. At this point, General Wavell heeded the urgent call for more troops from General Platt. In a quick decision, he transferred the Indian 4th Division to the Sudan. The 4th had born the brunt of the Sidi Barrani attack and its troops were now confident seasoned veterans. They were strengthened by a battery of six inch howitzers and a company of I-Tanks. This would give General Platt two full Divisions, raising the strength of his forces to nearly 35,000 men.

The 4th Division moved to the Sudan by two different routes, one by the Red Sea through Port Sudan and the other from Cairo up the Nile River to Khartoum. It established headquarters in the thick bush north of Kassala, thus strongly reinforcing the central Brigades under Brigadiers Mayne and Marriott. Commanded by Major General Beresford-Pierse, it was ready for action by mid January. The commanding General of the opposing enemy forces was General Frusci who had a strong record as a Divisional Commander from the Spanish Civil War. The anticipated attack from the British Forces reinforced by the enormous disaster in Libya, caused the Italian Command in Rome to order a protracted defence in the Sudan Frontier, hoping to avoid any further transfer of British troops from the North Africa Campaign. General Frusci had to admit that his was now a defensive action and thus, he prepared for withdrawal to the best available defensive line even before the British were ready for their frontal attack. This line stretched from behind Kassala and Teseney to the lip of the escarpment which led to the high plateau on which Keren and Asmara were located.

The military odds had now dropped to three to one, with the obvious advantage still on the side of the Italians who were now digging in for a prolonged defense of a vast mountainous area thought to be totally impregnable to the attacking force which had only limited air power.

The Preliminary Probing Attack

The first skirmish between the British and Italian forces took place on the 24th of October when a Colonel Rolle, fresh from Addis Ababa with a full battalion of colonial troops decided to attack the British offensive force that was threatening the Italian forts of Um Hagar and Metema. The Italian strength included 12,000 troops with several brigades for back up support. Colonel Rolle's objective was Rosierres on the Blue Nile. He broke out of the border bush to attack the newly formed battalion of the Sudan Defence Force which had the support of a RAF squadron of Hurricanes from Khartoum. Colonel Rolle was stopped in his tracks. His back up battalions failed to come to his support from their protective bases. Finally, on the 26th of October, suffering from the heat and lack of water, his retreat back to Beni Shunal became a rout.

The Italian prestige never really recovered from these frontier losses. Up until then, Italian propaganda had held the power of persuasion over the local tribal people. This was no longer true as the British advance was to learn. News of this first minor engagement quickly reached the Ethiopian Patriots in the Gojam, convincing them that help was finally on its way. Despair and discouragement were replaced with a new morale. The Italians were forced to realize that their enemies were forming on both sides of their defenses.

The Battle of Galabat

It is necessary at this point to move back to November to refer to the plans for the first serious frontal attack. General Platt had no intention of delaying his offensive until the reinforcements of the 4th Division had arrived. His initial force consisted of one full Division plus a number of separate units equal in strength to perhaps half of a second Division. Thus, on the morning of the 9th of November, he ordered the first initial action against the defending garrison at Galabat, some 150 miles south of Kassala, on the Sudan-Ethiopian frontier. Brigadier Slim was in direct command. The attack began with a flight of bombers from Port

Sudan at 5:30 a.m., blowing up the wireless station and bombing the Fort at Galabat. What the RAF missed in that first hour, a continuing barrage from the Royal Artillery destroyed. Captain Traino, commanding the 27th Colonial Battalion based at Galabat, retreated without delay across the river bed to the safer ground on the other side of the border facing Metema. The barrage followed him. At 6:30 a.m., the 10th Tank Squadron passed through the rubble of the Fort to clean up the last of the Eritrean Gunners of the 27th Battalion. The entire Galabat area had been taken successfully, land mines were cleared, and a counterattack by the 25th and 27th Colonial reserve battalions was repulsed — all in just three and a half hours. The brief engagement had taken its casualties — both in men and equipment. Five attacking cruisers and four tanks were out of action, the victims of mines and mechanical breakdowns. In the early morning as Brigadier Slims surveyed the scene of victory, he realized that he could not possibly continue the attack on the Fort at Metema which was his ultimate objective. Artillery had ceased at Metema but it was held by a strong defensive force which he could not expect to take, at least not that day. The official record of the War Office gives the intensity of this brief but vital action:

"The battalion was given the task of capturing the fort and, moving out during the night of the 5th/6th November, it reached the forming up place, 800 yards from the objective, without being heard. After a bombardment by our artillery for twenty-five minutes at first light, the battalion advanced to the attack, accompanied by tanks. Owing to the boulder-strewn nature of the ground, the tanks were foced to swing to the right and left and D Company had the task of forcing a way in, without direct assistance. The uncut wire was covered by two machine guns and two pack guns, firing over open sights. Fortunately, the wire was close in, and well aimed grenades, combined with light automatics fired point blank at the loopholes, silenced the enemy machine guns and forced the pack gunners to withdraw hurriedly. C Company was brought up on D Company's left and, with complete disregard of danger, two men (No 6620 Rfn Indar Sing Rawat and No 5483 Rfn Dalbir Sarki) dashed forward and cut gaps in the wire. About the same time, the tanks broke in round the rear of the position and started firing on the defenders from behind. The battalion, led by Lieut-Colonel S. E. Tayler, in person, then stormed the fort. Not many of the enemy awaited the assault, but those that did remain, fought well. A and B Companies, who had in the meantime been exploiting North of the fort, were twice heavily counter-attacked in battalion strength, but with the help of the supporting tanks beat off the attacks and inflicted casualties. Within two hours of the attack starting, the fort had been captured and consolidated. Two Italian Officers were captured, but the majority of the garrison fled to Metema, the Italian fort about one and a half miles from Galabat, just across the Ethiopian border. The battalion, together with the Essex, who were then moved up, maintained the position for the rest of the day and throughout the following day, during which time, both units experienced sustained air bombing attacks. Ten heavy, accurate and almost unopposed, attacks were carried out by Italian aircraft against a perfect air target. It was impossible to dig into the rocky ground and there was no air cover. Casualties began to mount up and, to avoid unnecessary loss of life, the troops occupying Galabat were ordered to withdraw to the outpost line. This was accomplished without incident after dark on the 7th November, by which time all enemy ammunition and equipment had been destroyed. The battalion's casualties, mostly from the air attacks, were 15 killed, and 48 wounded. The men showed great dash in this, their first attack, and also re-acted well under their first heavy air attack. For his leadership and courage in this action, Lieut-

Colonel Tayler was awarded the DSO. He led the battalion in person that stormed the fort. This fort was garrisoned by the 27th Italian Colonial Battalion a 'Banda' (native irregulars) with two pack guns, heavy machine guns and light automatics with a liberal supply of very effective anti-personnel grenades (no doubt the well known Italian 'Red Devils' encountered in the Western Desert). The whole battalion was officered by Italians and some Italian N.C.O's. Lt-Colonel Tayler was also mentioned in despatches for this action. He was later Killed in Action on Mount Sanchil before Keren, Italian Eritrea, 17th March 1941."[1]

In the meantime, Colonel Castagnola, the Italian commander at Metema had sent a wireless message to his Commanding General at Gondar requesting immediate aerial support. Fighter escorted bombers appeared before noon. Brigadier Slim, anticipating the arrival of the Regia Aeronautica planes called for support from the aged RAF planes based in Khartoum. In the ensuing action, seven RAF fighters were shot down compared with five for the defenders. The British support tanks at Galabat were destroyed. On the 7th of November, the bombers returned with a protective wing of ten fighter planes for a continuation of the aerial attack. They did the same thing on the 8th of November. The British forces now found that they had no alternative but to withdraw from the demolished Fort at Galabat and hold on to the ridge behind the Fort. For two months, the area in between became a no-man's land of patrol and skirmish without victory for either side.

The objective of this attack had not been reached but the assault was, by no means, considered a failure. In two hours, the major Italian Fort had been destroyed, as had one Colonial Battalion. Two others, the 25th and 77th Colonial Battalions, had been badly mauled. The defending Italians were now on the Ethiopian side of the border and not on the Sudan side. A more important result, although indirect, was that the Patriot guerillas operating in the Gojam area had been given further encouragement to participate in battles yet to come. The victory which lay in the weeks ahead certainly would not have been possible without the support of the Patriot guerillas from behind the Italian offensive lines.

The next action was to come at the centre front, as the 4th Indian Division established itself in readiness for a major thrust. The Gazelle units under Colonel Messerey had already begun a harrassing action against the Italian units to the north of Kassala. With experience and daring, the three Sudanese Motor Machine Gun Companies were in their element as they scattered one after another of the probing patrols of the defenders. In the meantime, caravans of supplies, arms and ammunition were dispatched to the leaders of the Gojam revolt and were mobilized into action by Colonel Sandford and the 101 Mission. Without question, the guerilla Patriot Forces were encouraged and strengthened in the knowledge that the British Armies were actually ready and able to defeat the hated occupying Italian forces.

By the time the two Indian Divisions were ready for a frontal attack on Kassala and on into Ethiopian territory, the military aspect of the planned stategy had undergone a complete change. It was now already evident that the Sudan itself was safe from Italian incursion. As a result, a calm had settled over Khartoum and a confident fighting force, diverse in nature, but with a coordinated and integrated strategy combined with brilliant field command, was without question ready for the big push.

The Frontal Attack Across the Frontier — Kassala and Teseney

The zero hour came on January 18, 1941. A single Brigade of the 4th Division attacked Kassala capturing it with ease, as General Frusci had already ordered withdrawal. Frusci had three Brigades from Kassala as well as the permanent defending troops that had been stationed there — all were part of the Italian second Division responsible for the defense of Teseney and Sabdaret. On orders from Rome, he had been instructed to establish a stronger defense line in the Keru, Briscia, and Alcota areas where sharp foothills begin to form the major points of the mountains behind, making a defense at Akordat and Barentu more logical than on the frontier plains between Kassala and Teseney. His orders were that they were to fight to the last man, never believing that the British could advance as fast as they did. In their withdrawal plans, the bridges were to be blown and all roads were heavily mined.

Elements of the 4th and the 5th Indian Divisions attacked simultaneously, with the Gazelle force leading the way. The Gazelle Units, mobile and fearless, slipped through Kassala and Teseney without even stopping, finding the defending troops already gone. This secret Italian withdrawal permitted the British artillery to take up new, aggressive positions near the opposing defense lines sooner than they had thought possible. At one point, a group of Italian native Cavalry, with the commander leading on a white charger, attacked the advancing Indian troops. They charged from the northern flank only to be decimated at point blank range. By the 23rd of January, just four days later, the Italian lines were penetrated. On the 24th of January, a frontal attack by the Highland Infantry and the Second Sudanese Motor Machine Group Company, spearheaded by the 10th Sikh Brigade, was made against Akordat and Barentu. By nightfall, the defending forces had completely surrendered, and more than 1,200 prisoners were taken including General Fangoli. With the capture of his troops, one sixth of the entire defending force on the frontier had been wiped out. Indian sappers quickly cleared the roads and the mine fields, particularly in the mountain passes. Even the Sciaglet Wells, some 130 kilometers from the frontier were now occupied by units of the Gazelle Force. This brought the elements of the 4th and 5th Division within eight kilometers of Akordat, in striking position. All of this had been accomplished in just four days, without air support.

A single Brigade from the 4th Division and two Brigades from the 5th Division with the Gazelle units in between had been too fast for General Frusci's plans.

Special note should be made of the "tin cavalry" of the Gazelle Force. On the morning of the 25th of January, they had taken the Sciaglet Wells, over 160 kilometers from the Frontier, and by nightfall had reached to within eight kilometers of the major fortifications of Akordat. In addition, a small detachment had struck southeast to cut the communication lines between Akordat and Barentu, the second major defense point of the foothill area. Desperately, 12 Italian light tanks were sent from Akordat to restore this vital communication link but they were also completely destroyed by the Gazelles. A battle involving all the heavy equipment both sides could muster was just ahead — but it was this daring and unprecedented four day advance, which penetrated to the very edge of the mountain fortress, that set the tone for the rest of the war.

The Battle for Akordat Turns the Tide!

Behind the lightning advance of the three Brigades and the floating Gazelles that had spearheaded the spectacular advance came the plodding foot soldiers of the 22nd Camerons and the 1/6 Rajputana Rifles. On their right, they were supported by the 10th Brigade of the 5th Division and together, they were able to move in their inadequate truck transport across trackless terrain and into positions to attack Akordat. Barentu, the second defensive area to the southeast, without a communication link, had already been destroyed by the Gazelles. The 10th Brigade immediately moved south to clear the Barentu area leaving the Akordat defensive open to a frontal attack both from the west and the southwest.

The blond hero of Italian notoriety, General Lorenzini, nicknamed the 'Lion of the Sahara', was now placed in command of Akordat under orders to hold to the last man. The Italians regarded this fortress as the key to the hinterland area beginning with Kassala but including Asmara. He had been promised full air support. For five days, he probed the gathering British attackers, only to be frustrated by the constant hit and run tactics of the Gazelles who were biding their time to allow troops behind them from the 4th and the 6th Indian Divisions to catch up. The 5th Brigade, just fresh from Libya, arrived to aid the 11th Brigade. General Lorenzini had four full Brigades consisting of at least 12,000 infantrymen, supported by 13 troops of artillery and a full company of medium and light tanks. The odds were at least two to one in favor of the Italians, in a mountainous terrain of the sort the Italians knew so well.

By the 28th of January, on top of the Cochen mountain table top plateau, the 3/14 Punjabi attacked. On the 29th of January, the 1/6 Rajputana followed up. On the 30th of January, the defenders, five Battalions strong, counterattacked, forcing the Indians back to the mountain edge. Recruiting even the sappers and the waterboys during the night, the Indians again attacked to regain the top of Cochen mountain overlooking Akordat below. The next morning, the 1st of February, the Cameron Highlanders overran the lower ridges of the Cochen, supported by the friendly fire, from the top ridges, of the victorious Indian Brigades. The Royal Fusiliers followed through on the northern flank, led by the new and untried I-Tanks. By mid day, six medium and five light enemy tanks were destroyed. Interestingly, several of these Italian tanks were manned by Nazi crews, sailors who had been taken as fugitives from ships in Massawa. Next, a wave of fresh 3/1 Punjabis with fresh tanks by-passed the weary Royal Fusiliers. Before nightfall, Akordat had fallen and the advancing troops found themselves chasing Italian soldiers fleeing up the road to Keren. In the meantime, the Barentu had been cleared. In just three days, these two fortresses yielded 9,000 soldier prisoners, 75 guns, 14 shattered tanks and thousands of local civilians who managed to survive by turning to looting Italian commercial and government stores.

The RAF and the Regia Aeronautica had to this point played only a preliminary and cautious role. The RAF had been strengthened in the latter weeks of January, both at Khartoum and Port Sudan, with elements of the South African Air Force, which had been transferred from Kenya and the southern campaign, and the RAF squadron from Southern Rhodesia. Several additional RAF Squadrons had come with the 4th Indian Division from North Africa. This enlarged the original miniscule air strength by five Hurricane Squadrons. Units of light tanks and a major number of heavy artillery pieces strengthened the ground forces. A full scale defense by the Regia Aeronautica had not taken place yet because of the nature of the approaching British forces. The RAF was able to distinguish itself in the fighting as it badly damaged both the airports at Barentu and Akordat, destroying the hangars and Italian planes based on the ground. At Akordat, a fleet of Caproni bombers was destroyed before they could take off. It was apparent that both air forces were waiting for bigger game at the pending attack and defense of Keren and Asmara.

The successful assault against the defending Italian forces across the frontier at Kassala, then into Eritrean territory at Teseney and on to Akordat had taken just 13 days. Against heavy odds, 6,000 soldiers and deserters had been taken, as well as 80 artillery guns, 26 tanks and more than 400 trucks. One General had been captured — Fongali. The British casualties were minimal, both in men and machines. British morale was high with the defending Italians demoralized in the realization that Eritrea was facing imminent collapse. There was, however, heavy fighting to come. Keren was basically a fortress surrounded by high mountains forming the last major natural obstacle. The British attacking forces were well aware that the battle ahead would be much more severe than the ones in which they had just been successful.

Through the Cliffs of Keren to the Italian Fortress
The winners of the Battle of Akordat did not stop to celebrate their victory. The ever aggressive Gazelles moved quickly forward the same day, only to discover that the retreating Italian troops had blown up the Mussolini Bridge which crossed the dry bed of Baraka River. The Italians had also sowed a mine field which had to be cleared to allow passage up the ascending roadway. It took the Gazelles a full eight hours to do this giving the retreating troops time to blow up tunnels and mountainous roads, and to join the forming defences of Keren. Without this delay there would have been no Battle of Keren.

In their despair, the Italian Empire in Eritrea had thrown into the mountains of Keren its final strategic reserves which included the Savoia Grenadiers and the Alpini Battalion of the 10th Division. The Italians even brought in elite military formations from as far away as Addis Ababa. On the very day that Akordat fell, these select troops were already deployed at Keren. Even while the Gazelles were clearing the Baraka River bed and the RAF was harassing the weary retreating columns of General Lorenzini's army, these disciplined formations were blasting down the cliffs to block the gorges and bearing their machine guns in readiness for the defense of Keren.

Keren was like a giant medieval fortress, its draw bridge raised in the face of an attacking enemy. This was the scene facing the 2nd Camerons and the 1/6 Rajputana Rifles as they followed the Gazelles on the narrow mountainous road toward Keren. In reality, it would take a whole month to seek a way around or through the natural defensive terrain, in the face of a vastly superior defending enemy who now had its back to the wall. This did not mean that the British attack would be stalled. Without hesitation, the field Commanders, on the 3rd of February, sent the 2nd Camerons up the mountainside to capture and occupy a secondary ridge, the Sanchil, which became and still is named the Cameron Ridge. The next day, on the 4th of February, the 3/14 Punjab Brigade was sent to occupy the mountain crown of Keren, still known as the 'Brig's Peak'. Passing through the Camerons, the Punjabis reached the very crown of this dominating peak of Keren. After holding it for a few hours, the heavy artillery from the distance and the percussion grenades of the Italian defenders drove them back into the valley, but the Camerons held. The 5th Brigade of the 4th Indian Division had now arrived at Akordat. A second offense was made led by the fresh 4/6 Rajputana Rifles, via secondary route. The troops moved at night, carrying their own machine guns, munitions, signal equipment and three days of rations, to capture a neighbouring peak, the Acqua Ridge, on their way to retake the Brig's Peak. On the hillside facing Keren, at the location of the Roman Catholic Consulata Mission, the defending Savoia Grenadiers were well dug in behind the crest and ultimately forced the attacking Rajputana Rifles to withdraw from the hill with heavy losses. On the 10th of February, the 4th Division tried again with protecting units on the left and right but the Cameron Ridge could not be held. The 3/1 Punjab Rifles attacked yet again on the 11th of February behind a heavy artillery barrage but once more the odds were also too great for them. It was here that the first Victoria Cross of the Eastern Campaign was won, posthumously, by Rifleman Subadar Richpal Ram of the Rajputana Rifles who with fantastic courage, fell before the intensive enemy fire. Prime Minister Churchill, a few days later, in giving tribute in the House of Commons at Westminister, gave the following citation which describes the courage and tenacity that was typical of the

Indian troops of the 4th and 5th Indian Divisions:

> "During an assault on an enemy position in front of Keren on the night of 7th February, Subadar Richpal Ram, who was second in command of the leading company, insisted on accompanying the forward platoon and led an attack on the first objective with great dash. His Company Commander having been wounded, he assumed command of the company and led the attack on the final objective. In face of withering fire, about 30 men, with this V.C.O. at their head, rushed the objective with bayonets and captured it. Here, although completely isolated, they beat back six enemy attacks between midnight and 4:30 in the morning. On the 12th of February the Subadar led another attack on the same position. He pressed on fearlessly and with the greatest determination though met by very heavy and accurate fire. By his personal example he inspired the company with his own resolute spirit, but nearing the objective his right foot was blown off. He then suffered further wounds to which he ultimately succumbed. Even while lying wounded on the battlefield, he had no thought for his own wounds, but waved forward his men. His last words were, "We will capture the objective.""[2]

The Critical Strategy Takes Shape for the Final Attack on Keren
The small but stubborn British army was bleeding badly as its casualties mounted, but it was still aggressive. The British realized now that there was no way around the escarpment facing Keren and that it had to be pierced by sheer frontal attack. They knew more casualties were inevitable, but the Indian troops were courageous and determined. Though the ratio of strength had dropped to not more than 3 to 1 in favor of the defenders, even to hold was costing lives daily. Yet, the advancing forces held as a new strategy was formed.

The Royal Air Force kept up daily action, now strengthened from the North Africa and the Southern front, particularily with light bombers added to the Hurricane fighter squadrons. Every Italian Aerodrome in the area was destroyed in a 3 day period, including the ones in Asmara, Guri and Makalle. Most of the Regia Aeronautica planes were destroyed on the ground. As the final days of the major offensive against the mountain fortress of Keren drew near, the RAF concentrated on the batteries at Keren and on the enemy supply lines from Asmara. Propaganda leaflets dropped from the RAF planes under the seal of the Lion of Judah, Emperor Haile Selassie, told the Italian Colonial troops that future resistance was useless because the country was about to be liberated. This propaganda tactic was not without results as more than fifteen hundred Colonial troops deserted to the British lines before the next major attack.

During the lull before the final storm, reinforcements were gathering at Akordat. To the north of Keren, two battalions of the 7th Indian Brigade which had operated for some time directly under General Platt were detached and moved into fighting position. They were joined by a Free French Battalion from the French colony of Chad. A Battalion of the French Foreign Legion on the Red Sea Coast crossed the Frontier and captured the smaller port of Karora bringing pressure on the Italians from the north of Keren. On the 11th of February, this combined force captured an Italian outpost at Kubkub and two weeks later broke through the Mescelit pass 15 miles north of Keren.

This Brigade-sized force under the command of Brigadier Briggs, now some 500 kilometers away from Port Sudan, had moved down the coast maintaining constant pressure on General Frusci in Asmara, but particularly on his coastal defence at Massawa. Another interesting development was the arrival of two Cypriot Mule Companies speeding up the overland approach as they moved southward towards Keren.

Back at the escarpment dividing the British attacking force from Keren, the heroic and most effective Gazelle force was now divided into several units. In a way, it was almost tragic to see them disbanded, never again to be reassembled as a unit, but they were to perform a very special role in smaller units in the preliminary hours before the final attack. At Aressa and at Adi Ugri, they harassed the defending troops to the point where reinforcements were not able to reach Keren from the south and the southwest. Their constant reconnaissance, now as small units, kept a continuing probing pressure on the Keren defenders while the major force assembled back in the Akordat valley.

The road to Asmara beyond Keren was clear, as was the cross country road southwest to Metema which had not yet been taken by Brigadier Slim. Thus General Frusci had been able to move the 6th Colonial Brigade from Metema and bring his best 11th Blackshirt Legion from Asmara. This had increased his manpower strength to 21,000 at Keren in addition to his heavy and light artillery and tanks.

The forces defending Keren, Asmara and Massawa were held to a much smaller strength than General Frusci would have liked to have had. This was a critical weakness, as the simultaneous fronts to the southeast, the south and the central west were now in full action, pinning down many of the Italian forces that General Frusci would have preferred to have moved to Keren.

By the middle of March, the Italian Empire had lost all of its former Italian Somaliland, and the former British Somaliland was under heavy attack from General Cunningham's lightning thrust of the north. The two Ethiopian Irregular Divisions had crossed the frontier at Moyale, taken Mega and were moving northward into Sidamo. The losses of the Italians now included the major seaport of Mogadishu which opened a direct supply route for General Cunningham's forces. To the west, the 101 Mission under Brigadier Sandford had succeeded in forming a truce between the two leading Patriot guerilla leaders in the Gojam. Also, Brigadier Sandford joined Emperor Haile Selassie and Colonel Orde Wingate to form the Gideon Force which then frontally attacked the Italian forces in the Gojam, with tremendous help from the supporting Patriot forces. This Gideon offensive had moved to occupy Debre Markos, the capital city of Gojam, by the time the last attack on Keren took place. The Patriots were on the warpath from Sidamo to Gojam, northward even to the area of Keren and through Tigray to Asmara. General Frusci was well aware of his precarious position but he was determined to hold Keren, Asmara and all of

Eritrea. He was almost successful.

General Platt, in his holding action, was now ready for the final thrust on Keren. He knew well that the taking of Keren was the crisis point of the whole campaign. The Commander-in-Chief of the British forces in North and East Africa, General Sir Archibald Wavell, flew down from Cairo for a brief visit with General Platt to review the plans for the final assault on Keren. While he realized that the mountain fortress, defended by a stubborn enemy, was as forbidding a challenge as had ever faced a British army, he gave his assent that the assault must move forward.

The Final Assault and Victory at Keren

Preceded by martial music, the final assault came on the 15th of March. The ground assault was preceded the evening before by an air attack from RAF Wellesley Bombers on the rail connection between Asmara and Keren that destroyed a train carrying forty trucks loaded with some 30,000 artillery shells. The next morning, the attacking troops followed with a heavy artillery barrage. At 07:00 hours, elements of the 4th Division attacked the Sanchil and Samanna peaks and the fortresses embedded on them. They quickly overran the defenders on the Samanna but they failed to retake the Sanchil. The plan had been for the units of the 4th Division to capture the Ridge and Brig's Peak with units of the 5th Division to take Mt. Ziban and Fort Dologorodoc, which guarded the entrance to the narrow Dongalas Gorge.

The 5th Division leading the attack on the Cameron Ridge was delayed by heavy automatic fire from the defenders who were dug in and fortified. It was evening before the 3/5 Mahrattas were able to gain a foothold just below the heavy fortifications of Fort Dologorodoc. Before daybreak the next morning, the 16th of March, the 9th Brigade, led by the West Yorkshire Regiment, took the defenders of the Fort by surprise capturing more than 400 prisoners. It was backed by the 29th Brigade of the 5th Division. The defenders, however, called in new units from Asmara and Gonder, including Eritrean units with light tanks. These forces counterattacked eight different times in the next ten days but each assault was driven back and followed by counter assaults. The artillery guns ran out of ammunition. They received supplies by air drops from the old Vincent and Wellesley aircraft bombers of the RAF. It was in one of the concentrated artillery barrages that the flamboyant Italian General, Lorenzini was killed.

On the 17th of March, the Garhwal Rifles of the 4th Division led a renewed attack on the Sanchil as a follow up to the unsuccessful attack on the 15th of March. They suffered heavy casualties in savage hand to hand fighting with the defenders who effectively used anti-personnel grenades. The Commander, Lieut. Col. S. E. Tayler, D.S.O, the hero of the Galabat action, was killed, leading his men as he had done on the desert facing the Galabat Fort. Every British officer except one was killed that day. The battalion was now commanded by a Punjabi Subedar, Man Sing Negi, and later by a Major Murray. This remnant force of three companies managed to hang on to Sanchil. The bravery of these gallant men, British and Indian alike, was rewarded only with new orders telling them to again withdraw from the Sanchil in face of the very heavy casualties.

At this point, General Platt adopted a new strategy. Keeping a constant artillery barrage on the fortified mountain sides, he ordered fresh infantry to attack through the valley dividing the peaks. The infantry shouldered its way through the range, subjected to heavy fire from above on both sides. However, with the constant artillery barrage on these fortifications, the fresh troops were successful in bi-passing them all, including Brig's Peak, Sanchil, Flat Top Hill and the Cameron Ridge.

The ten days of incessant attack and counterattack had inflicted heavy losses on both sides. The deaths of men such as Lieut. Col. Tayler were serious losses, as his fearlessness and persistent cheerfulness had been an inspiration to all who served with him. Both the 4th and the 5th Indian Divisions were bleeding badly but the surviving troops were determined and optimistic about victory.

It was a different story with the defending Italians and their colonial troops. In five days of the heaviest fighting, they had suffered more than 3,400 casualties. Another 1000 or more had been taken prisoners, including deserters from the colonial units. Overall, morale was at a low ebb. Perhaps this was not fully realized at first by the attacking forces of General Platt, but they were soon to learn this as victory moved closer.

At 04:45 hours on the 25th of March, zero hour came for the final attack. The 10th Infantry Brigade attacked through the Gorge and by noon had reached the north side capturing Lieut. Col. Fabiani, Commanding Officer of the Savoia Grenadiers, and most of his men.

Simultaneously, the 9th Indian Brigade took Fort Dologorodoc and advanced to clear the southern road block. In 24 hours, they had captured another 600 Italian troops. A weak counterattack failed as the I-Tanks passed through carrying explosives to be used by the Sappers and Miners to blow open the last locked doors to Keren.

General Frusci's game was finished! He had lost a General, five senior officers, and more than 3000 men. At dawn on the 27th of March, the white flags of surrender flew on the Sanchil and on the Cameron Ridge and even at Keren itself. The Bren gun carriers and the I-Tanks quickly departed through the town, headed for Asmara, even before the formal surrender took place.

Along the way, they met the tanks of the French Foreign Legion from Chad who had cut through the mountain peaks from the north, just east of Keren. Four thousand Italian prisoners surrendered on their own at that time — the Colonial troops deserted even in larger numbers, often sitting by the roadside waiting to be taken.

It had not been an easy victory — more difficult than any in the African War. The two Indian Divisions had lost between 4000 and 5000 men. The 4th Division had been particularly hard hit losing nearly 3000 of their numbers including three Battalion Commanders. Had it not been for the magnificent performance of the artillery and the out dated aircraft of the RAF, casualties would have been much higher. However, even with the odds heavily stacked against them, General Platt's forces had, by sheer determination and loyal fighting, shattered the strength and will of the defending Italian forces.

The Capture of Asmara and Massawa

The road between Keren and Asmara was not an open highway by any means. The last mountain range before the

An Italian Lieutenant captured at Keren.

Lieutenant Colonel Tayler the hero of Gallabat and Sanchil. He was killed while leading his Indian troops in the Battle of Keren.

plains of central Eritrea had yet to be pierced. The defenders had been reinforced by the two remaining battalions of the Savoia Grenadiers which had moved from Addis Ababa, some 1000 kilometers to the south, and the 80th Colonial battalion from Gonder. The narrow valleys and the tunnels, which gave passage under the highest mountains to both rail and highway, could have been blocked but were not. If they had been, the demolition treatment could have made the last mountain obstacle more formidable than even Keren had been. The major difference was that the 'heart of the defenders had turned to water.' The Italian forces did not relish a repeat of their Keren experience. On the opposite side, the British were so confident that the major part of the 4th Division returned to Khartoum for deployment to North Africa where it had come from in the first place and where it now became a vital reserve in blocking the German counterattack at Cyrenaica.

Thus, the 5th Division, led by a squadron of I-Tanks, Central Indian Horses, and Sudan Defence armoured car units, was left the task of completing the takeover of Eritrea. There was some resistance but the spirit of defence had departed from the defenders. They even forgot to blow up the key mountain tunnel at Ad Teclesan. On the 31st of March, Major General Heath sent the West Yorkshires and the bearded Punjabi Sikhs to lead the assault at Ad Teclesan, but they faced only token resistance. All that was left of the central Italian East African Empire in the north had been either destroyed or captured.

The next morning, the 1st of April, the occupant of a small passenger car, flying a huge white flag, met the advancing British troops to negotiate the surrender of the city of Asmara, where two battalions of Italian Colonial troops were already rioting. General Platt took nothing for granted. In a matter of hours, he had given orders to Major General Heath to take over Asmara and then ordered his troops to move beyond Asmara, down the escarpment to the key port of Massawa and south towards Tigray to the defended towns of Adigrat and Adwa. The RAF continued to strafe and bomb the defending remnants along the way both down the escarpment to Massawa and south across the Eritrean plains to Tigray.

Back in Asmara, a homemade Union Jack was mounted on

the headquarter's flag pole as all traffic on the streets moved from the right to the left in true British fashion. There was no resistance to the takeover of Asmara. The signal sent to military headquarters in Khartoum on that 1st of April announced the capture of Asmara. In order to convince headquarters of the victory, the message read, "This is NOT repeat NOT an April fool joke."

That same day, a mobile reconnaissance force named FLIT, (after the anti mosquito remedy), replaced the desert Gazelle Force, which in the early weeks had served so successfully, and moved southwards to clear any pockets of resistance in the towns and villages of the plains area. FLIT also ordered the release of prisoners who were held in a prisoner of war camp at Adi Ugri. Simultaneously, the troops which were left to complete the occupation of Asmara headed eastward to complete the takeover of the vital port of Massawa.

General Frusci, the commanding General in Eritrea, and a small number of his headquarter's officers had escaped to the south ahead of the occupying British forces. Rear Admiral Bonnetti, commander of the Italian naval forces in the Red Sea, and General Tessitore, the officer commanding all Italian troops in Eritrea, took refuge in Massawa. The naval force included seven destroyers which Admiral Bonnetti had ordered out to sea. The ground forces defending Massawa numbered approximately 10,000 troops, including some of the survivors of Keren. There were a number of servicable artillery guns and tanks assembled for the defence.

One of the defending destroyers was sunk by the Royal Navy before it could get away from the port area. Two were sunk by aircraft of the Fleet Air Arm near Port Sudan, and two were sunk at Port Suez, with the last one running aground at Jedda on the east coast of the Red Sea. From Asmara, Major General Heath notified Admiral Bonnetti that if he decided to scuttle the commercial ships in Massawa Harbour, the British could not be held responsible for the 40,000 Italian civilians left in Asmara. Rome intervened by refusing Admiral Bonnetti permission to surrender. By the time the advancing troops could take Massawa, all 19 ships in the Harbour had been scuttled. However, the Italians even bungled their attempts to scuttle the ships properly. As a result, most of the sunken ships in Massawa Harbour were refloated again in a few days.

The 5th Division, led by its tanks, broke through the defenders, blocking the road down to the Massawa port, and the 7th Infantry Brigade united with the Free French Battalion from the coast from Port Sudan to join the 5th Division. Without any serious defence, Admiral Bonnetti mounted a white flag of surrender and asked for a negotiation of terms. However, he was suspected of playing for time so he could complete the destruction of the Harbour. Refused by the attacking forces, the white flag came down. At 04:00 hours on the 8th of April, the Allied forces went in for the kill. The Highland Light Infantry, led from the left, the French Foreign Legion from the right, and the 7th Brigade from the north. There was no organized resistance.

General De Gaulle and his Free French Navy, taking over Djibouti from Vichy France.

Admiral Bonnetti was found sitting moodily in a deck chair at the Harbour front. He attempted to break his own sword, but it only bent, so he threw it into the Harbour. It was later retrieved and has become a museum piece of the British army. The cranes in the Harbour had already been blown up, but nonetheless, the occupation was achieved that afternoon.

It was a major accomplishment, completed long before the heavy rains expected in June. Eritrea had been taken in just three months, with the exception of the sandy and poorly developed port of Assab, some 450 kilometres down the Red Sea coast.

In Retrospect

It had been a hard fought battle for the 4th and 5th Indian Divisions, the supporting Sudan Defence Units, the French Foreign Legion from Chad and the Free French out of Djibouti. The fighting was by far the most severe of the entire East African campaign, and even, perhaps, of the entire African campaign. While the casualties had been high, they were still comparatively light in view of the heavy mountainous terrain and the strongly fortified defences. It was admitted, also, that the defending Italians had put up the most stubborn and hard fought resistance of any of the Italian forces in the entire World War II. By the time of the capitulation of Eritrea on the 1st of April at Asmara and on the 8th of April at Massawa, the entire Italian Army in Eritrea had been demolished. This army had included the best of Italy's colonial troops, the 1st, 2nd, 3rd, and 4th Colonial Divisions, the Savoia Grenadier Divisions and eight Blackshirt Battalions. This added up to a total of 65 Battalions. More than 40,000 prisioners, and 300 artillery guns were captured. The Regia Aeronautica had been shot to pieces, losing more than 100 aircraft — in fact, 70 Italian aircraft were demolished either in the air or on the ground in the last days of the attack on Keren.

The amount of materials taken was tremendous. The booty included equipment and clothing for the entire Italian army in East Africa which numbered up to 300,000 men in the fall of 1940. This equiptment included 500,00 artillery shells, 3 million rounds of small arms ammunition, tanks, trucks, and medical supplies. The vital seaport of Massawa had been completely destroyed and blocked, but the Red Sea once again became an open sea lane.

The logistical problem for the victorious army was tremendous. Forty thousand Italian civilians were left in Asmara, plus those in Massawa and in nearby cities and towns. They had to be fed. They had to be protected from possible reprisals from the Eritrean population. In addition, there were 40,000 prisoners of war and there were at least 50,000 Askaris Eritreans who had deserted. Many were destitute, although a majority of them were able to go back to their own villages and farms very often dresses in the discarded Italian uniforms.

A major prisoner of war camp was immediately necessary and was established at Adi Ugri some 50 kilometres south of Asmara. This had been the site of the Italian prisoner of war camp where British prisoners taken the June before at Kassala and British Somaliland on the Ethiopian Sudan frontier, were housed.

A significant event had taken place in the Italian prisoner of war stockades at Adi Ugri as the liberating forces approached to assume control from the Italian military. A white bed sheet had been crudely painted with red and blue ink to make an improvised Union Jack. It was mounted in place of the Italian flag to the joyful shouts of both the British and Colonial KAR's alike, and to the dismay and grief of their former guards who stood silently by.

It was, to say the least, a very congested prisoner of war camp with more than 40,000 Italian occupants. The logistical problem of meeting the needs of more than 80,000 Italians, civilian and military, was very crucial and difficult. The local Eritrean people, who had for the most part welcomed the liberators, were better able to care for themselves, as the market had not been seriously affected, by any earth sorching tactics of the victors or the vanquished. There had been no heavy military action in the cities of Keren, Asmara, or, for that matter, Massawa.

An interesting note showing the concern of the British for the welfare of the citizens of Asmara was that when General Platt's personal plane arrived, it brought not only the General from Khartoum, but also hundreds of cases of canned milk for the children of the city. With General Cunningham came British political officers to take over the responsibility of governmental administration. While General Cunningham dismissed many of the Italian minor officals, it was impossible to avoid allowing civilian Italians who appeared to be trustworthy to continue with their normal duties. This often caused consternation amongst the Eritrean public. On the whole, however, the establishment of a provisional military government went smoothly. There were problems in spite of traditional British justice and efficiency, but they were handled by a reasonable and gentle military occupying force.

For the most part, Italian colonial administration had been bloated and was riddled with inefficient bureaucrats. In spite of the vast problems inherent in the takeover, the new administration received the enthusiastic support of the Eritrean public. With a war yet to be won farther to the south, the occupying forces did an admirable job.

The Ramifications of the Eritrean Victory

There were three major contributions made to the overall Allied cause in North Africa and beyond as a result of the success of the Northern Campaign in Eritrea. The first was that the entire battle-hardened 4th Indian Division and most of the RAF squadrons, with some of the Tank units, were immediately transferred to North Africa from the battle of Keren. They did not even wait for the takeover of Asmara, leaving that to the 5th Division and their attached units. General Wavell, the overall Commander in Africa, was being blamed for miscalculations in the second phase of the North African campaign. After his victorious sweep against the Italians in the earlier months, he now faced an almost overwhelming onslaught from the German forces which had moved eastward from Tunis and now threatened the security of Egypt. Yet, it was his foresight which allowed the 4th Indian Division, with supporting artillery as well as additional squadrons of the RAF, to be transferred to the East African Campaign. Having destroyed the threat from the south, they returned to assist in blocking the new turn of events as far as the German forces were concerned and the Axis plans for the takeover of all Africa.

The British military record stated it well, "Not a man, nor a gun, nor an aeroplane, nor a tank was left one moment too long on any one battlefield." The second contribution was that the Italian defeat in Eritrea and soon after, the Italian East African Empire, completely destroyed the Italian contribution to the world ambitions of the Axis powers. Mussolini was no longer the Saviour of Italy, nor was he the valid partner of Hitler. His star was moving to be completely eclipsed. Another interesting sidelight was the fact that the South African Air Force were moved from Ethiopia, with the South Rhodesian 250 squadrons, to North Africa and then on through Sicily up the peninsula of Italy. These squadrons were to play a strong support element for the British and Canadian forces who were now facing the combined Italian and Ethiopian forces in Italy. One of the lead Hurricane pilots of the Rhodesian 250 RAF Squadron from Salisbury was Ian Smith who, after being shot down behind the German lines in Italy, joined the Italian patriots and went on to capture Mussolini and his mistress on the day of the complete collapse of the Mussolini Empire.

The third contribution of the liberation of Eritrea, and the one with the most long range effect, was the clearing of the Red Sea to yield a safe sea lane for Allied shipping. This meant that American reinforcements and war materials intended to relieve the British in their defence of the Middle East and the Near East could now move up the Red Sea. This fact gave an incalculable impetus at this crucial point to the war in Crete and Syria, and later on to the India and Burma Campaigns. In fact, even the Colonial troops repaid the British and the Indians for their assistance in later months when the KAR's became a vital part of the Burma campaign against the Japanese.

The Patriots — now a Major Fighting Force

Another major effect of the liberation of Eritrea was the impact that it had on the Patriot guerilla forces who were now moving en mass to support the liberators. One such Ethiopian leader, who had under Italian pressure more or less aligned himself with the Italian rulers, was Ras Seyoum, the old ruler of Tigray who came from Adwa to Asmara to make a formal and contented act of submission to the liberators. There has been much controversy in studies of Ethiopian history over the part played by Ras Seyoum during the war. He was considered to have been a puppet of the Italian who, very quickly, made his real loyalties known to General Platt. Another was Haile Selassie Gugsa, who explained to General Cunningham how much he regretted moving over to the Italians at Mekele, the capital city of Tigray in 1935. There were others. In fact, across the whole countryside, down to Gonder where there was still a major Italian force, and south towards Dese into the whole province of Welo, the patriot forces were realizing that liberation was near at hand, and they moved unanimously to assist the liberating forces whenever they could. There is no questioning that this shortened the final months and weeks of the campaign to complete victory.

However, in the war in East Africa, the 101 Mission, having now joined with the Gideon force, was making excellent progress from the west. The South African and Colonial Brigades from Kenya, Nigeria, and Ghana were making rapid gains from the southeast — in fact, three days before the fall of Massawa on the 8th of April, General Cunningham's forces, led by the South Africans and the King's African Rifles, entered Addis Ababa, the capital of the East African Empire of Mussolini and the modern capital of Ethiopia. The final collapse of the Italian government and the military forces of the Viceroy, the Duke d'Aosta was coming to a close. In retrospect, the overall Campaign was in reality a joint operation. General Platt could never have taken Keren as he had if it had not been for General Cunningham's rapid progress from the south.

The "other" front was not underestimated or overlooked by Generals Platt or Cunningham. General Platt was reluctant at the beginning to give Emperor Haile Selassie too much say in the formation of strategy. However, he slowly came to realize that the support of the Patriot guerillas and the potential of wholesale defections from the Italian Colonial forces could have a major impact on the eventual victory. This caused him to relent on his initial opposition to the 101 Mission and to give much credance to Orde Wingate's "guerilla" plans. Wingate had been looked down upon as a bit of an "Indian Scout"

The Keren Memorial to the Allied Soldiers who fought in the Battle of Keren.

officer from the colonial days in North America, and certainly as an unorthodox, perhaps unreliable officer, not really qualified to lead a Battalion or a Brigade. His spectuacular success and close liason and cooperation with Colonel Sandford and the Patriots made him a legend with the Ethiopians. The British had no alternative as the Gideons entered Addis Ababa on the 5th of May with the Emperor but to give both Wingate and Sandford the equivalent rank as that carried by Brigadier Pienaar, Commander of the 1st South African Brigade, and Brigadier Fowkes, Commander of the 22nd East African Brigade.

Thus, having followed General Platt's forces from Kassala through to Asmara and Massawa , we must now turn to see how General Cunningham, with the South African Division, the two Colonial Divisions and the Ethiopian Territorial Division, was making out on the Southern Front, and what was happening with the Gideon Brigade to the west.

END NOTES

[1] 1 W.G.E. Jackson, **The Battle For North Africa** (New York, Mason, Charter Publishers, 1975). pp. 41f.

[2] British War Office, **The Abyssinian Campaigns** (London, His Majesty's Stationery Office, 1942), pp. 41f.

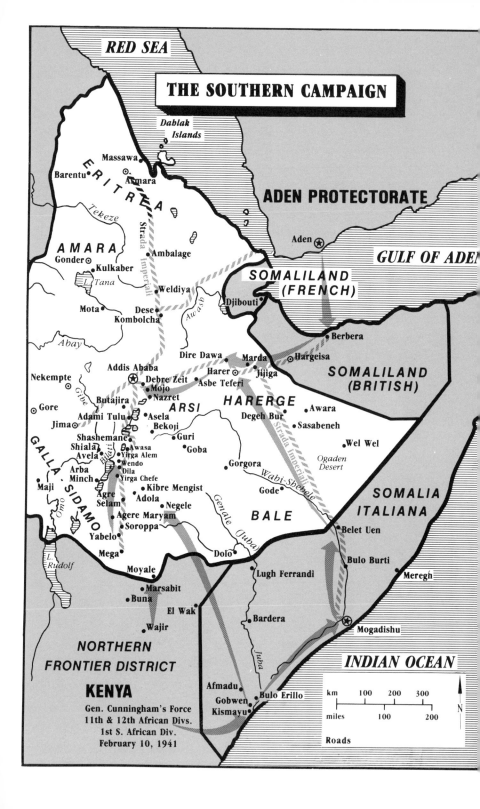

6

THE SOUTHERN CAMPAIGN

The southern frontier had many similarities to those in the north. A vast stretch of desert reached from Kismayu on the Indian Ocean past Lake Rudolf to Juba on the Nile, in the Sudan, a distance of more than 1,200 kilometres. Nairobi, the capital of Kenya, was just as exposed to a takeover by Mussolini's forces out of Ethiopia as was Khartoum, the capital of the Sudan. In June 1940, when Italy declared war on Britain, the minimal defence forces in Kenya consisted of four companies of King's African Rifles and a hastily formed East African Reconnaisance Squadron made up of British settlers using open Ford trucks. This 'Reccie' outfit was not as well equipped or as well trained as the Sudan Motor Machine Gun Companies on the Sudanese frontier facing Ethiopia, although their daring probing and skirmishes with the Italian forces in the northern frontier were comparable.

Within two weeks of the declaration of war, a Brigade of strong Italian forces had attacked the Kenyan fort of Moyale on the Kenya border but were held at bay for five days by a single King's African Rifles (KAR) Company which withdrew only when their water supply ran out. There were no major confrontations during the months of July, August and into September, except for a few occasional forages and skirmishes into Kenya at a few water holes and frontier settlements. The Italians established a military post at Buna and El Wak as they had done at Galabat and at Kassala in the Sudan.

The only major action in the south on the part of the Italians after the declaration of war was the takeover of British Somaliland and its Indian Ocean port at Berbera. These minor naval bases did not even extend towards the north Red Sea base at Port Sudan which, at that point, they could easily have taken and which would have assisted them in their claim to complete control over the Red Sea. Thus, the most significant factors of these months, both in the north and in the south, were the heat and the vastness of the frontier and the failure of the Italians to mount any full scale invasion of British territory which Mussolini had boasted to Hitler as being his objective.

While the military situation and the expanse of the two desert frontier areas had many similarities, the actual terrain in the south was very different. In the north, the high mountains of Ethiopia quickly tapered off into a narrow band of foothills, covered by dense bush, to fade into the swampy desert sands, right up to the banks of the Nile River. In the south, the low coastal plain facing the Indian Ocean on the east is covered by thick bush. Farther inland, the bush thins out into the physical features of semi desert which stretches across the vast area of the northwest frontier district of Kenya, even up to the western borders of British Somaliland to include the settlement areas on the Kenyan side of Dalo, El Wak, Buna, Wajir and Garussa. Further west of this desert, the scrub turns into the white sands of the desolate Chalbi desert, broken on the west by the beautiful volcanic Marsabit Mountains. The Chalbi desert in the dry season displays a surface comparable to a speed track, but becomes a sea of mud in the rainy season. It is virtually uninhabited. To the north and west of the Chalbi desert towards Lake Rudolf, the terrain turns into a lava desert, beautiful to behold, but devoid of permanent population except for the Tana and Wasa Nijiro river valleys. In this vast southern desert wilderness, both the British and Italian military seemed to be but lost wanderers without any major strategy apart from the occasional skirmishes when they came into contact with each other.

There were no actual fronts as this wilderness and desert area kept the opposing sides apart. The Italians hesitated for fear of facing a frontal attack from the fertile and developed parts of the central and southern parts of Kenya. If the strategy of the Italian Generals had been to move southward in the month of July, or August, no military defence would have been able to stop any full scale advance. The British were just not prepared for the scale of military action in the area that Italy could have mounted with their forces of some 300,000 well equipped men. The situation, however, changed quickly. The Nigerian and the Gold Coast (Ghanaian) and North Rhodesian Battalions (Zambian) arrived in August to join several full Brigades of newly recruited KAR troops. Two South African Brigades also arrived in August, with the transferal of more support units throughout September and October. The first South African Air Force Squadrons joined the 237th Squadron of the RAF from Southern Rhodesia. The presence of this Air Force kept the Italian Air Force, the Regia Aeronautica, from crossing the frontier other than for an occasional patrol. A recruitment and training program amongst the thousands of Ethiopian exiles in Kenya, resulted in the formation of two Divisions of what came to be known as the Ethiopian Irregulars. There was also a Somali Force patrolling in the north eastern part of the frontier, made up of recruits and trained into two Companies under British officers. The Turkastan tribesmen west of Lake Rudolf were also trained into an effective Company. Thus, a colonial force of amazing strength arose almost miraculously under the threatening clouds of an Italian invasion, which never materialized into a storm.

The British officers, who commanded these troops, often asked themselves about what might be going on in the minds of these non-Europeans who made up this polyglot colonial army. Three articles from three diverse African soldiers, whose thoughts were typical of the thousands of their non-European fellow troops who had volunteered to take part in this European War, give some ideas of their thoughts:

Profession of Faith
by A Cape Coloured Transport Driver

"Sometimes I wonder what this is all about. Sometimes I think that civilization is not all it claims to be. Everything seems 'topsy-turvy' in a world full of 'topsy-turvy' politicians. I am no politician, but as an everyday man in the street I cannot help being aware of the trend of everyday events. To me at least it seems that civilization is entering a new era. My hope is that the end of this struggle, culminating in a victory for the Democracies, will be the stepping stone to a second, and the greatest, renaissance period for civilization — a civilization that would spell peace and plenty for every race, creed or colour.

War, poverty and death know no colour bar. It is for that reason that the non-Europeans have decided the fight is theirs too. In war at least it seems as if all men are truly brothers.

The young coloured men from the Union have not been slow in answering the call. We are up here in our thousands putting our shoulders to the wheel of VICTORY. We have put our political differences aside for the time being and are showing the world in general, and South Africa in particular, that we are not one mite inferior. We have proved again and again that where any kind of duties were concerned we were never found wanting. We are doing our best, hoping that by our self-sacrifice, our peoples in the Union and elsewhere would be given a better, fair-deal, a full share of the rays of the Union's sun of prosperity. We would go through hell merrily for the realisation of wishes dear to the heart of each and every non-European.'

Why We are Fighting
by A West African Soldier

"The British Commonwealth of nations had grown up in an atmosphere of freedom and developed on this principle and practice of self-government. The Nazi system, on the other hand, was bondage — bodily, spiritually, economically, morally, and otherwise. Truth, conscience, mercy, honour, justice and love were regarded by Hitler as offensive things and the world under his so-called NEW ORDER would be divided into Germans as masters and the other nations as second class peoples.

We are presently concerned not only with physical but moral invasion. We are fighting the aggressive powers to save our freedom — the world's freedom from being murdered, as it had been murdered in Czechoslovakia, Poland, Norway, Denmark, Holland, Belgium, France, Yugoslavia and Greece. If all the men serving in the East Africa Force had not sacrificed their lives and everything they possessed best in fighting and conquering the Italians at this end, what would have been the fate of our people in the Gold Coast on the arrival of the Italian and German armies on our soil? Total destruction and everlasting slavery would have certainly been our lot. Good luck and good courage to every one of you till we meet again.''

Remembrance to our Brothers Behind Us
by an Infantryman of the King's African Rifles

"We all of 2nd/6th Bn. K.A.R., we are sending our compliments and thanks to all those who stay in Tanganyika and Kenya for the gifts they have awarded to us.

To the Information Officer, Dar Es Salam and to the Editor of Baraza, we are much pleased with their work. Because they are somehow fighting like men, and of course, we have been feeling very bad for not having heard what is happening in our country, and at last the above people have cured the disease amongst us. And now all our faces turn bright whenever news comes from our behind in a paper called "Baraza" (Gazette). All those who do not know how to read are being told what is in the Gazette by the other soldiers. And of course we are very much pleased with the pictures in these papers.

Everyone of us will see in the "Baraza" as all civilians have got a fixed mind as below:
1.   British Government always deal with the

truth and he never take part in telling lies, as is practiced by Hitler and Mussolini.

2.   British Government is having part of small nations, and he is fighting for the independence of these nations (Think of Poland).

3.   Government of freedom to his people is known as 'Father and his Son.' Wealth and Unity brings good understanding. Without unity there is no understanding.

4.   Well, my friends, soldiers and civilians who are remaining, please take in your daily prayer 'The Union Jack should remain as it is,' as we are quite sure that we will win tomorrow. And with the aid of our prayers will strengthen the heart of our King till he wins.

All of us of the 2nd/6th K.A.R. are having conversation that though we are very far, miles and miles, but our brothers behind us are still remembering us, and surely they are looking after us properly."[1]

The Frontier Comes to Life as a Colonial Army Moves into Action

By the time Lt. General Sir Alan Cunningham, in command of the Southern Campaign, had arrived in Nairobi on the 1st of November, a formidable colonial army had taken shape. In September 1940, the 237th RAF Rhodesian Squadron had already been transferred to Khartoum to continue its strafing and bombing, which had been so helpful in Kenya during July and August. The South African Air Force had increased in size with the arrival of two more squadrons as well as the 2nd and 5th South African Brigades. General Cunningham was able to consolidate the forces into three Divisions, enabling him to plan a two pronged stategy. At first, these three Divisions were not up to standard strength but had a degree of mobility between them, particularly with the South African units, which proved to be a most practical and functional arrangement as the campaign progressed.

The first Division to take formal shape was the 1st South

African Division, made up of three South African Brigades and a number of smaller units, under the command of Major General G. E. Brink, CB, DSO. The 11th and 12th African Divisions were made up entirely of Colonial units commanded, for the most part, by British officers. One of the South African Brigades was used as a floating unit attached at times to one or the other of the African Divisions, and at other times returning to their own Division. They even performed on individual assignments as was the situation at El Wak. Several South African artillery and engineering battalions were attached and detached as the need required. This proved an excellent strategy!

South Africa's vital contribution to the Southern Campaign and, more centrally, during the Battle of the Lakes and north on to Dese and Ambalage, cannot be over emphasized. The Air Force, wherever they were located, soon assumed command of the skies. The Engineers bridged impossible rivers, cleared difficult blockages in the mountains, built water supplies, laid out roads where none existed and with their transport drivers, supplied the troops. The South African Infantrymen, whether of Dutch or English backgrounds, including the coloured transport drivers, were courageous, efficient and willing to act on their own initiative in complete harmony with the African troops.

The planning of General Cunningham was conditioned by the timing of the early rains which came in late February and March, particularly in the highlands. He orginally thought he would have to delay any major attack until May or June. In the meantime, his strategy was to improve training, strengthen communications; maintain vigorous patrolling actions and, perhaps, local offensives in the frontier as the situation arose.

The West Africans settled in quickly, particularly the KARs who didn't require any settling in; albeit they faced many new situations and experiences. Without exception, they proved themselves credible soldiers, fearless and obedient to commands. Their descriptive letters home tell of their reactions to their new surroundings. Three descriptive letters written by these West African troops tell some of their impressions:

Extract from a Letter of a Nigerian Soldier

"On the 10th of October, I saw a wonderful thing called a 'Tank.' I saw a war motor. It was constructed like a tortoise, with wheels of rubber enclosed in chains. There are two men inside it and one machine-gun in front. When it starts moving it appears like a crocodile chasing a man. Neither trees nor rivers nor hills are a hindrance to its progress and all roads are alike to it, and I even entered it. It is very hot inside. It is indeed a thing of wonder to all Africans."

Extract from a letter of a Ghanaian Gold Coast Soldier

"We were at Wajir Camp when we first saw about six Armoured Cars and some Tanks going on patrol, when luckily they stopped for a few minutes at our area and many of us gathered round to see how the lorries were made of, as they appear unlike the ordinary lorries with which we travel. We discovered that the whole body of each of the cars have been covered with thick plated-iron with the exception of the tyres, which we found to be rubber. The tanks were all made of iron and they appeared to be very heavy. We were anxiously looking steadfastly at them when one of the soldiers exclaimed, 'Oh these cars and tanks are very good for this war. If one company of this Battalion get about fifty of the cars and another company get about the same number of the tanks, I think we fit finish the war in East Africa for one week, because if you are in this car or tank you fit shoot the enemy and they can't fit to shoot you. You can kill them plenty. No you won't die from rifle fire or machine-gun fire at all.'

Extract from a Letter of a Nigerian Soldier

"On Monday the 28th November in the evening, about 6 o'clock, we were sitting down and we heard a noise like a 'dimm-dimm-dimm.' Together we lifted our eyes towards the sky; suddenly we noticed three Italian aeroplanes, and they were throwing bombs on our soldiers guarding a bridge in front of us, about twelve miles away. We could see flames and fire like you would see a big bush fire. Instantly our fighter pilots started up their engines, they climbed up in the air, and almost immediately they joined battle with the enemy. We could hear the sound of 'Ra-da-da-da.' That was the noise of machine guns and Bren guns. Had there been thunder, one would not have been able to hear it. In a short while one could see one Italian aeroplane falling towards the ground. The two other aeroplanes had to fight hard, and just managed to make their escape. Our aeroplanes were not damaged in the slightest. Truly the King of England has real fighting men in the air. We pray to God to give our King victory in this war. Amen.''[2]

The Proving Ground at El Wak
    The first local attack was at El Wak on the 15th of December. The 1st South African Brigade and the 24th Gold Coast (Ghanaian) Brigade were used against this frontier junction that the Italians had established in Kenyan territory. It was defended by one Italian Battalion, in addition to several Banda Battalions (Italian native troops). There were 16 artillery pieces and a number of armoured cars defending the Fort. This raid, as General Cunningham described it, was actually a full dress rehearsal for the Southern Campaign. On the night of the 14th of December, the troops were moved 160 kilometres from Wajir, the most northerly of the Kenyan outposts. They took the Italian troops at El Wak by complete surprise. The Italians had the smug belief that the road to Rogier was too rough to allow passage of tanks or any mechanical transport. So devastating was this early morning attack by the combined South African/Ghanaian troops in the 106 degree heat, that within hours the El Wak settlement and the Fort were completely destroyed, as were the surrounding villages. One South African

spotter Aircraft was given the credit for shooting down a Regia Aeronautica Caproni bomber which had attempted to harass the attacking forces. With only two fatal casualties, the El Wak raid was completely successful. The most important outpost the Italians had on the Kenyan frontier was razed to the ground! The impact of this victory was much wider than the defeat of a single Italian frontier post on Kenyan soil. The first result was the tremendous morale boost for the waiting British troops, who knew all too well that their fighting days were yet to come. In this sense, it was a trial run for the attack on Italian Somaliland and on into Ethiopia. It also served as a lesson not easily forgotten; the Italians had little stomach for a fight to the finish. Most important of all, the El Wak did severe damage to Italian morale. It was from the incident at El Wak that the collapse of the Italian momentum is dated. While not part of the main offensive in the Southern Campaign which was to begin in a few weeks, it was regarded as a significant prelude to it. From the El Wak area, the Italians withdrew their forces to what is called the Juba line, with only a scattered screen of Banda troops and one larger armed Fort at Afmadu west of the Juba river, well within Italian Somaliland.

A South African signaller summed it up with these quotes from a letter that he had written home:

"It was just getting light. The Infantry was in front of us and I was in the signals, sitting waiting; there was nothing we could do. We just sat in the truck in the dark, and we couldn't smoke, because it would have made a glow, and we couldn't eat because there was nothing to eat. The kitchen van was miles behind us — it had got stuck in the sand and we couldn't wait.

The village was about three miles away and we were on a bit of a rise, but even after sunrise we couldn't see it properly, because it was in a sort of little bowl and all we could see was a few round Native huts. Just as it was getting light, the planes came over. That was what we had been waiting for. There were four of them — Hardebeestes, and they got into line and attacked one behind the other. First one would go over and as he came to the village he would dive right down on it and drop his bombs, machine gunning at the same time, and go up again, and then the next would come down. It was the first air bombing we had seen, and we were very glad to be this side of it.

Soon the village was burning. There was smoke, thick black smoke — and now and again you could see the flames leaping up out of the valley. Then the planes flew back to the drome, and the Sergeant Major walked down past each truck and said, 'We're off,' and hit on the side of the truck to wake us up because half of us were asleep.

The bush was so thick that we never knew where the Italians were, and we didn't see how anyone could possibly fight in it. We thought we'd meet trouble on the road though, and we fully expected to be fired on at any moment.

The Natal Carbineers were going along close ahead of us, spread out, and the first thing we knew was when three machine guns opened up on them.

There were only two people killed in this extraordinary battle of El Wak — we never understood how there were so few — and they were killed about fifty yards from me. But we didn't see anything of it at the time, because when you are being shelled you don't watch the shells burst. You just lie on your tummy and you cover your head, because, although you hear the stuff whistling over you, you don't really know where it is going to burst — so if you look up you may cop it.

There's been too much fuss made about this action because it was the first. There wasn't a battle really. When the Carbineers got near enough they fixed their bayonets and charged, singing an old Zulu war song which means 'Here comes the Mothers' Son's, 'and there was another thing they sang, 'Juga Malloya' — I don't know what it means.

The Italians hadn't known that we were coming — they thought it was going to be Native troops — and when they saw white men with bayonets, they just bolted — their Commanding Officer first!" After El Wak, General Simone, the Commanding Officer of the Italian forces in the Juba area sent this message to his waiting and uneasy troops:

"In some units there is little zest. In some parts of the front, the defensive organisation has been carried out with a rudimentary conception that calls to mind the primitive military arts of the Negus. This bears witness to the incapacity, the indolence of the men or, even worse, the incapacity of the responsible commander. Training in most cases is not observed; at the most it consists of a few haphazard hours of instruction in the use of Company or Platoon, a little arms drill badly carried out, and a little theoretical teaching in obvious and monotonous subjects. Nobody pays any attention to the war training of Company or battalion. There are many who know just enough to keep their Ranks and that is all. This war which we are at this moment fighting against the English calls for the most sagacious and intelligent application of the latest tactical principles as evolved in the great modern armies and not those of primordial systems of guerilla warfare against Abyssinian rebels, unled and like hunted gazelles."[4]

The Opening of the New Front

The real offensive for the drive through Somaliland and on for 3000 kilometres through to Addis Ababa did not begin until the first week of February. It was proceeded by an important large scale thrust northward from Marsabit, the beautiful mountains of the north, through the Chalbi Desert in mid January. The objective was limited. It was intended to clear the last remaining Italian troops from Kenyan soil, and then take the major Italian fortified outpost at Mega, which is some 40 kilometres inside of the border in the Galla/Sidamo area of Ethiopia. It was also intended to let the Italian command know that the main thrust to Addis Ababa was being planned by a major force directly up from the south on the route that was taken by this lead attack, instead of through Somaliland. It was the shortest route through to the capital, Addis Ababa, through Borena and the Lake Country.

The attacking force included the 2nd and 5th South African Brigades, two KAR Battalions and a Division of Ethiopian Irregulars. The latter were assigned to do the advanced scouting, probing and skirmishing, with the heavier equipment and troops to follow. This also allowed the Ethiopian Irregulars to make contact with the Patriot forces, who were active all along the Kenya border.

It should also be noted that General Platt's strategy in the north was that no action anywhere in East Africa should be considered isolated. All were considered an integral part of the overall campaign. For this reason, General Cunningham agreed that any action in the Galla/Sidamo area would prevent the Italian enemy from concentrating reinforcements in the defence of the northern campaign or the anticipated attack through Somaliland. As a result, not one Italian battalion was moved out of the Galla/Sidamo area — not even later on, when the 12th African Division replaced the South Africans who were sent to join in the Somaliland-Harer forces and were already in action as far as Mogadishu.

From the lush slopes of Mount Marsabit, two roads ran northward into Ethiopia. The easterly one ran across the northern frontier desert to Moyale. In a more direct route, the second crosses the Chalbi desert to El Sardu and El Yibo. The westerly road was really non existent in many places and unreliable at the best. The advantage was that it offered an easier way of piercing through the Moyale-Mega escarpment which ran parallel to the Ethiopian/Kenya border.

The enemy fortifications at El Sardu and El Yibo were quickly overrun, clearing the last Italians from Kenyan soil. Most of the Ethiopian Irregulars had already infiltrated across the border travelling between Mount Dibbandibba and Mount Murdur. On the second day of their route northward, they reached the Hobok-Gore road which ran parallel to the border. The 2nd Brigade then moved to the west with the intention of stimulating the Ethiopian Patriot forces. They crossed the border to occupy the first Ethiopian village at Dukano. On a road running through Dukano, parallel to the Kenyan border, the two South African Brigades separated, after spending their first night on Ethiopian soil between Mount Dibbandibba and Mount Murdur. As they separated, one went to the west for an encircling manoeuver and one to the east. The plan was to reach Mega from two different directions. The armoured cars were able to force their way over difficult trackless roads, often through heavy bush. Their first action was at Lake Gore, the military Fort to the east. It was situated on the southern lip of a crater, 400 feet deep, with a clear line of fire in all directions for the defenders. By mid afternoon, the attackers had circled the crater mountain blocking any escape roads to the east of the Fort while a company of infantrymen climbed the slopes on the western side. An armoured car climbed up the long eastern slope, broke through the wire and entered the Fort with the infantry charging with fixed bayonets! Within an hour the Fort was taken, with a loss of only two lives.

Moving to the west, the 2nd Brigade reached El Gumu by 14:30 hours and, in a brisk encounter, overran the Fort which was in reality a military post at a road junction. The next morning, the Brigade advanced to Hobok, a well constructed fort on the edge of Lake Bulal with the green foothills of Ethiopia as a backdrop. The situation appeared formidable to the advancing South Africans and the Ethiopian Irregulars with them, but the enemy was less determined and fled before the arrival of the armoured cars.

These engagements convinced the attacking forces, as had been the case at El Wak, that the Italian defenders were not only incompetent, but also had no determination to stand and fight. The defence in each of the three conquered fortifications was both costly and ineffective as far as the defenders were concerned, but with a minimal number of casualities for the attackers.

Following the fall of Gore and Hobok, the 2nd and 5th South African Brigades moved for a joint attack on Moyale. The 2nd Brigade made a circuitous detour northward and then came directly east to cross the Mega-Yabelo road, cutting off any escape route to the north. This prevented any reinforcements coming from Yabelo and Soroppo to the north. Mega was attacked from the west and the south and southeast, leaving part of the force on the north to block the road to Yabelo. This was an important strategy because before the attack on Mega itself began, 15 tanks from Yabelo moved southward, but they failed to break through the South African forces holding the road blockade. The attackers on the Mega Fort were assisted by three days of heavy rain, resulting in mud and cold temperatures at the 1000 metre level where they now were. It was very difficult for the troops who were used to 110 degree desert heat and who were now short on rations and facing difficult bush barriers; yet on the final day, the infantry charged with fixed bayonets! A cloud concealed their approach, and the defenders mounted a white flag after only twenty minutes of resistance. Again, it was a case of incompetent defenders lacking the spirit and determination to fight. Some 600 Italian prisoners were taken while more ran for the bush.

The remaining battles in this centre-northward thrust were brief. The Ethiopian Irregulars occupied Moyale without resistance on the 22nd of February, while a joint force of South Africans fought a brilliant action at Soroppa after taking Yabelo without resistance.

At this point, the South African Brigades were withdrawn leaving the entire Galla Sidamo area to the Ethiopian Irregulars for what was now the beginning of the heavy spring rains.

General Cunningham now had his confidence strengthened. He withdrew the 2nd and 5th South African Brigades from this initial engagement of the Southern Campaign. The 2nd South African Brigade was posted to Berbera, in order to occupy and to guard communications and supplies coming in at that port. The 5th South African Brigade was then released for service in Egypt. These two Brigades had completed a short but difficult assignment extremely well. They were now to leave the East African scene, except for two battalions. These battalions were to be involved in the Battle of the Lakes and, ultimately in April, they were to join again with Ethiopian Irregulars, who had worked their way up from the south across the Borena to complete the defeat of the Italians in control of that Southern area of the country.

The main front up through Somaliland was now well on its way in their 3000 kilometer planned advance to the Ethiopian capital. General Cunningham had considered that it would take a number of months to reach his objective, but he was now convinced that the final capitulation of the East African Empire in Somaliland was going to take place much more quickly than he had planned!

The Capture of Mega
Excerpts from a report by a South African Corporal

"I was in "C" Company of 1st South African Irish, 13 Platoon, commanded by Captain Cochran. We had waited at Mega for about a week before the battle started.

On the Saturday night we were pushed off from the outpost and slipped on to another ridge, where we slept in our greatcoats, one blanket, and groundsheets. We got up early next morning, about 5 a.m., had breakfast, which consisted of bully beef and biscuits, and left everything with the truck on account of the heat — greatcoats, blankets, groundsheets — everything bar ammunition, webbing and rifles.

It was terribly hot on that Sunday morning when we started out, like it had been all the way across the N.F.D. and in Abyssinia so far. We'd no idea that in addition to climbing thousands of feet, the getting to Mega meant the end of the weather. The truck took us as near our objective as it could — a hill where it couldn't go any further. Then we debussed and started climbing on foot. The hill went up in steps. You climbed for about twenty minutes — then you got to a sort of flat bit — then you went up again. All during the first morning we were busy cleaning up outposts. The riflement didn't fire — the Bren gunners did, and their fire was returned by the enemy. Some mortar shells came over, which went well overhead out of range and fell in the road. They were trying to stop the trucks getting supplies through, you see, and they were being pretty successful. Our artillery and mortars were not in action yet.

That afternoon it started raining, and from then on it rained all the time — all that afternoon and night — and we coulnd't get blankets, greatcoasts, anything, because every time the trucks tried to get through to us, the roads were shelled and they had to turn back. We retired five hundred yards to get a better place to sleep and there we were told to dig in. We only had short entrenching tools, but the ground was fairly soft, so we got dug in all right, which didn't stop us getting drenched — officers and all. Meantime the enemy were still firing, mostly mortar fire. Some bully did come through, but not enough to go round, so we all gathered round and the Company Sergeant Major ladled it out with a tablespoon — one spoon to each man's hands. We also managed to get some cigarettes and matches, and put the cigarettes in our pockets. But in the morning it was raining again and, when we wanted a cigarette, it was all drenched and none of us could smoke, unless you happened to have a celluloid tobacco pouch.

It was 12 when we got to the landmines. We were waiting for orders, standing under some trees to shelter from the rain, about fifty yards from a gully we had to cross, and one of our majors and a sergeant walked down to have a look at it. The sergeant was called back, and the major went on alone, and as he went through the gully he put his foot on a landmine, and the next thing we saw him go up in the air. The landmine smashed one of his legs badly, and two stretcher bearers ran down to pick him up. They carried him away to the C.C.S. and then a machine gunner walked down the gully, and he went up in the air too. Then the two stretcher bearers ran down to pick him up, and both his legs were useless, so they asked him if he could crawl a bit closer, and he started crawling on his elbows, and the stretcher bearers couldn't bear that, so they ran forward, picked him up and put him on a stretcher. They started walking back, and the back stretcher bearer, he trod on a landmine, and the three of them went up in the air. The fellow already on the stretcher, he was killed outright.

The other chap was just chucked away for 10 or 15 yards and he rolled over. Nothing seemed to be the matter with him bar shock — he started running away, then came back and asked for assistance. One of our chaps — a fellow, who had been our company cook, went to help and picked up the stretcher bearer with the smashed legs and the machine gunner and put him on the stretcher. Then we were all afraid to go through the gully for fear of landmines, but Captain Cochran, he said he'd go through first and we'd walk in his footsteps. So we all got into single file and we tried to walk exactly in his footsteps. We got safely across — no one was hurt. Apparently we did walk on landmines — the engineers found out afterwards, but the fuses were wet and they didn't go off.

We were then told to look out for booby traps. One man who had been a soldier in the last war said, 'Watch out for such things as bully beef tins, Italian bayonets and old motor cycles lying around.' Fat lot of motor cycles there were there.

The next few hundred yards were mud, and you couldn't walk more than a few paces at a time, you got so bogged in it. We then came to a hill we called 'Shivering Hill,' and on the right of the hill was another very, very big one which would take an hour to climb. We were going up the whole time.

There was an Italian observation post on this hill, and the Major asked the men of 'A' Company for twelve volunteers to blow it out. He asked a platoon of 42 men, and all stepped forward. The Major said he only wanted twelve men, so he selected them, and together with a corporal they started off to climb the hill. They had twelve rifles and two Bren guns, and there was lots of cover on the hill. And they approached to within 30 yards of the enemy. The enemy could see them coming and fired all the time, but they didn't fire back till they were in a good enough position, when they opened up. They fired for about ten minutes when the enemy stopped firing and put up a white flag.

The Major, being an older soldier, said, 'Don't get up.' He got up himself. An Italian officer got up too. The Major called him over (We could see all this from our hill.) The Italian officer spoke to his men and we saw him pointing on the ground, so we thought he'd told them to ground arms and surrender, and then he suddenly dropped down and they opened fire again. So our Major, he said, 'Next time they put up a white flag, let them have it.' Our men went on firing, and up came the white flag again. So as soon as the Italian officer showed himself, they let him have it and he fell. Some of his men jumped up and started running away; a few were killed and the rest were taken prisoner.

At 11 a.m. that day we came to a place where we would have to be in the open for 200 yards. So the Captain, he called us together and said, 'It will take a bit of an effort. You'll have to race across. When in the bush, cut over to the left for 200 yards, then to the right for 200 yards, then right again for 200 yards.'

Well we did this — it was difficult going in the bush — and we had not quite reached our spot, where we wanted to be, when the artillery opened up barrage after barrage on the spot where we'd entered the bush, but by that time we'd gone, so the shrapnel didn't get us.

Then right in front there was another hill, on which was a blockhouse, and we advanced at that.

There were four Breda guns firing at us. We'd good cover and, when we got the word to advance, we'd dash and land up behind some rock. Sometimes they fired rifles at us, but we did not fire back because we couldn't see them. Our artillery was firing at the blockhouse.

We had two aircraft by then and they tried to blow up the blockhouse, but at first they were pretty wide off the mark. Then one plane went straight up in the air and dived, and we thought it was going to go right into the blockhouse, but instead he landed a bomb in the middle of it.

The mist came up dark. You couldn't see a thing. In the end it started clearing and, as it cleared towards the Italians, we advanced. We heard our corporal was wounded, and we thought a lot of him, but eventually we heard it was only in the calf, and the mist kept on clearing. I remember we were told to be very cautious in case of traps. Then suddenly the mist cleared and we saw the fort and the flag come down off the fort and all the enemy coming out surrendering. They came with great big white flags, and they came without arms or anything, but we got down and lay ready with our rifles in case of monkey tricks.

They sent a man to speak to our commander and he said 'We're surrendering.' After that we were told to clean out all M.G. nests, etc.

I must say the Italians were masters at camouflage — you had to be right on top of a place before you recognized it. Most of them were Breda posts, and there were cases of ammunition, food, water, everything. Only in one place did we find one of the enemy. He crawled out with tears rolling down his eyes, and he whipped out a photo and said, 'Wife, wife.' We said, 'Did you see us coming up the hill?' He shook with fright and said he had seen us crawl a little, yes. He said, 'Are you going to kill me?' and we said, 'No.'

We slept in the fort that night. The prisoners were in the part with the roof, and we had the part without, and it rained again too, but now we were beside a great big fire, and the trucks had been getting through, you see, and we got food and tea and were quite happy."[5]

The Big Push Moves Out

On January 23, 1942, Lieut General Sir Alan Cunningham sent the following message to the 11th and 12th African Divisions on the eve of the drive northward:

"The Victories of Imperial troops further north have filled us in East Africa with pride and excitement though no doubt the ensuing period has been touched with envy and strong desire to emulate achievements stop Change is now before you to prove what I well know that East Africa Force is no whit behind in dash courage and endurance stop In this confidence I send to South African East African West African and Indian troops taking part in operation a message of good luckstop Hit them Hit them hard and hit them again."[6]

The first major objective was Afmadu, intended to clear the area between the Tana and the Juba Rivers. The two Divisions included four motorized Brigades which were to lead the attacks against six Italian Brigades and six Banda Battalions; all based in the Juba River Valley with Afmadu as the key defensive base. The distance from Garussa, which was the jumping off point for the 11th Division, to Afmadu was 425 kilometers, over wilderness desert country. This was approximately the same distance which separated the 11th Division from their base at Bure through to Kismayu, the first Italian Somaliland seaport. The roads were not more than trails across the desert and all movement was made at night to avoid air attacks from the Italian Air Force, which was still active in the area. The plan was to move swiftly as support was available; supplies having to be moved from the Garussa and Bure bases in Kenya. The take off for both Divisions was in the evening of January 23, 1941. The timing was also important, as it was considered necessary to coordinate the attacks on all three fronts — north, south and west. In the north, General Platt's forces had taken Kassala on the Sudan side of the border and Teseney on the southern side on the 19th of January. On the 22nd of January, the attacking forces had split at Biscia, one heading south to Barentu and the main force heading towards Akordat. Akordat was captured on the 1st of February, and Barentu on the 2nd. In the west, Emperor Haile Selassie crossed the Ethiopian frontier on the 20th of January and was united with the 101 Mission at Belaya on the 6th of February. Mussolini, back in Rome, as well as Italian commanders in the East African Empire, were well aware that they were under heavy attack on all fronts.

After the sham offensive drive from El Wak toward Bardera on the upper Juba, the 11th and 12th African Divisions left from Garussa. Both Divisions crossed the Italian Somaliland border the next morning. Headed by the 22 East African KAR Brigade, the border post of Liboi was taken the same day. Haiveina was captured on the 27th of January and Beles Gugani five days later on the 5th of February. Immediately, they were face to face with the heavily fortified base of Afmadu! Artillery shelling and aerial bombing by the South African Air Force broke the morale of the defenders and the KAR Brigade entered Afmadu on the morning of the 11th of February. The entire garrison had fled to the bush for a trek to Juba which few were able to reach.

On the 14th of February, the 1st South African Brigade moved southeast from Afmadu to capture Gobwen on the banks of the Juba. The Gold Coast (Ghanaian) Brigade had taken Bulo Erillo the day before, in the face of heavy resistance. Both of these towns were on the banks of the Juba River which, at these points, was nearly 200 meters wide with heavy foritifications on the opposite side at Kismayu and ahead at Jelib.

The South Africans found no resistance at Kismayu. A Captain Frost in a South African Hurricane, in one afternoon, had shot down three Fiat fighters and three Caproni bombers. Fortunately, the South African Air Force had now complete command of the air. At the beginning, travel from Bure and Garussa was only by night. Even then, there had been heavy strafing and bombing by the Regia Aeronautica. Now, not a single enemy aircraft appeared as the South African Air Force had moved aggressively against the Aerodromes at Afmadu and Gobwen, destroying the Regia Aeronautica in the area.

Before the Italians had evacuated both of their military and civilian population at Kismayu, they had destroyed most of the military installations. The Somali population, however, gave the occupying forces an enthusiastic welcome, in spite of a heavy artillery barrage from across the river which had preceded the South African takeover.

It was a different situation at Bulo Erillo which was heavily fortified with tanks, troops, land mines and wire, behind which were artillery and machine gun emplacements. It was here for the first time that casualties were heavy. The attacking Ghanians were fearless under fire, although they lost many of their troops including most of the British officers. The final attack was at the point of the bayonet. In addition, the attacking troops were under heavy fire from across the river.

It took three days for the South African Engineers to construct two crossings of the Juba River — one at Kismayu, and the other some 40 kilometers upstream at Bulo Erillo. On the opposite side, both the 11th and 12th Divisions counted their losses and regrouped. Fortunately, they had captured supplies of food, fuel, water and ammunition — even armoured cars. Besides this, they had reached their objective five days ahead of their timetable. Mussolini had now lost his southern territory, most of which had been ceded to Italy after World War I for their part in the European struggle which took Kenya away from the Germans. The capture of Juba land for the British forces was to prove the most decisive action of the East Africa Campaign!

The Juba River was the only natural defence in all of Somaliland. Three days later, the capital and major port of Mogadishu was captured. The Italians had concentrated most of their Somaliland forces in the Juba area. Both the Italian military commanders and the government officials did not believe that the British could penetrate and overrun their defences. Again, their ability to withstand the pressure of attack was shown. Leadership was weak and general morale was low.

The advancing forces of the British now saw the road opening — well ahead of the dreaded rainy season.

The following quotation from the diary of a captured Italian soldier is indicative of the morale and conditions which prevailed amongst the Italians defenders:

The Evacuation of Kismayu from the Italian Diary of a Captured Italian Soldier

"Nervousness is spreading among the battery. We have heard that the Viceroy arrived at 2 o'clock last night and that it has been decided, after a council of war, to evacuate the town. We are all sorry to leave this place. The English have given us no trouble during three months of war. In fact, when their aeroplanes came to pay us a visit, the break in the monotony of our lives was pleasant, and we used to amuse ourselves by shooting at them being absolutely convinced, among other things, by our knowledge of mathematics, that only a miracle could lead to the destruction by anti-aircraft fire of an aeroplane travelling at 250 m.p.h. I say a miracle because our guns were rather too old, weighed down by 26 years of hard life, with no adequate sighting apparatus, and with a traverse useless against fast modern aircraft. During the 24 reconnaissance raids we have had, we have fired off our guns mainly to make a bit of noise and introduce a little variety into our dull existence in the bush.

At 4 in the afternoon we received the order to evacuate. At 10 o'clock in the evening a truck is sent to take our machine guns and ammunition. Our personnel are also to be sent to Jumbo. We load the lorry with 53,000 round and nine machine guns. I send the chief gunner and the other members of the crew with the guns, with strict orders not to abandon their weapons on any account. The rest of our personnel of about 50 are formed up and, at 11 o'clock, they leave for Jumbo. I stay with the battery with ten men. We are supposed to await orders for the destruction of the guns. Those who are going take their leave of us on the beach, and I then return with my ten men to the battery. I go back to my quarters, but as soon as I come in, I realise that the room has been ransacked. I visit the other quarters and find the same thing everywhere. The soldiers who have gone have taken advantage of my absence to steal or destroy everthing they can find. It has taken only a few minutes to produce the effect that Attila himself has passed this way."[7]

The Phantom Australian Division

When the attack on the Juba was in its final stages, the 1st South African Brigade was closing in on Mega. There was a gap of some 500 kilometres across the southeastern Ethiopia as it faced the Northern Frontier District of Kenya. The most northerly bases were at Wajir and El Wak on the Kenyan side, both firmly now in British hands. In this vast area, the Italians could have staged a dangerous counterattack from their bases on the upper Juba River, such as from Dolo and Lugh Ferrandi which was the home base of the 101 Italian Division. In this entire area, there was only one KAR Battalion and one troop of South African Armoured Cars jointly responsible for the security of the entire Northern Frontier District all the way to El Wak.

General Cunningham, in planning his strategy for the attack on the Juba area, devised a feint offence out of El Wak headed by a newly arrived 'PHANTOM DIVISION FROM AUSTRALIA'. Using a communication code which the Italians had been able to break, a series of communications were initiated to convince the Italian command in the Juba district of Somalialand that the opposing forces were even much larger than the already exaggerated estimate of the British forces at the beginning of the campaign at El Wak. The story is best told by the Captain (Acting as a Major General) who was chosen to head the Australian Division that didn't exist:

"The first I knew of what was afoot was when I

received brief orders at a rendezvous at Nanyuki appointing me, to my horror and amazement, the Commander of a Division consisting of three youthful Captains, acting Brigadiers, a number of wireless sets, a handful of British and African signallers, and sixty dummy light tanks made of canvas. The Commander of the tank 'Battalion' was a very gallant young Captain in the 8th Hussars, who was speechless with rage and shame at the degradation of his command.

The following day we made all speed for Wajir and contacted our scanty forces in that area. Their platoon outposts were rapidly converted into Brigade Headquarters by the addition of one of our wireless sets and a suitable quantity of dummy wireless traffic, and our dummy tanks were pushed, more in hope than in anger, under the nose of the enemy.

Division soon settled down to normal routine, and the Italians were offered messages by wireless to show that leave had been stopped, the supply of N.A.A.F.I. stores was unsatisfactory as usual, Sergeant Hucklebuery's wife had presented him, after an anxious few days, with a son and heir, and the G.O.C. was furious at the loss of his bedding through the carelessness of his A.D.C. All this, in addition to such messages a orders as would still further convince the Italians of our existence and intentions, should they have better knowledge of our cyphers than we hoped.

Meanwhile the Tank 'Battalion' Commander, who had been looking for someone on whom to work off his temper, had rounded up a number of local Somalis and terrorised them with tales of great battle impending, and, through inefficient blindfolding, allowed them a glimpse of our great concentration of armour. These badly scared informers fled to El Wak, where the Italians were reported to have a W/T set, and doubtless their stories lost nothing in the telling.

The first three days were uneventful, except for a little enemy air reconnaissance, which persistently refused to see what was offered. Our wireless traffic had, however, already been intercepted, as we discovered later, and the enemy was busy building up our order of battle.

13th February was our big day, when two Italian reconnaissance planes flew straight into our 'armoured force,' and from the rapidity with which they beat it for home, it was afterwards we discovered that General de Simone, the Italian Commander on the Juba, gave orders the following day for troop movements to counter our impending advance.

Emboldened by success, our meagre patrols pushed out and made contact with the enemy outposts, and the Brigade and Divisional Headquarters commenced their advance into Italian territory. The 101 Division opposing us eventually withdrew without being finally engaged, and the Commander claimed to have performed a magnificent military feat in stemming our advance.

The successful crossing of the Juba by the 11th and 12th (A) Divisions coincided with the arrival at Wajir of the remainder of the K.A.R. Brigade, to which 4 (A) Division handed over the further conduct of the battle, after a hectic but most exciting and highly entertaining fortnight. To carry the story to its conclusion, the existence of the Australian Division was maintained by propaganda and occasional indiscreet wireless messages. Prisoners and deserters stated it was common knowledge that we had an Australian Division in the Field, and, after the occupation, the Italian authorities in Addis enquired of us when the Australians would arrive; others insisted that we should take a firm step to keep the blood-thirsty New Zealanders in check.[8]

As far as it was known there was not a single Australian in the Southern Campaign. The ruse had worked well.

The Road North Divides — First To The Northeast

General Cunningham quickly became aware that he was facing a demoralized and confused enemy which was in no condition to counterattack. He even saw that Harer and Dire Dawa, still 1500 kilometers ahead to the north, and Negele, to the northwest, could both be reached before the onslaught of the heavy rains in the Ethiopian highlands. Receiving clearance from General Wavell, GOC in the African theatre, he divided his forces and immediately planned a two-pronged attack. The 12th African Division, inactive in the thrust as far as the Juba River, crossed the path of the successful and eager 11th Division at Jelib. It was headed by the Gold Coast (Ghanaian) Brigade and the 21st KAR Brigade and moved northward up the Juba valley. The fortified Bardera base was taken on February 26th. Leaving the Juba River valley, the Division veered to the northeast, and after a rapid two day 180 kilometre advance through the foothills of the 'outback', captured Iscia Bardoa two days later on the 28th of February. Three days later, on the 3rd of March, travelling a similar distance in a northwesterly direction, they captured Lugh Ferrandi on the Juba River, with only minimal resistance. On the 5th of March, the entire Division was inside Ethiopia at Dolo which proved more of a mopping up exercise than a battle.

The 12th Division now faced two extremely difficult problems. The first was the extended supply route from Jelib, which became longer and more difficult with each kilometer gained. The much needed supplies of food, ammunition and fuel were not always available on schedule. The second, and most crucial problem, was that they had now reached the Ethiopian highlands where the heavy rains had started in full force. Dry river beds were now raging torrents and trails became a muddy morasse making mechanized travel laborious and sometimes impossible. The reckless advance slowed down to a grinding and groaning pace. Most of the defending Italian military, both Italian and Banda units, had taken to the hills, becoming more of an elusive nuisance than a defending force. Yet, in spite of these seemingly insurmountable obstacles, slow but steady progress was made up the Juba Valley. These forces moved forward towards what proved to be the heaviest battle of the entire Southern Campaign.

Spectacular determination and bravery was the key to success as the Ghanaian and the KAR Brigades proved themselves, again and again, in a terrain and under conditions totally foreign to what they had known in their homeland. The Patriot forces and the general population gave assistance wherever possible.

Leaving the river valley, the advancing Division moved through the mountains towards Negele, the location of the major aerodrome of the Regia Aeronautica in the southern central part of Ethiopia. It took the entire month of March, with heavy slogging and numerous skirmishes, for the 12th African Division to reach Negele which surrendered without a struggle. The defenders withdrew northward towards the major base of Wadera. It was here, again, that the South African Air Force played a decisive role as they bombed and destroyed the air base, and in so doing, made progress easier for the ground troops who reached Negele in early April.

The heaviest fighting of the entire southern front was yet to come in a three week battle for Wadera. This was defended by two Italian Divisions with a forward defense line made up of five Colonial Brigades centered in the slopes of a great ravine dividing Negele from Wadera. The entire country seemed one great tangle, difficult to traverse, and difficult to fight in.

And Then To The North

In the meantime, the 11th Division had completed their 3,000 kilometer dash through the Somalilands, and eastern Ethiopia, to reach Addis Ababa before the battle of Wadera began. It is necessary now for us to retrace our steps down the length of the Juba River to Jelib and then to follow the grand thrust northward and westward to Addis Ababa. The glory of the most spectacular, lengthy and speedy advance in military history was left to the 11th African Division, which included the 1st and 2nd South African Brigades. They reached and captured the capital of Somaliland at Mogadishu in just three days, where a great amount of supplies were awaiting them. The haul included some

(From The Abyssian Campaigns, British War Office, London, His Majesty's Stationery Office.)

STORES OF A BEATEN ARMY. Checking Italian ammunition at Mogadishu. The haul so far was 500,000 square kilometers of territory, 30,000 prisoners, 1,500,000 litres of petrol, rations to feed 10,000 men for six months, weapons and stores of every kind in perfect condition.

30,000 prisoners, 1,500,000 litres of petrol, rations to feed 10,000 men for six months, weapons and stores of every kind in perfect condition.

It was a short six weeks after the patrols crossed the border at Liboi, and only two weeks after forcing the Juba Line, that the entire southern half of Somaliland was in British hands. The enemy had lost their last port on the Indian Ocean and there was hardly an organized enemy force surviving in this colony that

Italy had possessed for nearly 50 years. The 102nd Italian Division, and nearly the whole 101st Division, had now been destroyed. In addition to the 30,000 Italian prisoners taken, several thousands more had been killed or had fled in panic into the waterless bush, where many of them died. Many of them also came staggering back begging to be allowed to surrender. The words of Major General Godwin Austin to the 12th African Division under his Command, before the Battle Jelib, were so very true and deserve mention at this point:

"At last, after weary months of waiting, we have now been given in Mr. Winston Churchill's policy of 'tearing and continuing' — to tear Mussolini's much vaunted Roman Empire to tatters. The operations on which you are to be engaged will give you the chance of achieving very decisive results. If relentlessly conducted, there is likelihood of our starting the complete demoralization of the collapse of the Italian forces in East Africa. I do not disguise from you the fact that in these coming days, you will have to fight hard and live hard, but in you, I have the highest confidence. Fight fiercely, shoot low and quickly. If any enemy escape you, I hope very few will do so, let them be missionaries of terror whose tales to their comrades will unnerve them for their meeting with you when the time comes."[9]

(From The Abyssian Campaigns, British War Office, London, His Majesty's Stationery Office.)

The 30 ft. wide tarmac surface of "Strada Imperiale."

Trucks crossing a grassy plain.

END NOTES

[1] Kenneth Gandar Dower, **Abyssinian Patchwork** (London, Frederick Muller, 1949), pp. 38f.

[2] Ibid., p. 61.

[3] Ibid., pp. 90f.

[4] Ibid., p. 96.

[5] Ibid., pp. 102-7.

[6] British War Office, **The Abyssinian Campaigns** (London, His Majesty's Stationery Office, 1942), p. 77.

[7] Dower, **Abyssinian Patchwork**, p. 112.

[8] Ibid., pp. 202f.

[9] War Office, **The Abyssinian Campaigns**, p. 87.

THE EXTRAORDINARY ADVANCE THROUGH THE SOMALILANDS TO ADDIS ABABA

It is said that the goal of any offensive is not only to exhort pressure on the enemy, but also to sustain pressure. This goal is very seldom realized because of supply and administrative difficulties. In this case, however, the Italians had been routed on the Juba by an enemy which they had come to believe, through their Commander's propaganda, was decadant and not to be feared. Instead, the advancing British forces did not even give the Italians time to rally their forces or their morale as the race northward continued.

The British now had three ports on the Indian Ocean — Kismayu, Merke, and Mogadishu. Each of these ports had been sabotaged but not very efficiently as they were soon back in working order. In Mogadishu, there was unexpected assistance from the 200 officers and men of the British Mercantile Marine who had been held as prisoners for six months. Upon release, they immediately volunteered to assist in reconditioning the ports. In a matter of a few weeks, it was soon possible to land as many as 500 tons of supplies a day.

Until these shipping facilities were available, the handling of supplies had to be done through mechanical transport from Kenya. The roads were long enough already, but those through the desert between Natanu and the Juba Rivers were in no shape to bear continued heavy traffic. Here it was the South African Engineers who deserve praise as they bulldozed animal tracks into motor car roads and maintained and kept a road connection back into Kenya that was far superior to anything that they had found when they first came in.

The drive ahead began on the 1st of March with a Nigerian mobile column leading the way. This time they had a beautiful Italian hard surfaced highway, the Strada Imperiale, which was a road that was reasonably well completed, all the way from Mogodishu northward to Asmara, Eritrea, over a 3,000 kilometer route. Every 20 kilometres, they found a flamboyant kilometer post bearing the name of some celebrated general who had helped to create the empire, and nearly every five kilometers, there was an overturned Italian lorry bearing witness to the collapse of the work. The troops and their vehicles moved on through the undefended town of Bulo Burti and then on to the oasis of Belet Uen where they found tall palm trees providing shade even at mid day. They moved onwards to the Sciaglet Wells where thousands of goats and camels of the Somali tribesmen gather, again, without any resistance. It was here that the Strada Imperiale faded out and the roads grew rapidly worse, but the Nigerians never paused. They passed through a desert area, past a broken statute of Mussolini which had been bullet ridden by their advancing troops and continued to cross a sea of desert sand that lies beyond Degeh Bur, and finally on to the broad green plains on which Jijiga is located. It was a journey of nearly 1,200 kilometers and, in the last stages, there was little resistance apart from many Italian land mines. However, in spite of these obstacles, the Nigerians continued in hot pursuit.

The only real delay to the advancing troops was caused by the necessity of having to pause for a day or two to wait for supplies. In spite of this, the lead troops had averaged 80 kilometers a day. The 1,200 kilometer journey had taken only 17 days.

The next objective was to retake Somaliland.

The rapidity of the advance of the 11th Division, led by the Nigerians, caused the Italian high command to order the evacuation of British Somaliland. The 70th Italian Brigade began the withdrawal but on the 16th of March, a force from Aden, organized by Air Vice Marshall Reid, sailed into the Berbera Harbour and occupied the town with very little opposition. This surprise attack, plus the rapidity of the Nigerian thrust, resulted in the 70th Brigade being caught between the force that had taken Berbera and the Nigerians who had now turned towards Hargeisa, the capital town of British Somaliland, cutting off any hopes of retreat for the Italians.

They found themselves in a terrible situation. The commanding officer, General Bertello, had already left his troops, driving through to Dire Dawa a few hours before the British had arrived at Jijiga. He managed to escape into the Ethiopian hinterland where he was taken prisoner some weeks later. Nothing more has ever been heard of his Brigade. It simply melted away.

Berbera, the seaport of British Somaliland, is just 300 kilometers from Jijiga. For this reason, it was more satisfactory to use this port to supply the advancing army into Ethiopia. Without delay, the port and the route were opened up, a great feat of the type seldom seen in modern warfare.

The surrender of some 10,000 Italian troops in Somaliland, overseen by one tank and a truck convoy.

On the 20th of March, a small column of Nigerians occupied Tugwagale on the British Somaliland border. Two armoured cars, led by a chief engineer of the East African Forces, motored to Hargeisa to make contact with the troops that had landed at Berbera. There was great rejoicing in British Somaliland with the return of the British. The welcome given by the population indicated that the British had been very popular with the local Somalis, much more so than had the Italians.

With the collapse of the resistance in British Somaliland, the most next important objective ahead was Harer City and Dire Dawa which was the main base of the Regia Aeronautica.

On to Harer and Dire Dawa

Jijiga is the last town on the plains in the lee of the foothills that lead on to the plateau on which the city of Harer is located. From the start of the northward thrust, from Garussa and Bure in the northeast corner of the North Frontier District of Kenya and on into Italian Somaliland, the level terrain had made it possible to attack the enemy from either the right or left flanks as well as from the front. Fighting in the foothill country was much different. The road ahead passed through Marda Pass and the advancing troops knew that the Italian defenders would be hard to dislodge from their positions in the hills on either side of the highway — in fact there was no reason they could not have held back the advance for many weeks.

The hilltops had been mined, tunneled and wired on a six kilometer front. For three days, the Nigerians and the South African artillery paused on the Jijiga plain, eyeing and planning how best to advance. The direct assault was planned for 23rd of March. However, intelligence and patrol reports indicated that the Italians were planning a withdrawal and as a result, the attack was moved forward to 21st of March, just after noon. Four fortified hilltop defences guarded the Marda Pass, Observation Hill on the left, the two breasts of Marda and Camel Saddle Hill on the right. Supported by a heavy artillery barrage, the attack was led by the Nigerians who were under continuous fire for some five hours. In the frontal attack, they quickly took command of the first Marda Hill. Observation Hill was taken more easily when the South African artillery shells ignited a grass fire. This was followed by smoke shells, forcing the defending Italians out of their positions without a battle.

Casualties had, however, been heavy as artillery from both sides was accurate, and the final takeover of the two defending hills had been hand to hand struggle. Darkness gave time to gather the dead and the wounded and to plan for the next day. In spite of the cold at the higher levels, the attackers who wore only the clothing required in the desert heat used the respite of darkness to ready themselves for the early morning attack — an attack which did not take place because under the cover of darkness, the Italians had withdrawn. By noon, the road through the Marda pass had been cleared of mines and demolitions and the Nigerians and the South Africans were on their way through the beautiful hills, expecting to face heavy opposition at the Babile Gap and the Besdimo River.

Any determined defence should have been able to completely fend off an attack at any one of the three natural barriers. However, after the rapid advance of the attacking forces, the Italian morale was completely shattered.

The Babile Gap appeared even more formidable than the Marda Gap. The huge granite boulders and the precipitous walls which gave passage for the impressive Strada Imperiale appeared impregnable to any attack. It had been evident all through the East African Campaign that the Italians were not able to anticipate in advance the alternative routes open to the attackers, or to judge the speed of the advance. At the Babile Gap, two approaches were available to the attackers. One was the old road which had been used before the new highway had been built. This was the route of the attack by the South African Royal Natal Carbineers. This secondary attack diverted some of the strength of the Italian defenders the from well-placed positions which already had made the Nigerian advance on the main highway very difficult. A costly two day battle followed through road blocks, under heavy fire from the heights on both sides. However, facing the prospects of still another day of attack, on the third morning, the Nigerians and the South Africans both found, as they had at Marda Pass, that the enemy had withdrawn during the night — the Italians were gone.

The defence some 15 kilometers farther on at the Besidimo

River was also firm. The attackers, however, were able to approach from both flanks. Through most of the 27th of March, the fight for the last hurdle before the city of Harer saw the attackers with the support of the South African heavy artillery making slow progress. Finally, the forward troops effected a crossing of the river to take up new positions on the opposite side. Further action was not necessary, as a truck racing down from Harer city appeared on the opposite side with a huge white flag, indicating surrender and declaring Harer an open city, to take effect at 07:00 A.M. the next morning. This would have allowed General de Simon's forces to evacuate. Major General Wetherall's reply was simple, "Either you go back to the town while we continue our attack and fight for the town and take it victoriously or we will send you in an armoured car with the same infantry who will take over the town as surrendered by you".[1] In a few minutes, the armoured cars with the Italian envoy riding in the second vehicle followed by the first armoured car flying the white flag, entered the city of Harer. They received a tumultuous reception by the Ethiopian population and several battalians of the Italian Banda troops.

The booty captured at Harer included two batteries of 105 m.m. guns, the first to appear in the East African campaign.

The Fall of Dire Dawa

The South Africans took the lead from the Nigerians at Harer City, advancing to the important junction and military base of Dire Dawa. The first half of the road was across the beautiful 3,100 meter high plateau, while the second half was a 1,800 meter drop to Dire Dawa town, via a highway effectively closed by demolitions. There were two rivers also that had to be crossed. The defenders present at Dire Dawa estimated that the rebuilding of the blown out mountain sides and the bridges would stall the advancing forces for eight to ten days. Instead, it took just 36 hours. Working night and day, the 1st South African Brigade and the 54th East African Field Company, assisted by a back up Nigerian Regiment, cleared away the debris. The Italians made no significant attempt to defend themselves at Dire Dawa, with the exception of a bitter but short defence by two Italian companies at the approach to the town. It was two companies of the Transvaal Scottish infantry which entered Dire Dawa unopposed on 29th of March.

General Cunningham, officer commanding the Southern Front, paid tribute to the troops for their extraordinary advance,the fastest ever made in military history. Thirty-five thousand prisoners had been captured.he praised in a message he sent to the Ticons now in Dire Dawa:

"In thirty days, you have covered 1,700 kilometers, an average of 56 kilometers a day. The final 100 kilometers to Harer entailed an advance through the most difficult country in face of opposition from three strong positions, yet, the distance was covered in three and one half days. The Nigerian soldier, unaccustomed to cold and damp, fought his way from the hot and dusty bush to the wet, cold highlands of Ethiopia, where he maintained his cheerfulness and courage in spite of strange conditions and the strenous climbing operations made necessary by the terrain."[2]

Addis Ababa — Here We Come!

From Dire Dawa to Addis Ababa is 468 kilometers, across plains, over the deep Awash gorge and up 2000 meters to the Addis Ababa plateau. In effect, the advance proved to be no more difficult than any section experienced in the long journey from the Juba River to Jijiga. The morale of the attacking troops was at an all time high as they sensed victory was near. The air base at Dire Dawa was a great asset as the South African Air Force moved in after the ground troops had cleared the runways. Even the Djibouti-Addis Ababa railway proved to be an asset to the advancing troops.

Italian morale had been completely cracked. The inevitability of collapse was no longer limited to the colonial troops — even the Blackshirt battalions were in despair. At many defensive positions, the Italians surrendered rather than resisting. The masses of Italian prisoners offered important intelligence information to the attackers. The fall of Addis Ababa was now a foregone conclusion.

There are two roads west from Dire Dawa towards Addis Ababa. The first is the northern one to Miesso, across the plains parallel to the railway. The southern route is through the foothills. The retreating Italians followed both. The South Africans gave them no respite. In three days, the Duke of Edinburgh's Own Rifles had occupied Asba Tafari on the southern road. On the northern route, the rest of the South African Brigade reached Miesso and the 22nd East African Brigade reached the Awash River gorge in the same three days. The rail bridge across this last major natural obstacle before Addis Ababa had been blown up by the Italians the night before. The highway bridge had also been destroyed. It was a logical place for a major defensive action and, in this case, a number of machine gun posts were located on the far side. The impetuous South Africans attacked frontally, as well as on two flanks, fording the river in the space left by the broken span now down in the river. It took them just one afternoon and one night to complete the task. By the end of the day, the full Brigade was on the other side in the town of Awash. Fifty kilometers beyond, they stopped, waiting to see what might happen as they approached the capital city.

As the troops rested, a convoy of Italian motor vehicles appeared, escorted by an armoured car flying a huge white flag. The escort included a squad of military police on motorcycles. The request was to meet Brigadier Fowkes and ask for an immediate takeover of the city. There was fear that there would be a major reprisal mutiny in the city and it was necessary to protect the civilian population. The Brigade immediately moved on to be met at Nazret by masses of jubilant Ethiopians, waving white flags.

The Italian military, based at Nazret, had left on the side roads to the west and to the south. Gunfire could be heard coming from both directions and a company was assigned to follow in pursuit. The South African Air Force had been active during these days in strafing and bombing and thus the roadway to Nazret was strewn with burnt out military and civilian vehicles.

The Surrender of Addis Ababa

The situation was unusual in the extreme. Never in the annals of modern warfare had there been anything like it. Here a liberating army was being escorted into the capital city by the defending army at the request of the civil authorities! Fifteen kilometers away, at the suburban town of Akaki, the Chief of the Addis Ababa police force was waiting to formally surrender the city. It was decided to delay that surrender until the next day allowing for a full representative force to share the occupation honours and the arrival of the Division Commander. Major General Wetherall arrived the next morning to lead the entrance into the city and to accept the official handover.

The next day turned out to be an extraordinary climax in this extraordinary war. In the first place, Addis Ababa was declared an open city. Secondly, the streets were lined by thousands of cheering Ethiopians — even Italian civilians were interspersed in the throngs, all giving friendly Italian salutes. Thirdly, there was no trace of hostility even on the faces of the senior Italian officers — more often they showed amazement rather than anger. There were no tanks present. The oncoming military came as infantrymen, riding in trucks or on foot.

At the actual ceremony, there was a Fascist Guard of Honour to receive the three senior British Officers and their senior staff, all arriving in Italian civilian cars at the Viceroy's palace. The senior officers were Major General Wetherall, commanding the 11th African Division, Brigadier Pienaar, commander of the South African Brigade which had captured the Juba River territory and Dire Dawa, and Brigadier Fowkes, commander of the 22nd East African Brigade, which had captured Afmadu, Brava, Merke, Jijiga, Harer and had now led the way from the Awash. General Mambrini, the military Governor of the capital city, in full Fascist uniform and supported by his senior officers, gave the official surrender. One armoured car carrying a homemade Union Jack appeared on the scene. The Italian flag was lowered from a 12 meter flagstaff and the Union Jack was raised as the armoured car withdrew to the shade of a mimosa tree.

The authorities withdrew into the palace to sign the formal documents. Upon completion, they all came out to receive a formal salute from a Fascist Honour Guard. It had all been done with typical British promptness, efficiency and courtesy.

Only one error was made in the whole proceedings and that revealed the true chivalry and manners of the victors. The Italian flag had been lowered ahead of time and the Union Jack mounted. General Wetherall ordered the flag reflown so it could be lowered at the correct time, after the signing of the surrender, with a full salute, which was repeated as the Union Jack was raised in its place. An Ethiopian flag appeared almost simultaneously, hoisted above what had been the Emperor's Palace and which now waited for his return.

The situation in Addis Ababa was most unique. It had been a beleaguered city, ringed by 53 concrete blockhouses, joined together by heavy strands of barbed wire fences. Patriots had repeatedly attempted to force entrance to the city and gunfire could be heard from the perimeters almost every night through the years of the Italian occupation. Every male citizen of Addis Ababa was secretly armed. Ten thousand soldiers and police guarded the city from inside the fence. Each blockhouse was manned by 30 to 40 Italian soldiers and armed with five or six machine guns.

The new occupying conquerors were much fewer in number than the defending Italians. That customary scene had now been replaced by masses of people, all joyous, friendly and peaceful, as Ethiopians and Italians, mixed with the South Africans, Kenyan, Nigerian and British soldiers. The Ethiopians showed remarkable restraint towards their previous masters. When a Company of KAR troops reached the airport, they found the wreckage of thirty-two burned out military aircraft strewn about the airport confines. Just two days before, South African airplanes operating out of Dire Dawa had completed this raid. Now they were met by more than 1,000 Italian soldiers and airmen, all waiting in trucks for someone to receive their surrender.

Countless other Italian soldiers shed their uniforms to become instant civilians. Even patriot forces from the surrounding areas infiltrated into the city to be rejoined with families and friends or to mingle with the crowds. Food supplies were ample for the civilian populace as the marketplaces scarcely missed a day.

The captured booty of war at Addis Ababa was tremendous,

Giorgis Cathedral, Addis Ababa

far exceeding that taken at Mogadishu, the capital of Somaliland. It included more than 2,250,000 litres of gasoline and 1,350,000 litres of diesel fuel. There was sufficient military supplies to feed and clothe an army of 10,000 for more than a year. The collection of small arms rifles and handguns numbered into the tens of thousands. Signal equipment and medical supplies were valued into the millions of dollars.

More than these physical gains, the liberation of Addis Ababa was welcomed by the entire Allied and free world. The consciences of British, American, Commonwealth and European nations still burned with a sense of guilt and shame at the negative response of the League of Nations in the 1936 takeover. The two leading members of the League of Nations commission on the Ethiopian/Italian crises, Sir Samuel Hoare of Britain and M. Laval, had decided that no action would be taken which would risk war with Italy. Sir Samuel Hoare made this announcement on the 11th of September to the League

Assembly. This betrayed Ethiopia and gave the green light for Italy's takeover of the country. The result was the loss of a half a million Ethiopian lives at the hands of the Fascist. The nation was now, six years and eight months later, about to be freed. BUT THE WAR WAS NOT YET OVER.

END NOTES

[1] British War Office, **The Abysinnian Campaigns**(London, His Majesty's Stationery Office, 1942), p. 97.

[2] Ibid., p. 98.

THE TAKEOVER
FROM THE WEST

The Triumverate — Sandford, Wingate and Haile Selassie
The infiltration and conquest of western Ethiopia focuses
on three men. One was a British farmer turned military; the
second was the Ethiopian Emperor returning from exile; the
third was an Indian born British career officer. The story of the
101 Mission and the Gideon Force is a book in itself. Because
this front was timed and integrated with the northern front
through Eritrea and the southern fronts from the northwest
district of Kenya through Sidamo and the Somalilands, it was
part of an overall strategy. These fronts cannot be separated,
but the climax of the successful campaign came on May 5, 1942
when the three main actors and their troops, from the western
thrust, entered Addis Ababa to restore the Emperor to his
rightful throne. Not that this was the end of the war in East
Africa, but what had to follow was, in reality, anticlimactic.

Colonel (later Brigadier) D. A. Sandford led the 101 Mission
from the Sudan, inflitrated the western province of Gojam and
united the Patriot elements who prepared the way for the
Gideon force and the return of the Emperor to Addis Ababa. As
a young man of 30, he had come to Ethiopia in 1913 to establish
a modern farm. He returned to Britian to serve in the British
Army as an Artillery Officer during World War I, coming back
to Ethiopia after the war to resume his pioneer farming
operations. He and his wife, Christine, became close friends of
the Emperor and the Government. In 1936, they were expelled
from Ethiopia by the Fascist rulers. In the interval, he became a
trusted authority on Ethiopia, its culture, geography and
peoples. He had learned to speak the language of the Court and
Government, the Amharic language. In 1940, he was selected by

the British Government, at the suggestion of the Emperor, to lead the 101 Mission with the rank of Colonel.

Sandford, then 58 years old, was respected by the Ethiopians and was affectionately known as 'Fikre Mariam' which in the Ethiopian language means the 'Love of Mary.' To his troops and the Italian military, he became known as the 'uncapturable Englishman.' As the Emperor entered the capital city, the Emperor appointed Sandford military and political advisor to the re-established government. Later, when the government had been re-established, he returned to his beloved farm and lived there for the rest of his life in retirement.

The second actor in the Western campaign was Haile Selassie I, Lion of Judah and Emperor of Ethiopia. In 1930, he was declared Emperor with the name of Haile of Selassie I, King of Kings of Ethiopia. Exactly one year later, Ethiopia had its first constitution which was intended to set the basis for the implementation of a democratic government.

He established diplomatic connections with most of the major countries of the world. He brought Ethiopia in as a full member of the League of Nations and first drew attention there in 1925 when he declared that the practice of slavery would be abolished. However, as progress moved forward, Italy initiated a long series of border incidents which came to full military action in the 1934 attack at Wel Wel, some 100 kilometers inside Ethiopia. As briefly mentioned in Chapter 2, this confrontation came before the League of Nations arbitration commission, formed on September 4, 1935. As a committee of five, it was charged to examine the crisis situation. However, France and Britain reneged on its support of the Commission and Italy refused to recognize it. Ethiopia had already agreed to abide by the findings of the Commission. One month later, on the 3rd of October, Italian troops invaded Ethiopia simultaneously from Eritrea and Somaliland. Haile Selassie appealed directly to the League of Nations in 1936. When there was no possibility of League support for sanctions, his final words were,

"We now demand that the League of Nations should continue its efforts in order to ensure respect for the Covenant, and that it should decide not to recognize territorial extensions, or the exercise of an assumed sovereignty, resulting from an illegal recourse to armed force and from numerous other violations of international agreements." [1]

On the 30th of June, in his final message to the League, he closed with the statement, "God and history will remember your judgement." History and God did not forget!

Orde Charles Wingate, unorthodox in his behaviour and strategy but brilliant in mind and speech, was dedicated to suffering people whom he came to love and who, in turn, made him their hero. In 1940, he was selected by General Wavell, Commander in Chief of the African/Middle East Theatre to lead the military force into Ethiopia from the west. He was at the time a Major, but through a series of rapid promotions, he entered Addis Ababa, less than a year later, as a Brigadier. Wingate named his troops the Gideon Force as they were outnumbered by at least fifteen to one in manpower and more than that in firepower.

Wingate had mastered the art of Guerilla Warfare, using harassment, hit and run tactics, infiltration and ambush. His small, but courageous force, made up basically of Ethiopians and Sudanese, led by British officers, pestered and gave the Italians no rest or respite, and finally broke their nerve so that in the final battles, the enemy collapsed.

Wingate became a close friend and confidant of the Emperor as he commanded the loyalty of all the troops serving under him. Sandford did not always agree with Wingate, but the two men were equally courageous, daring and wise in their judgment. Their common abilities and instincts kept them close together as they honed their mutual skills of guerilla tactics to a fine cutting edge.

The strain of the Gojam Campaign took a heavy toll on Wingate's health, but after a troubled six months of recuperation in Cairo, he was called again by Wavell, now a Field Marshall, to take full command of the guerilla campaign against the Japanese in Burma.

Sandford, Haile Selassie and Wingate became an inseperable triumvirate as they fought for the downfall of Mussolini's East

Colonel Orde Wingate in the Gojam Offensive

African Empire and the restoration of Haile Selassie to his throne.

The preliminary plan of action for a military thrust into Ethiopia and the activation of the patriot causes in the central western part of the country was conceived even before Italy declared war on Britain. The old province of Gojam, which bordered the Sudan on the west, Lake Tana on the north, and Addis Ababa on the east, was an area where Patriot activity had been kept alive right from the formal takeover of Ethiopia by Fascist Italy on May 9, 1936. Revolt against the Italians simmered through 1937, 1938 and 1939 under the leadership of patriot warriors such as Ras Abeba Aregai and Dejazmatch

Gerassu Dukai. There were also those elements within the country such as those led by Ras Hailu who cooperated with the Italians and acted as the puppet leaders of this part of Ethiopia.

The Emperor had managed to keep in touch by letters and by occasional messengers with the Patriots who were disappointed that Italy was not directly in the war at the beginning of August and September, 1939. They were extremely frustrated and discouraged when Hitler's Nazis overran France in 1940.

During the exile, the roots of a Government had been formed in London led by a group of younger Ethiopians who formed a committee which they called the 'Union and Collaboration.' Some of these younger men had been at Geneva with the Emperor, others had been in Britain and France as students, and still others had filtered out of Ethiopia through the Sudan Frontier. At the same time, he maintained contact with the survivors of the Italian occupation in the country who were sustaining guerilla activity. It had been a bitter blow to the Emperor when his own son-in-law, Ras Desta, was murdered at a village near Butajira, following a formal agreement of surrender in the southeast of the country. It was at a time when armed resistance was brought to a futile halt in the southern east of the country and in the central north where Ras Imersa's armies were forced to surrender.

One of the first direct contacts with the Patriots came in the fall of 1938 when the Emperor sent one of his trusted young men into the Gojam, travelling through Khartoum, to meet with the leaders of the Patriot forces. He returned to London in the early months of 1939 to report that the fires of revolt were smoldering, waiting to be fanned into flames. He had travelled openly, dressed in an officer's uniform. His valuable report was delivered directly to the British Middle East Headquarters in Cairo as he returned to Britain. This was actually the very beginning of the strategy used by General Platt who was later appointed as the officer commanding the East African Campaign based in Khartoum.

In the early months of 1940, General Platt appointed Major Cheeseman to be the special Intelligence Officer for Ethiopia and Colonel Sandford to lead a direct mission into the Gojam, later to be known as the 101 Mission. Both of these men were familiar with the people and the terrain of western Ethiopia and were respected by the Patriots.

So definite were the contacts with Ethiopian Patriots that on the very day that Mussolini declared war on Britain, General Platt sent a message to eleven of the Patriot chiefs in the Gojam, Armachabo, Wolkait, and Gonder areas. The message was sent in the name of the United Kingdom's Government and read as follows:

> "Peace be unto you. England and Italy are now at war. We have decided to help you in every way possible to destroy the common enemy. If you are in need of rifles, ammunition, food, or clothing, send as many men and animals as you can spare to the place which our messenger will tell you. We can help you with your requirements. Also it would be a good plan to send your personal representative to consult with us and to arrange the best means of attacking the common enemy." [2]

The message was sent in sealed envelopes to the District Commissioner at Gedaref where they were held until the night of the 10th of June following Mussolini's declaration of war, when the seals were broken and sent by messenger to the eleven Patriot Chiefs inside Ethiopia.

The Emperor's personal representative to the 101 Mission was Azazh Kebada, who later became the Afa Negus or the Lord Chief Justice in the new Ethiopian Government. In addition, a call went out to exiled Ethiopian young men who were living throughout the Middle East and to others within the country who were able to find their way out across the frontier. The plan was to train a Frontier Battalion under the command of British officers. Even before the declaration of war, five depots of arms, food and Maria Theresa dollars had been established on the frontier under the guards of the early elements of the Frontier Battalion, for distribution to the Patriot Forces across the frontier. The first of the Patriot Chief to use the weapons received at Gedaref was the one-eyed guerilla Chieftan, Gerazmatch Werku, who almost immediately wiped out an

Italian patrol working out from the fort at Kwara. There is no doubt that the Italian officials were now becoming increasingly nervous about the unrest amongst the Ethiopians and the mounting guerilla activity. In all fronts, the opposition of the Patriot forces was to prove a significant factor in victory.

In the early planning of this strategy, Emperor Haile Selassie, on the 3rd of July, appeared in the Sudan at Wade Halfa, without previous warning to General Platt. Colonel Sandford was immediately dispatched to escort the Emperor to Khartoum. In the meantime, arrangements for the Emperor's accommodation were made. In Khartoum, he was met by General Platt and the senior government officials, as well as by a number of Ethiopian leaders such as venerable Ras Kassa and the Itchegi, the senior Ethiopian Bishop in the Coptic Church. They both had travelled to Khartoum from Palestine. Meanwhile, the answers to the eleven letters to the Patriot Chiefs in the Gojam and Begemder were arriving in Khartoum. Many of the Chiefs went themselves, accompanied by units of their own Patriot soldiers, and equipped with the arms they had collected from the Frontier Battalions. After giving their reports to the Emperor, they returned home with the message that they had met Jan Hoy (His Imperial Majesty), that he was still alive and would soon be returning to their midst. The Italians had reported through the years of their occupation that the Emperor had died in exile.

In the meantime, large numbers of Ethiopians, anxious to fight for the liberation of their country, continued to arrive in Khartoum. A camp was set up at Shoa, which was easily accessible from Khartoum. An officer's training school was established. These trainees were supplemented by the arrival of a Battalion of Ethiopian soldiers who had already been trained in Kenya where they had been part of the two Divisions of Ethiopian Irregulars. Out of these recruits came the 2nd Ethiopian Battalion which was to become a vital part of Colonel Wingate's "Gideon" force.

During the months of June and July, the 101 Mission was readied for action. There had been a number of unexpected delays, the major one being that the Emperor himself wanted to be part of the Mission from the beginning. He was finally convinced that this was impractical, dangerous and premature. Instead, Azazh Kebada was selected as the Emperor's personal representative to accompany Colonel Sandford. His appointment proved to be an excellent addition to Sandford's miniscule force consisting of five British and five Ethiopian officers, a small mule caravan carrying two wireless sets, money, clothing and food supplies for a month, as well as letters addressed to the various leaders of the Patriots.

On the evening of the 12th of August, the 101 Mission slipped across the frontier and quickly disappeared from view in the tall grass and brush. They were not heard from for three weeks because of the slow and dangerous journey they were making into the highlands. One British officer was captured by an Italian patrol and was never heard of again. The medical officer was forced to turn back because of the shortage of mules caused by the fatal mule fever. Three weeks later, the first wireless messages was received in Khartoum from Col. Sandford to the effect that he had established headquarters at Sekela, due south of Lake Tana in the heart of the Gojam highlands. He reported that he had met with many of the Gojam chiefs, such as Dezmatch Negash and Dejazmatch Mangasha Jembari, all of whom had promised full cooperation. Sandford asked for and received ammunition and supplies, dropped by the RAF planes based in Khartoum at his Sekela headquarters. By keeping away from the roads and Italian fortifications, he had avoided direct clashes with the Italian Patrols, although they had narrowly avoided capture, on several occasions. Later, it was learned that Sandford, in a fusilade of rifles and machine gun fire, had narrowly escaped being taken prisoner and death. He hid in a cave within earshot of the Italian patrols who searched vainly for the "uncapturable" Sandford, as the Italians came to call him.

In mid September, Negash and Mangasha, along with minor chiefs and an entourage of two hundred soldiers, under the command of Shialeka (Major) Mesfin Sleshi, who was one of the outstanding Patriot guerilla commanders, reached Gedaref. Here, the entourage was met by the Emperor who was flown in from Khartoum. There was a great celebration in this first meeting of the Emperor with the Patriot leaders. On the 27th of

September, the Feast of Maskal (Feast of the Cross of the Coptic Church) was celebrated in Khartoum with several thousand Ethiopians present. These meetings proved to be of great propaganda value in a positive way for the Patriots and of great concern for the Italians who were now strengthening their forces in the Gojam with fresh units drawn from Addis Ababa.

The Italians, nervous about the growing strength of the Patriots and the presence of the 101 Mission in their territory, countered with a heavy propaganda campaign, using leaflets dropped from aircraft in the marketplaces. Their propaganda containing a forged signature of the Emperor, announced that the Dejazmatch Mengasha Jembari had been appointed as Governor of all Gojam in opposition to Ras Hailu, the puppet governor in the Italian Empire. This false announcement aroused tribal jealousies and it was only thwarted by Colonel Sandford and Azazh Kabada who convinced the Patriot population that it was propaganda forged by the Italians, the mutual enemy.

During October and November, the RAF, based in Khartoum, began a series of bombing raids on the Gojam Italian military centres of Dangla, Bure, Bahir Dar and Debre Markos. This, combined with the 101 Mission ambushes and raids, caused increasing anxiety for the Italians. General Nasi, who held the position of Vice Govenor-General of the East African Empire stationed in Addis Ababa was placed in command of the military post in Gonder, the capital of the Italian Amara province. He was the outstanding senior Italian in his ability to hold the confidence of the Ethiopians. This large military force, with sizeable detachments in all of the surrounding towns, was unable to capture or destroy the 101 Mission menace or to suppress the growing hostility of the general population. In fact, four Italian Brigades were held paralyzed in the Gojam area alone by the threat of the 101 Mission with their Patriots.

On the 28th of October, Anthony Eden, Churchill's Foreign Minister, arrived in Cairo. After consultations with General Wavell, he moved on to Khartoum for further discussions with General Platt. The result of these visits came quickly. General Platt was promised reinforcements in the form of the 5th Indian Division and several additional RAF Squadrons. The attack plan was to proceed from the north and the south simultaneously. Wingate's force with Haile Selassie was also to move in from the west to join up with Col. Sandford. Eden, who had great respect for the Emperor, met with him and informed him that zero hour was finally approaching.

On the 20th of November, a vintage RAF Vincent aircraft landed on a backwoods airstrip near Sekela, which Sandford and his men had prepared. The lone occupant was Colonel Wingate who came to meet Sandford. He brought word that the time was now ripe for a frontal invasion of the area. It was to be made up of a mixed Sudanese/Ethiopian force, travelling with a huge camel train carrying ammunition and supplies adequate to break the Italian strongholds of Dangla, Bure and Debre Markos. A first base would be established at Belaya, which was already occupied by the Patriot Chief Tafarra Belaya. An airstrip was to be built at this point and the Emperor would join Wingate's forces. This was later changed as the building of the airport was not successful and the Emperor came instead with the ground troops. The fighting spearhead of the attack was to be the No. 4 Patrol Company of the Sudanese Frontier Battalion which would first proceed up the Blue Nile River from Roseirses.

That same evening, Wingate returned to Khartoum. The pioneer work of the 101 Mission was now nearing completion.

Within ten weeks of Eden's visit with Wavell, Platt, and Haile Selassie, all was ready. On the 17th of December, the attack from the west moved into action. There were no roads, no bridges from Roseirses or from Umidla to the frontier, nor was there any adequate water supply. The 150 kilometers from the frontier to Belaya were first attempted by a motorized transport column, planning to travel at least to the foothills. This proved impossible after a month long attempt. The Emperor planned to leave Umidla on the 19th of January. On the previous day, General Platt's army had crossed the frontier at Kassala. General Platt's forces moved into Somaliland on the 24th of January. Haile Selassie crossed the frontier on the 20th of January. This significant occasion was celebrated by the raising of the Ethiopian flag on Ethiopian soil for the first time in nearly five years. It was accompanied by a proclamation by the Emperor:

"A new era has arrived when all will be able to serve their beloved Ethiopia in their different spheres with greater zeal and surer strength. Gracious God who has turned His merciful face does so on each one of us. Therefore we now forgive those of you who have worked against the interest of your Emperor and your country, whether you worked from force, or from your own free choice: under Italian control, or whether you worked from outside Italian control.

I reason with you to receive with love and to care for those Italians who fall into the hands of Ethiopian warriors, whether they come armed or unarmed. Do not mete to them according to the wrongs which they have committed against our people. Show that you are soldiers of honour with human hearts. Especially do I ask you to guard and respect the lives of children, women, and the aged."
3

After repeated attempts through the trackless bush, it was decided to abandon the motorized vehicles and to resort entirely to a camel train. The Emperor was accompanied by nearly 2000 men, made up of the Frontier Battalion, and working in harmony with the Patriot forces. The first base to be established at Belaya was a high mountain halfway point between the frontier and the Gojam escarpment. The road up proved an impasse for motorized vehicles, and even the Emperor's own vehicle overturned with him in it. He, with his senior men, often worked with the troops to carry rocks and brush in an effort make the way passable. Finally, the decision was to resort entirely to camels. A huge camel train was made up of 15,000 animals. All of these animals were expected to be sacrificed along the way as there was no way of feeding them or returning them. They were driven without mercy. Halfway to Belaya, the original force with the Emperor was joined by the Sudanese Frontier Battalion, under Colonel Boustad. They had made easier progress for the first part of their journey, as they had travelled up the Blue Nile. They led the way into Belaya, on the 6th of February, to be met by Tafarra Belaya and Colonel

Sandford who had walked some 100 kilometers from his base at Sekela. He arrived without proper shoes, as his original boots had worn out.

The presence of the Emperor at Belaya became a magnet for the Ethiopian population and for the Patriot forces. From all sides, the populace of the area came to meet him in the mountain cave which served as his 'field' residence. Any doubts about his popularity or his ability to command the loyalty of the Patriots was cast aside by the tumultous welcome at Belaya.

The 101 Mission joins The Gideons

It was at Belaya that the 101 Mission completed its mission. As Col. Sandford and his guerilla forces joined with those of Wingate, the combined forces became known as the Gideon Force. The military attack was under the command of Col. Wingate, as Col. Sandford, now promoted to a Brigadier, became the political and military advisor to the Emperor. It was essential as the troops moved forward into the Gojam territory that some form of stable administration take over the occupied territory. This was not an easy task and Sandford remained close to the Emperor to advise in this regard.

Zeleka Birru, who was the important chief of the Matakal area of the Gojam escarpment, submitted to the Emperor with his full force Patriot warriors. Wingate and Boustead left Belaya with a force of 600 men and 4 pieces of mortar artillery. Supplies were also now being dropped to them by the RAF. Their first major test came at Injabara. The fort was taken without difficulty as the Italian defenders had fled a few days before. Injabara was a vital point as it was on the road built by the Italians coming south from Bahar Dar Giorgis through Dangla and Injabara and on to Bure, Dembacha, Debre Markos and finally to Addis Ababa. At Injabara, a company of Sudanese Patriot forces moved northward to take Dangla unopposed. Bahir Dar, on the shores of Lake Tana, had now become a major base for the Italians. Because of their few soldiers, the single company of Sudanese were able to blockade any counterattack or any road escape until late in May, but were unable to take Bahir Dar until Gonder on the north side of the Lake was taken by General Platt's troops coming south from

Tigray.

Wingate's main force now moved quickly down the road to Bure. They marched at night in single file with 700 camels and 200 horses and mules as they had no air support. The RAF was heavily involved in the fighting at Keren. The column was 6 kilometers long and received a rousing welcome from each village along the way. An automobile and several trucks had been taken from the Italians and messages were sent back to the Emperor and Sandford to come forward immediately to Belaya to meet the motorized transport waiting for them west of Injabara.

The commanding officer at Bure was a Colonel Natale who had more than 5000 troops in a well fortified position, with artillery, cavalry and heavy machine guns. His Intelligence reports told him that a huge force was approaching. Little did he know that Wingate's Gideon force now counted 450 men with four mortars. On the 27th of February, Wingate engaged the outer forts of Bure with the four mortars and two platoons. A cavalry counterattack was easily repulsed. The main Fort was harassed each night by successive single platoons. The entire defending garrison evacuated Bure on the morning of the third day. The terrier-like attacks of the Frontier Battalion took the eastern Bure forts the same day.

An interesting side light of the guerilla attacks on Bure included two older ladies who slipped into the town on the second night to open the gates of the cattle enclosures, driving the entire cattle herd into the arms of the waiting Patriots.

The Emperor, following in the wake of the advancing troops, was using several captured Italian vehicles. He moved quickly on to Bure in follow up of Wingate's victory. Here, he established his next headquarters. Again, the entire population gave instant support and welcome to the Emperor who was occupied from morning until after nightfall in meeting with the local area chiefs in planning an occupying administration. The Emperor dispatched Ras Biru, with his Patriot forces, to engage the Italian Fort at Debre Tabor to the north and east of Lake Tana. Only the outposts at Bahir Dar and Mota remained in Italian hands. The attack on Debre Markos was made by the Sudanese Frontier Battalion consisting of 300 men.

The Gideon Force did not rest. Boustead's Frontier Battalion of 300 men followed close on the heels of the retreating Italian forces under Colonel Natale. At this point, if there could have been any strong air support mounted, the entire Italian Gojam force would have been liquidated in short order. However, the RAF were not available, due to the extremely critical position facing General Platt's forces in their attack on Keren.

In guerilla fashion, the 2nd Ethiopian Battalion moved through a short cut to establish a road block in a dry river bed just west of Dembacha. Here they were nearly overrun by the retreating Italian horde and the small force was not able to stop the retreat. Finally, they hid by the roadside to watch the retreat move by. Completely demoralized, Col. Natale abandoned Dembacha on the 8th of March and Fort Emmanuel two days later. This left the entire Gojam army of Italians concentrated in Debre Markos, numbering more than 12,000 men under the command of a Colonel Maraventano.

The attacking Sudanese employed the organized guerilla tactics of which Wingate was an acknowledged expert. At night, they sniped at the enemy's campfires, from close range with light automatics. They rested in the daytime, then attacked with platoon or company strength, only to withdraw and attack again the next night. As the small guerilla force neared Debre Markos, they bombarded the enemy positions and forts with mortar fire. The main force of the Italians now withdrew across the Blue Nile, leaving many deserters behind. On the 4th of April, two days before General Cunningham's troops entered Addis Ababa, Emperor Haile Selassie and Brigadier Sandford, entered Debre Markos to establish their Gojam headquarters. It was here that Ras Hailu, the betrayer of the Gojam, bowed to the ground, pledging allegience to the Emperor. The 70 year old man was graceful, with his chest bemedaled with Ethiopian and Italian decorations. Again, Haile Selassie forgave him and accepted his support for the inevitable victory. The Emperor kept Ras Hailu "close" to him until his death!

Colonel Maraventano escaped with only half of his Gojam forces, across the Blue Nile and moved northward towards Dese. On the 6th of April, Addis Ababa had capitulated. A few days later, Dese had fallen, so Maraventano moved to the northwest, hoping to reach Debre Tabor instead of Dese. There were 100 men of the Frontier Battalion and 60 men of the 2nd Ethiopian Battalion, supported by 2000 Patriots under Ras Kassa, who pursued him and pinned him down at Agibar with spirited attack through a day and night, until Maraventano put up the white flag for the biggest haul of the Gideon force. 7,000 infantrymen surrendered, 120 light machine guns, 50 heavy machine guns, seven mountain artillery, two mortars, 15,000 mules, 300 horses and 700 civilian officials were taken by this Gideon force of less than 200 men, carrying three Bren guns. While the Patriot forces jeered and cheered the surrendering Italians, Wingate, at this point, earned a bar to his D.S.O.

In the meantime, Mota, to the north, remained the single military garrison not taken. Three hundred men of the Frontier Battalion moved to take this fort which was located on a 4,000 meter high plateau. Two platoons, made up of 60 men, completed the job as the rest of the troops were recalled to join the forces in pursuit of the remnants from Debre Markos. The British Lieutenant in charge of these two Ethiopian platoons, dressed himself as a major to receive the surrender of the 400 defenders.

"Gideon" had now done its work and had done it well. With some help from the RAF and a friendly countryside, the outnumbered Sudanese and Ethiopian Irregulars, supported by the Patriot forces, had defeated the Fascist Goliath. They had pestered the Italians, giving no chance for rest or sleep, forcing them in the end to go on to an ignominious defeat. Too late, the Italians had come to understand the strategy and tactics of a guerilla warfare, perfected by Col. Wingate.

An aftermath of the Campaign, which left the bones of more than 14,000 camels marking the 600 kilometer route of the Gideon force from the Sudan frontier, was the slaughter of the last 50 of the camel train on the approach to Addis Ababa. There had been no way to send any of the camels back to the Sudan, and there was no further need of them. However, without the camels, the Gideon force would never have accomplished its objective.

The Emperor, with Sandford and Wingate, now prepared for the victorious entrance to Addis Ababa. The transportation problem had suddenly been solved with the takeover of Debre Markos and the late arrival of a fleet of new American trucks which had been manhandled up from the Sudan. The engineering for this feat was spectacular and, in some places, the support follow up for the Gideon forces literally carried the vehicles through the impossible terrain. Likewise, the supplies for both the Gideon troops and the Patriots were now in abundance. In Debre Markos, as in Injabara, Bure and in Dembacha, Italian supplies were found in great quantity, much in excess of the needs of the Gideon force. All that was left was the grand entry into the capital.

The Emperor Arrives Home

The gates of Addis Ababa were open wide to receive the returning Emperor. It was indeed a moving scene. Driving down from the Blue Nile Gorge at Debre Markos, the Entotto Hills surrounding the city of Addis Ababa were visible from 100 kilometers. Rising to a height of 3,000 meters, these hills obscured any trace of the capital city except from the top of the hills. A halt was called at Fiche northwest of Addis Ababa in order to make arrangements for the formal entry into the city. This pause allowed for a visit to the ancient monastery of Debre Libanos where a remembrance ceremony was held for the treacherous shooting of two of Ras Kassa's sons-in-law and the execution of 200 monks who had been charged with concealing rifles and sheltering the Patriots.

Finally, the last stop in their approach to the city was at the Church of St. Mary, at the summit of the Entotto Hills. At this point, a delegation of senior British officers sent by General Cunningham met the Emperor's entourage to receive him into the city. They waited as the Emperor went to the church to give thanks to God for the mercies given to the Gideon force in their difficult but successful assault at the Sudan frontier. With Wingate, astride a white horse, leading the 2nd Ethiopian Battalion, the procession moved down the roadway fringed by the graceful eucalyptus trees. Next came the Emperor and his senior officials, including Brigadier Sandford who had worked so well with him, and last but not least, the Sudanese Frontier Battalion who had fought so magnificently along the way.

Lining the road into the city were the Patriots, their leader, Ras Ababa Argai who had fought and waited for him for five long years. Standing on the podium at the old Menelik Palace with the Emperor was Lt. Gen. Sir Allan Cunningham, GOC of the East African Force facing a Guard of Honour of the King's African Rifles. It was here that Haile Selassie made his famous victory speech as he reclaimed the throne which he had abdicated five years before. It was an historic occasion.

However, there were more battles yet to come. The South Africans, with units of the KAR Battalions, had already moved northwards to Dese as General Platt's forces moved southwards for the final surrender of the Duke d'Aosta at Ambalage.

END NOTES

[1] Christine Sandford, **The Lion of Judah Hath Prevailed** (London), J. M. Dent, 1955), p. 79.

[2] Kenneth Gondar Dower, **The Abyssinian Patchwork** (London, Frederick Muller, 1949), p. 87.

[3] Sandord, **The Lion of Judah Hath Prevailed**, p. 93.

AMBALAGE — THE LAST STAND OF THE DUKE D'AOSTA

The assault to the north had begun on the 12th of February at the Northern Frontier District outpost at Bure as the 11th East African Division moved forward towards the Italian Somaliland border. On the same day, the African 12th Division left Garussa, some 70 kilometers upstream on the Tana River. The 12th Division had carried the brunt of the fighting as far as the Juba River at Bulo Erillo, Kismayu, and Jelib. It had taken just ten days to take over the lower third of the Italian Somaliland, a distance of some 300 kilometers. As the two Divisions crossed the Juba, the 12th separated to move north and northwest up the Juba River valley into the southwestern heartland of sourthern Ethiopia.

The 11th Division moved north east up the coast to Mogadishu, Jijiga, Hargeisa, Harer and Dire Dawa and then westward to Addis Ababa. On reaching the capital, the victorious army had travelled some 2,800 kilometers (1750 miles). Divisional headquarters had moved 21 times for an average distance of 130 kilometers a day. Fatal casualties for the 11th Division had been less than 30, while the Italian casualties numbered into the several thousands. A total of 22,082 Italians had been taken prisoner and several thousands more had disappeared into the bush. General Cunningham had achieved a triple victory against: a vastly larger enemy, the weather and the approaching heavy rains, and a long and difficult supply route. The loss of one of these struggles would have meant the loss of all three. As it was, defeat for the Italians, now with their backs to the wall, became inevitable.

The Italians refused to concede ultimate victory to the British. As the pressure increased, the surviving commanders became more determined to resist, which the attackers had not entirely anticipated. Perhaps the victorious counterattack by the German forces under General Rommel in North Africa gave Mussolini the hope that the German Army, after defeating the British in Libya and Egypt, would come up the Nile River to relieve the beleaguered Italians in East Africa. This hope was obviously the motivation behind orders from Mussolini's command in Rome to resist the enemy as long as possible, in spite of the fact that most of the Italian troops and civilians in East Africa doubtlessly preferred surrender over fighting.

The greatest feat of the Italian administration between 1936 to 1940, a period of just over four years, was the engineering and construction of new roads radiating out in five directions from Addis Ababa like spokes of a wheel radiating out from the hub. The first highway, the Strada Imperiale, began in Mogadishu, went northward to Dese and then on to Asmara, a distance of some 1,000 kilometers from the Capital. A second highway went northwest to Debra Markos and Bahir Dar on Lake Tana and then on to Gonder. The third went westward to Nakempte and Gambela on the Sudan frontier. A fourth went southwest to Jima and then on to Bonga and Maji, near the frontier of the Sudan. The fifth highway went southeast to Mojo and then divided into two branches one going on to Shashemane, Dila and on to Negele and Mega, the other going eastward to Dire Dawa, Harer and on to Mogadishu.

The Duke d'Aosta, Viceroy of the Italian East African Empire, had led the evacuation out of Addis Ababa to the north. His goal was to establish major defensive fortifications at Kombolcha Pass and Dese and to strengthen the fortification of Ambalage on the highest mountain in Ethiopia at more than 4,000 meters, where General Frusci had already dug in. After the fall of Asmara on the 1st of April, General Frusci had fled southward with the "FLIT" mobile force in hot pursuit. On the way, he ordered strengthening of the defensive position at Quorum and a speed up of the digging in on Ambalage. He greeted the Viceroy, the Duke d'Aosta as he arrived from Addis Ababa. They would soon be trapped here at Ambalage by General Platt's forces moving south from Asmara and General Cunningham's attacking force moving northward from Addis Ababa.

The 1st South African Brigade, under the command of Brigadier Pienaar, having been recalled from the start of an assault to the southwest towards Jima, was selected to lead the events northward. The Brigade was now at half strength with a total of 1,500 men. After the takeover of Ambalage, this remnant eventually kept moving north, having been assigned to Egypt. Once there, they were to reinforce General Wavell's forces in a new counterattack move westward to finally defeat General Rommel and his Panzer Divisions.

The forces from the north totalled approximately 3,000 men from the 29th Brigade of the 5th Indian Division. The enlarged Brigade, now under the direct command of Major General Mayne, included the 1st Worcesters Regiment, the Garhwal Rifles, the Frontier Rifles, the Skinner's Horse, a Jewish-Arab Unit, and elements of the Sudan Defense Corps. Working in close liason with the British troops, from both north and south, was a major force of battlewise Ethiopia Patriots, under the command of Ras Seyoum Mengasha and the boy Commander, Dejazmatch Zeudie Gebre Selassie.

The first objective of General Mayne was to clear the Strada Imperiale to provide clear passage between Addis Ababa and Asmara. There were two major defensive fortifications to be taken before this could be accomplished — one at Kombolcha Pass and Dese, and the other at Ambalage.

At Kombolcha and Dese, there were twelve Italian Battalians strategically placed behind high mountain defenses with the major pass of Kombolcha below them. On the first day, the 13th of April, Brigadier Pienaar's South African Brigade travelled 180 kilometers to the Mussolini Tunnel, which he had expected to be blocked by demolitions. Such was not the case, as the Italians were content to leave this monument to their road building expertise intact. It turned out to be an excellent air raid shelter, as the Regia Aeronautica based at Dese kept up an aerial strafing action. Just beyond the tunnel was a roadblock which was quickly cleared. A brief engagement at the village of Debre Sina followed. From here, the South Africans moved quickly on up to the Kombolcha Pass, 50 kilometers before the city of Dese where they faced heavy opposition beginning on the 17th of April. The enemy's positions were strong, well located behind dug in mountain fortifications, and he had much greater manpower than did the attacking South Africans. The terrain was steep and mountainous, the weather cold and wet, and transportation extremely difficult. Being greatly outnumbered simply compounded the problems of the attacking South Africans. The decision was to move in frontal attack up the mountain sides with the final Italian defenses high in the clouds. The Duke of Edinburgh's Own Rifles, assisted by the European led Patriots, nicknamed the "Campbell Scouts," battled for five days. They faced heavy Italian counterattacks which in each instance were repulsed with heavy losses. Every spare driver, cook, clerk or stretcher bearer was pressed into action. Finally, joined by the Natal Carbineers and the Transvaal Scottish, the attacking soldiers forced the Italians to withdraw from Kombolcha and flee to Dese. The capture of Kombolcha on the 27th of April was substantial, as 46 abandoned diesel trucks, and six new guns were obtained, plus an excellent airstrip which the S.A.A.F. quickly put to good use. Furthermore, the branch road to the northeast at Kombolcha, which led to the port of Assab, was an excellent supply route, particularly as the Campbell Scouts quickly and completly took over control of the area.

After losing at Kombolcha Pass, the Italians at Dese quickly surrendered. An artillery barrage exchange preceded the South African attack. One direct hit on the main Dese fort resulted in the raising of a white flag. The Transvaal Scottish accepted the unconditional surrender, arriving in captured Italian lorries on the 28th of April. The ten day battle from Addis Ababa was over. The battle-hardened South Africans had mastered mountain fighting efficiently and effectively, with minimum casualties. They had collected 8,024 prisoners and a fabulous tonnage of stores, supplies and ammunition, including artillery and more transport vehicles. The most surprising loot of all was 44 boxes of clothing and personal possessions belonging to the Duke d'Aosta.

The next objective was the capture of the mountain fortress of Ambalage. On the 30th of April, the Natal Carbineers left Dese, and by the 1st of May, had occupied Waldea. For the next four days, the Carbineers faced strong roadblocks and tunnel and road demolitions. The Campbell Scouts circumvented these road barriers and defenses and skirmished their way onwards, taking Alamata on the 5th of May. The entire South African Brigade reached the foot of Ambalage on the 8th. In doing so, it completed its formal task. The attack on Ambalage was now passed to the command of Major General Mayne of the 5th Indian Division to the north. General Mayne answered directly to General Platt, the G.O.C.

Ambalage was an impressive fortification. For some six months, the Italian engineers had drilled tunnels and passages connecting caves and gun pits. Mine fields and barbed wire guarded every approach, and in the last days demolitions blew up every sharp curve on the engineered road which led up to the top pass of the mountain. On the southern descent, there were some seventy-two hairpin curves and almost every one had been blown away by explosives. Some 5,000 crack Italian troops guarded the mountain fortress. General Frusci had brought with him, from Keren, two battalions of the 211th Infantry Regiment, as well as the artillery of the Savoia Division, including the heavy machine guns of the Savoia Grenadier Machine Gun Battalion. Their orders from Rome were to resist to the last man!

From the north, Major General Mayne had only part of the 5th Indian Division, as a full Brigade was left in Eritrea to maintain internal security and to garrison the Eritrean area from Massawa to Akordat. The 4th Division had left directly from the battle of Keren for urgent duty in Egypt. This left only the 29th Brigade, a motorized Cavalry Regiment, the Royal Engineers, and the artillery of the Division as well as a Jewish-Arab Commando unit and two Cypriot Mule Companies which arrived too late to be involved in the Battle of Keren.

From the south came the overworked and undermanned 1st South African Brigade. To the east and the west in the mountain country were the Patriots, all ready for the final kill. They included those from the north under the command of venerable Ras Seyoum, and the Campbell Scouts coming from the south where they had been so effective at Kombolcha Pass.

Lacking brute strength and long supply lines, both Pienaar and Mayne knew they would have to use ruse and deception if they were to succeed, which they did on several notable occasions, depending on the Patriots for continued guerilla activity. Frontal attack was simply out of the question because of the defenses of the enemy on one hand and their own limited forces on the other. The attack which began on the 1st of May was led by Skinner's Horse, the Commando's and the Frontier Force Battalion. They battled towards the Falaga Pass to the east of the Strada Imperiale and at the same time, attacked the fortified positions known as Commando Hill, Wireless Hill, and Enda Medeni Alem. For five days, the forces of General Mayne continued aggressive probing, taking one position after another and avoiding heavy casualties. On the 4th of May, the Garhwal Rifles took Fort Toselli at bayonet point, and the Brigade finally captured Middle Hill which directly faced Ambalage. This placed General Mayne's forces directly in front of Ambalage at Castle Ridge and gave them open sights from three different directions. This advance was backed by a heavy artillery barrage and supported by strong forces of Patriots, particularly on the west.

The South African Brigade had taken to the hills, travelling parallel to the Strada Imperiale, with a strategy to take the Italian fortifications on the hilltops. The Transvaal Scottish, backed by the Duke of Edinburgh's Own Rifles and the Patriot Campbell Scouts played leap frog with the South Africans as they took first one fortification after another. The Royal Natal Carbineers came up the middle to take the fortification at Valdea on the main highway in the late afternoon on the 3rd of May. Early on May 4th, the South African Artillery began shelling the various hilltop fortifications which were now in sight. During the next day, first Sandy Hill, then Pyramid Hill, Whaleback Hill and Elephant Hill were captured. Middle Hill was taken in the early morning of the 4th of May, as well as Bald Hill. Thus, all the surrounding fortifications of the great Ambalage had been taken expect for one: Castle Hill. The attacking forces were regrouped in order to strengthen their positions for the final assault. Finally, on the 11th of May, General Mayne flew over the top of Ambalage and the Italian forces to meet with Brigadier Pienaar on the south approaches below Castle Hill. Here, it was decided that the 1st South

African Brigade should lead the final assault of the main fortress aided on both sides by the Patriots. The pincers from all four sides were about to snap shut.

What followed was one of the strangest of all modern military attacks. The South Africans had depended upon civilian three ton trucks, with "home" built armoured plate boxes, to act as troop carriers and mobile machine gun vehicles. Several hundred of these had gathered on the south side of Ambalage with Triangle Hill in front of them. Up the highway, almost every sharp turn had been blown away by demolition. Taking several thousand empty 200 litre oil drums, the South Africans chiselled off one end and loaded the empty drums on the trucks, with several of the drums dragging behind to make as much noise as possible in the intended night climb up the mountain side. With lights off when exposed to fire from above, but with lights on when they were hidden by the mountainside, they moved to the first demolition. Here, the sappers were waiting to unload the empty barrels to use them as building blocks. They were filled with rock rubble and then the gaps were filled in. It is an interesting note that this unique way of bypassing the demolitions stood as a memorial to this unusual action for many years until more proper construction was possible. The trucks would then go back down dragging their empty drums behind them, making a tremendous noise both coming and going, only to return to the sappers at the next demoltion who were waiting for another load of empty drums for the next build up. In the meantime, all through the night as this process went on, the artillery, from their new advantageous positions, kept a steady barrage on the Italian fortifications above. By daylight, the road up the Triangle was passable and then, with the Bangalore torpedoes blasting holes in the barbed wire entanglements, the encirclement of the top of the Ambalage fortifications became complete. The defending Italians were convinced that they were now facing a full tank Brigade and flew the white flag.

It was on the 16th of May that the Duke d'Aosta indicated that he wished to discuss surrender. Because of the turmoil in which he found himself, he had to send a wireless message to General Nasi at Gonder, who was in overall command, requesting a plane to drop a surrender message to General

Mayne below Castle Hill. When this happened, General Mayne gave acknowledgement by ordering a cease fire.

The Duke d'Aosta then sent General Valpini to negotiate a surrender. However, without sufficient guard, Valpini was attacked and killed by impatient Patriots waiting along the way. The next day, further negotiations continued admidst a delicate and almost ghostly standstill.

On the 18th of May, the act of surrender took place. The Guard of Honour was made up of the Transvaal Scottish playing "The Flowers of the Forest" on their pipes. General Mayne took the formal surrender salute as some 5,000 Italian troops traipsed by, placing their arms in huge heaps. These stood in contrast to the grey background of menacing Ambalage, surrounded by its dozen or more lesser peaks. It is an interesting footnote that the Duke d'Aosta insisted, as his last act before marching off to a prisoner of war camp, that his personal dress sword be given as a final act of surrender to the seventeen year old boy General of the Patriot forces, Dejazmatch Gebre Selassie, who was the stepson of the Crown Prince of Ethiopia.[2]

For General Platt, G.O.C. of the East African campaign, this surrender completed a historic four month campaign, which began with the British forces moving from the frontier fort of Kassala, then in Italian hands, to cross the Ethiopian frontier. Without exception, the odds were heavily against the attacking British forces — always in a David and Goliath ratio. It had not been easy, as when one Battalion was battered, another had to quickly take its place. Yet, the British Command, once in motion, never relinquished the initiative. For the most part, the British Command was made up of Colonials whose courage, tenacity and morale never once wavered. The mountains, heat, cold, casualties and supply difficulties were all overcome by sheer determination and loyalty to the cause ahead, and by the able, fair and determined British officers in command.

It was the end of the Ethiopian Road for the 1st South African Division. From Ambalage, as they were slowly joined by the other elements of their divisions from the south, they headed for North Africa to play a key role in repelling the counter onslaught of the German armies of General Rommel. The official war record of the British War office had this comment to make about the role of the South African Brigade and its attached units:

"No history of the East African campaign is complete which fails to pay tribute to the work of the South Africans. Their infantry brigades acquitted themselves with distinction on every occasion when they were in action, and their technical units, which assisted both East African and West African brigades, played an important part in almost every battle. Every soldier who fought in Kenya, Italian Somaliland or Abyssinia knows how much our victory owes to the work of the South African artillery, the South African engineers and the South African medical units. He also knows how much it meant, during the weeks of advance across coverless deserts and congested passes, not to be subjected to relentless air attack. For his freedom of movement, which was so largely responsible for the record-breaking achievements of that remarkable two months, he has to thank the South African Air Force."[1]

Before the Duke d'Aosta left for his ignominious defeat and final imprisonment and death in 1944 in a Kenyan Prisoner of War Camp, he took special care to express, in perfect English, his gratitude to the South Africans for delivering his trunks which they had found at Dese. It was an emotional ending to one of the final chapters of this first victory of World War II.

END NOTES

[1] British War Office, **The Abyssinian Campaigns** (London, His Majesty's Stationery Office, 1942), p. 117.

[2] The author has this sword of the Duke d'Aosta as one of his momentos of the demise of Mussolini's East African Empire.

10 CLEARING THE PROVINCIAL POCKETS

Liberating the South and West
     If the occupation of Addis Ababa by the East and South African troops was not the climax of the campaign, then surely the return of Emperor Haile Selassie to his throne should have been. If however, there was still any doubt left that Mussolini's Fascist forces in Africa were not in total defeat and disarray, then the surrender of the Duke d'Aosta, should have convinced all of the world that the East African war was over. While these three very significant events must, at least, be considered a three tiered climax, the fact remained that a major part of the Italian army was still in the field and the casualty lists from the last half dozen battles would continue to grow.

     One after another of the remaining provincial armies of the Il Duce capitulated, but not without a spirited battle and unnecessary loss of many lives. In retrospect, it is difficult to understand why the Italian forces did not surrender with the capture of their Commander-in-Chief and Governor of the Empire. It was generally conceded that the morale of the Italian soldiers was very low and that neither the troops nor their officers really believed victory could be theirs, particularly after the fall of Keren, Asmara and Massawa in the north and Mogadishu in the southeast. It was also conceded that the Italian army had been outgeneralled, outfought and destroyed by a mixed Colonial British force — outnumbered in most cases, but always courageous and tenacious in battle. The attitude of several hundred thousand Italian civilians and an equal number of Prisoners of War was universally one of relief and even satisfaction that the war was over. This could hardly be separated from the attitude of their friends and brothers who continued to fight half-heartedly, under the confused command of their officers.

What was it then that kept the war going? Why were thousands of Italians soldiers willing to give their lives in this hopeless cause, even fighting with as much or more determination as had their compatriots earlier in the war? Why did the Italian generals still in the field consider that continued resistance was the best way out? Already, the Italian forces in North Africa had been defeated and were treated with contempt by the German soldiers who were equally a part of the Axis. There are only two possible explanations. One is that Mussolini's military headquarters in Rome ordered a continued resistance, even after the fall of Addis Ababa and Ambalage, in the hopes that somewhere, somehow, the tide might turn in their favor, if General Rommel could win the day in North Africa, or if Hitler could defeat the the Communist hordes of Stalin. A second explanation is probably more likely. The senior officers of the Italian Army in Italy were committed to the Fascist hopes of the restoration of the Roman Empire — in spite of the fact that ordinary Italians had only a shallow image of such grandiose ideas. In their struggle to survive from day to day, most Italians could have cared less about the Empire or a Fascist ideology.

Whatever the reasons were, the fact was that the war was far from over in Ethiopia, particularly for those who were left to complete the work of the 4th and 5th Indian Divisions, the South African Brigades, and the majority of the British Colonial Units. Most of these now had been transferred as reinforcements to North African Divisions who still were locked in deadly battle with the Nazi troops of Germany. General Cunningham, himself, had been transferred to the north; Brigadier Wingate had gone to Burma; General Mayne and Brigadier Pienaar had moved northward with their re-assigned units. It was now left to Major General Wetherall and Brigadier Fowkes, who were left in charge, both upped in rank, to clean up the Italian resistance, along with a group of junior officers and their individual commands. As before, it was the African troops and the South African Air Force which, shoulder to shoulder with the Ethiopian Irregulars and the Patriots, carried the day to that final victory.

The first stage of these provincial battles started even before the fall of Addis Ababa when the 6th KAR Brigade and two companies of 5th KAR Brigade moved southward from Nazret and Mojo in pursuit of the Italian units who had left the main force and were now in full retreat towards Asela in the Arsi highlands and down the Rift Valley to the Lake country. It was General de Simone who led the retreat towards Asela intending to continue on to Bekoji and to Shashemane. Earlier, he had been in command of a large resistance force out of Dire Dawa consisting of several Blackshirt battalions, some Air Force, now turned into infantry, police and custom officers. The armament available to these Italian forces included a mixture of medium artillery and anti-tank guns. They crossed the Awash River Bridge at Maikaso, intending to reach Shashemane by the 6th of April, according to documents captured later. What they had not counted on was the heavy rains in the highlands turning the roads into a quagmire of mud.

The 5th King's African Rifles companies moved south from Nazret, only to find the bridge across the Awash River destroyed and a strong Italian defending force dug in on the south banks of the river. Two of the KAR armoured cars were put out of action by anti-tank fire. According to strategy, half of the KAR's kept up a steady small arms fire across the river while the other half moved unseen downstream, forded the river and then came back upstream with a successful flanking attack to capture the Italian artillery and force the main strength of the Italians farther south. Additional support came from units moving towards Addis Ababa, with the Nigerian Light Battery and a company of South Africans equipped with a 60 pound artillery. They were able to follow the retreating Italians with a shelling that reached at least 10 kilometers beyond the river. By this time, on the 7th of April, the 54th East African Field Company joined the forces on the north bank. In three days a Bailey bridge was constructed across the River, enabling the KAR's and their reinforcements to move with several armoured cars and anti-tank guns to capture the town of Asela without opposition. To their surprise, they found that the town was already under siege by roving banks of Patriot Guerillas. Brigade headquarters were established at Asela, while a small force of Henfrey's Scouts,made up of Ethiopian Irregulars, supported by armoured cars and heavy machine guns, continued some 140 kilometers south to capture Bekoji. Advance elements reached even farther down towards Kolfe where a number of Italian civilian officials were again rescued from the marauding Patriots. Because of the heavy mud, increasing rains and a shortage of fuel, these advance units had to return to Asela, leaving a small unit outpost at Bekoji. In the meantime, General de Simone's remnant forces had reached Shashemane.

At this point, Brigadier Fowkes, who was in command of the clean up forces in the south, decided to switch his main advance to a more passable road south from Mojo through the heart of the Rift Valley Lake country. A small force was left at Asela, while the Brigade Group went back to Nazret, then west to Mojo and south across the Awash River near Bole. Here they were stopped because the Machi Bridge had been destroyed by the retreating Italians. The river was quickly crossed again with another Bailey bridge in place, allowing an advance party to move southward to occupy the first major town south of Mojo, which was Adami Tulu, without any serious opposition.

When these advancing troops reached Lake Abyata, they found that the road divided to circumvent the lake on both the east and the west sides. They then divided their patrols so that they simultaneously moved on towards Shashemene and Butajira. When the western patrols reached Butajira, they found that roving bands of Patriot Guerilla troops had already scattered the defending Italian troops at this center. On the 21st of April both the British and Ethiopian flags flew over an improvised headquarters and cups of tea brought satisfaction to both soldiers and guerilla fighters.

Reports of that event state that whether the Ethiopian forces were formally trained Scouts, Irregular troops, poorly organized Patriots, or even just plain bandits, all were inherently excellent fighters. Travelling light, armed with only rifles or Bren guns, over familiar territory, they were able to live off the land. The main difference between the two groupings of Ethiopians was that the Patriots were not enrolled in any military organization, they received no pay and they fought skirmish battles or, at will, returned to their homes or villages. It was not so with the Scouts or with the formal Irregulars who were all enlisted, paid and disciplined soldiers, commanded by both British and Ethiopian officers. They had proved themselves over and over again as enterprising and efficient military units. Quite frequently, these Ethiopian soldiers were on the cutting edge of the battles in the south and west country, as they had been with the Gideon forces under Colonel Wingate and Brigadier Sandford. They brought in valuable information, attacking the retreating Italian forces from ambush positions as well as being part of frontal battles.

It is important here to recall that only a few KAR units, supporting the well trained regiments of the Ethiopian Irregulars, and the often uncontrollable Patriot forces were left to clean up the whole of the southern half of Ethiopia from the Italian forces. In this operation from Nazret and Mojo to Jima, 25,000 prisoners were taken. At no time did the forces under Brigadier Fowkes exceed 6,000 — in the early stages of the drive south his forces numbered less than 1,500.

Unfortunately for the 22nd KAR's the Gibe River was in flood delaying their forward movement for almost a week. Finally, on the 5th of May the KAR's were able to cross the river and ready themselves for the attack on Shashemane. At Shashemane, General Bertello, who had escaped from British Somaliland on a mule, was in control of the Italian forces. His plan was to move northward from Shashemane and block the 22nd KAR Brigade from moving south and, if successful, to drive the British forces back to Mojo. To further complicate the situation for the Allies was the 500 meter Mount Fike lying between Lake Langano and Lake Shala. The defending Italians had entrenched an artillery company on the slopes of this mountain which held the KAR forces on the northeast side of the Gibbe River and prevented them from crossing the swampy grounds below. To the east, the road led southeast towards Shashemane and to the southwest it joined with the all important Shashemane-Sodo road at Kolito and the Bilati River.

On the morning of the 1st of May the 22nd KAR Brigade, supported by the 18th Mountain Battery and a small force of Ethiopian Irregulars, moved in frontal attack on one side of

Mount Fike while a flanking attack moved from the opposite side. Just before dark, a bayonet charge settled the matter, as the enemy resistance petered out. In this attack Italian casualties were heavy and some 159 prisoners were taken, as well as a number of medium size artillery and Breda guns. The miracle of this operation was that the attacking KAR troops suffered only three casualties, all three wounded; no fatalities. The bravery of the King's African Rifle troops was illustrated in this particular attack when one of the stretcher bearers became so carried away in the excitement that he joined in the final assault. Having neither rifle nor bayonet, he used his stretcher to bash one of the Italians on the head. Then with the help of his assistant he rolled him on to his stretcher and brought him back to his first aid post as a Prisoner of War. It was this aggressive spirit that won the day for the British forces.

The advancing troops were now ready for an attack on Shashemane. This small town was located at a key crossroads and provided control of the roads that went west to Sodo across the Bilati River and southeast to Dila, 45 kilometers to the southeast from Shashemane.

The 22nd KAR Brigade, having given up a number of its units for duty along the way, was not, at this time, strong enough to mount the major attack on Shashemane and, thus, they waited until the 1st KAR and the 5th KAR Battalions arrived from Asela and Bekoji. The next day, this force moved on to Bubisa to cut off the escape of any Italian forces moving westward from Shashemane towards the Bilati River. The Brigade was now ready for the attack on Shashemane. In the advance on Shashemane, three rivers had to be crossed, the Awada, the Dedaba and the Little Dedaba. The first two were crossed unopposed, but the Little Dedaba bridge had been blown and the advancing Italian forces of General Bottello were entrenched on the tops of several hills and on the high banks of the river ravine. These positions invited a flanking attack which was the strategy of the British forces. On the 12th of May, the 1st/6th KAR and a heavy patrol by Captain Henfrey and his Scouts made a feint attack on the Italian left flank, while the South Africans attacked from the other side, sweeping around to the rear. With a very minimum of casualties, 800 prisoners were captured, along with 10 tanks and 18 guns. On the 14th of May the units coming down from Lake Shala moved in on Shashemane itself and captured another 150 prisoners.

Almost immediately, a mobile patrol force, consisting of one company of the Natal Mounted Rifles and the 6th KAR, with light tanks and armoured cars, moved forward towards the important town of Dila some 45 kilometers to the southeast. Almost to its own surprise, this scouting operation cut off the retreat of the 21st and 24th Italian Divisions, bottling them up on the east side of Lake Abaya. What had seemed to be comparatively slow progress in this southern area was much too rapid for the Italian defenders, who were either captured or fled in disorder towards Sodo.

The remainder of the British forces moved southeast to block the second and last escape road for the Italians who might be planning to move across the Bilati River to Sodo. This force captured the small town of Avela on the 16th of May, taking 500 prisoners, and went on to Dila where they took 300 more. At this point, divisional headquarters ordered the two South African Battalions and the First Natal Mounted Rifles to hold Dila, as the 22nd Brigade had already taken most of the Lake Country.

Having blocked the roads south to Sodo and Jima the next plan was to support the Division which had come up the Juba/Genale River and after capturing Negele, had become bogged down in the heavy rains and sea of mud. It is also necessary to pick up the story of the advancing Ethiopian Irregulars and the KAR units which had come up from Moyale, through Yabelo, Soroppa, Finchoa and Giabessire with the intent of clearing the Rift Valley around Lake Chamo and Lake Abaya to the north.

Up From the Juba

General Godwin-Austen, commanding the 12th African Division, including the Gold Coast (Ghanaian) Brigade, travelled up the Juba River, and captured Bardera, Lugh Ferrandi and Dolo without much resistance. However, as it climbed into the highlands of south eastern Ethiopia, it was not able to capture the important Italian defensive position at Negele until the last week of March. Beyond Negele, there were few roads in this heavily forested area, and due to the rains progress was almost impossible for both the troops of the 12th Division and the defending Italians. An officer of the King's African Rifles aptly described the situation:

> "Day after day it rained and the lorries, about a hundred of them sank deeper into the mud every time we tried to move them forward. We couldn't go back, for one thing we realized that it was probably worse behind than it was in front. The ruts became deeper, with the result that lorries sat fast on their axles, and in order to make any progress at all it was necessary either to cut away the middle of the road or fill up the ruts with bundles of brushwood. Hours were spent cutting brushwood and laying it in the tracks for the sake of moving the convoy a few hundred yards.
>
> It now became apparent that no further supplies of food would reach us till the rains stopped, so every man went on to half rations, hardly sufficient to support a full day's work.
>
> Daily progress varied from a few hundred yards to perhaps two miles for the whole convoy, but it was slow work manhandling every one of the odd hundred trucks. On occasions, river-beds normally dry became roaring torrents as much as ten feet deep which split up sections of the convoy and men from their food and bedding for hours and sometimes days." [1]

The Gold Coast/Ghanaian Brigade, with Ethiopian Irregular support, now moved to attack a vastly superior Italian force of five Battalions, covering a three mile front equipped with heavy guns, and protecting a natural fortress. The approach was across deep ravines, around steep cliffs and through dense forests — accomplished only in a vicious frontal hand to hand struggle, lasting three weeks as one after another of the Italian defensive positions was taken. One Sergeant Major described Bardera in North Africa as a skirmish in comparison to this bitter conquest of Wadara (Kebre Mengist). The final victory came on the 10th of May. No pages of history adequately record this military picture of hand fought victory by the Ethiopians and Ghanaians.

A huge supply of ammunition, guns and supplies, as well as several thousand prisoners were taken at Wadara (Kebre Mengist). The victorious African troops of the 12th Division hardly stopped to catch their breath as they followed in hot pursuit the retreating Italian remnants who never again turned to fight in the lake area.

Interestingly, in the 1936 invasion of Ethiopia, the best of Mussolini's forces were held at bay for eleven desperate months at Wadara, making it famous in Ethiopian history, and resulting in a post liberation name change to Kebre Mengist.

The defensive positions at Adola and at Hula were also quickly overrun, the advancing troops reaching Dila on the 17th of May and joining up with the KAR's and the South Africans who had already captured this important town the day before. It was a great coming together event, watched by more than a thousand confused Italian prisoners who were, for the most part, relieved that it was all over.

The capture of Hula and Wendo deserve special note. At Hula, the Italian garrison defenders numbered a full Battalion of approximately 1000 men under the command of a Brigadier. They offered no resistance, except that the Brigadier thought it below his dignity to surrender to a junior officer who was a mere Captain, who commanded the attacking unit of only double platoon strength. After being told that he had no alternative unless he chose to resist, which was rather uninviting in face of an eager force of black troops with trigger fingers at the ready, the Brigadier caught the point and gracefully accepted the indignity.

On the 22nd of May, the regional capital city of Wendo was taken. Wendo, located some 25 kilometers up the escarpment at an altitude of 2000 meters, overlooked the Rift Valley and the Lakes below. Vegetation was lush and the roads passable. Whether or not the Italian forces intended to resist was questionable. In fact, they did not. The South African armoured car unit, under the command of a Captain Styles, led a surprise dash into the town where the defending General formally surrendered to Colonel Bruce, the British senior officer. He feebly tendered the excuse that he was unable to offer resistance because he suffered a weak heart and he really didn't feel like fighting that morning. Not a single shot was fired in the capitulation of Wendo as the Gold Coast/Ghanaian troops and the South African armoured units took the surrender of another Italian Brigadier General and some 3,000 prisoners.

Up From Mega and Yabelo

The northward advance, following the capture of Mega on the 20th of February and Yabelo two days later, had been slow and difficult going for the 21st East African Brigade and a Battalion of Ethiopian Irregulars. They had floundered through mud to capture Soroppa on the 25th of April and Finchoa (Yrga Chafe post liberation) two days later. Here the road was so bad that it took ten days to travel 80 kilometers, making the transport of supplies almost impossible. As a result, two battalions returned to Yabelo with the motor transport vehicles, while one battalion continued the advance northward carrying the ammunition and food supplies by foot and mule pack. An attempt was made to join up north-eastward from Yabelo to Negele with the advancing 12th Division, but this proved impossible as floods had washed away bridges and road embankments. In the end, this did not really matter as the advancing combined battalions of King's African Rifles and the Ethiopian Irregulars were able to take the fortified town of Giabassire on the 11th of May without a fight, as most of the defending Italians, following the fall of Wadara, had pulled out for safer areas, hoping to make their way cross-country to Sodo and to Jima to the west of the Omo River.

Giabassire/Agere Maryam was another historical point in the 1936 war, as it was here that the Ethiopians had strongly resisted all attempts by the Italians to dislodge them, following the capture and murder of Ras Desta, son-in-law of Emperor Haile Selassie. This time it was a different story for the fleeing Italians who left their fortification to a much smaller, poorly equipped African force.

From Giabassire/Agere Maryam, the remnants of the 21st

Brigade continued northward over much easier terrain to block the southern escape of several thousand Italian troops bottled up east of Lake Abaya. At the same time the 22nd East African Brigade moved down from Shashemane and Kolito to close the pincers from the north. The Ethiopian Patriots were also now gathering in increasing strength, successfully taking care of an estimated 12,000 Italian soldiers, the remnants of the 21st, 24th and 25th Italian Divisions who had no where to go but await capture or hope to escape across the Bilati River.

The Curtain Falls in the Lake Country

Once Shashemane and Dila had been captured and the 12th East African Division had taken Wadara/Kebre Mengist and Wendo they joined with the Brigade from the south who had taken Soroppa and Giabassire/Agere Maryam. Thus, the trap from the southeast and the north had been closed, locking in the fleeing remnants of the Italian forces between Lake Abiata and Lake Shala. The 22nd East African Brigade, again supplemented by Ethiopian Irregulars and the 2nd Nigerian Regiment, swung west along the Shashemane-Sodo road to join with the units that had liberated the Bubisa area at Kolito. The Italians had evacuated the junction town, blown up the bridge crossing the Bilati River and established defensive positions on the opposite banks of the river.

The units taking part in this operation were the 1st/6th King's African Rifles and the 2nd Nigerian Regiment. Using a flanking strategy, which successive Italian units never managed to comprehend, the troops waded across the fast flowing Bilati, backed by an Artillery barrage, pushing the attack home with bayonets. In just an hour, they had subdued the defenders. At the last moment, a squadron of Italian tanks appeared to the dismay of the attacking infantrymen who had neither tanks nor anti-tank guns. The day was saved by a KAR Sergeant N. G. Leaky, who climbed aboard the leading tank, killed its crew and was last seen chasing the other tanks on foot. Posthumously, he was awarded the Victoria Cross. His extraordinary act of courage served to spur his troops on to victory in what is recorded as the Battle of the Bilati River.

After bridging the Bilati River with a Bailey bridge, armoured cars and light tanks swept on to take the important center of Sodo without resistance. Along the way, they took prisoners at each village. At Sodo, on the 22nd of May, after a minimum of resistance, the town surrendered. The loot included two Generals, Liberati with his 25th Division, and Bacarri with his 101st Division, including more than 4,000 officers and men, 6 medium tanks, 4 light tanks, 100 machine guns, ammunition and supplies. They also captured the remnant refugees of the 21st Division who had escaped around the north end of Lake Abijata. The offensive in the Sodo area had caught the Italians by surprise giving them no time either to fight or to fly — their only alternative was to surrender, which they did. Again, the surrendering Italians seemed relieved that it was all over.

The capture of Sodo was the final phase of the battle for the Lakes, which had been fought and won against impossible odds. It had been a combination of high courage, careful planning and excellent execution. The general collapse of the Italian morale also contributed to the overwhelming surrender. The evidence of collapse was everywhere; in orders not carried out, of Generals who did not follow through on their commands, and of a careless laisser faire attitude.

The victors had already learned that it was an easier task to defeat the enemy than it was to supply the needs of their own troops, or to manage the territory conquered and feed the thousands of prisoners of war.

Patrols radiated out from Sodo to take the various garrisons in the area. The major village was Chencha some 100 kilometers to the south. There were some 20,000 to 25,000 Italian troops wandering about to the east and southwest of Sodo. Most of these had found it impossible to cross the Omo Gorge and, as a result, were begging in desperation for food and protection from the harrassing bands of Patriots. Still more remnants of the 21st Division, under the command of General Gaffarti, having come cross-country from Dila, were taken prisoner on the 27th of May.

However, the remnants of the 24th Division, under General Parlormo, having fled westward from Giabassire/Agere Maryam, refused to surrender to three armoured cars sent out to intercept them. They refused to do so because of the miniscule force that had come to take their surrender. After a few days of repeated attacks by the Patriots, however, General Parlormo surrendered. A radioed message from the Italian General in command at Jima city to the English at Sodo had begged them for refuge from the Patriots. A patrol force of the Gold Coast/Ghanaian Regiment obliged on the 17th of June. This was an interesting aspect of military history.

Across the Omo to Jima and West

There were at least 30,000 Italian troops to the west and the north of the Omo River. It was known that some 12 Generals were present in the Jima area alone, well entrenched behind a deep and precipitous gorge of the Omo and the treacherous Omo River itself. There had been two crossings over the river, built by the Italians — one a bridge below Abelti on the Addis Ababa/Jima road and the other via a ferry and a cable foot bridge below the village of Sciola closer to Sodo. However, the Abelti Bridge, the Sciola Ferry and the foot bridge had all been demolished. The winding road down the approaching escarpment had been destroyed and was well planted with land mines. Wrecked Italian vehicles blocked the road in many places — the result of daily bombing raids by the South African Air Force based in Addis Ababa. Heavy gun emplacements, including 75 mm and 105 mm guns, were strategically placed on the high banks of the Gorge on the Jima side at both crossings, making any attempted crossing most difficult.

The Addis Ababa-Jima road was an excellent highway and, for the most part, was covered with asphalt. However, the 75 kilometer road from Sodo to the Omo River had to be cleared of mines and demolitions had to be filled in. Two bridges also had to be replaced before the crossing could be attempted. The road had been made passable by the 30th of May and the entire 22nd East African Brigade Group reached Sciola ready to attempt a crossing in face of the heavy defences on the opposite side of the Gorge. In the meantime, at the northern crossing of the Omo, a concentration of men and material had been assembled at Abelti ready to take the same action, coordinated with the Sciola crossing. This employed the last of 70 Bailey bridges that had been originally shipped from Kenya and had been assembled along the way, as river crossings were constructed in 69 different areas. The troops given this responsibility were the 23rd East African Brigade and the 1st and 3rd Nigerian Battalions. The latter included a number of boatwise sappers and assault boats. Ordinarily, the Omo River is about two meters in depth and some 30 meters wide, but now in flood time, it was 100 meters wide, from 5 to 10 meters deep and very fast flowing. It was not an inviting assignment for the battle hardened but weary Colonial and Ethiopian Irregular troops.

The Nigerians were equipped with heavy machine guns and supported by the 18th Mountain Battery providing cover from the eastern escarpment. The strategy again was to approach the enemy in a flanking attack. On the 2nd of June the Nigerians attempted a three pontoon crossing two kilometers downstream. However, all but one of the assault boats were wrecked or swept downstream. Only a small party of King's African Rifles managed to reach the westbank. They held their beachhead for three days in spite of repeated attacks from enemy patrols. On the late afternoon of the 4th of June and all that night, using rescued or repaired assault boats, three companies of King's African Rifles and two companies of Nigerians managed to cross the river. The King's African Rifles climbed the escarpment during the day and by 5:00 p.m. were above the 105 mm guns emplacements, quickly silencing them. As darkness fell, the battle was one of confusion. The King's African Rifles were, at one point, surrounded by Italian troops who, it turned out, were asking for surrender rather than vice versa. In the meantime, the Nigerians had moved upstream to a point 2.5 kilometers above the wrecked foot bridge. They then moved up the escarpment to join the victorious KAR's the next morning. To their amazement, they found that victory was theirs and the Italians who had not escaped were taken prisoner. A Captain, C.P.B. Maggeridge won the Military Cross for this operation and several non-commissioned ranks were awarded the Military Medal.

It had been a victory over difficult natural hazards, including the escarpment cliffs, the flooded river, mud and rain, even more so than over humans. In regard to the latter, 53 Italian officers and 1,147 other prisoners had been taken. As well there were 170 enemy fatalities. The rest of the Italian force had retreated towards Jima. The British losses were recorded as 2 officers and 7 soldiers killed and 24 others wounded. It was a heroic victory against almost insurmountable odds.

By the 7th of June, the engineers had built a ferry and by the 12th of June, a pontoon bridge was in place. With the help of the local people, the blown up roadway on the west side of the escarpment was rebuilt and the mines cleared, enabling the 23rd Brigade Group and the 1st KAR's to reach the top of the escarpment, ready for their march on to Jima city. The northern crossing of the Omo River below the town of Abelti, some 90 kilometers upstream was equally difficult. The one main advantage here was that the engineers and sappers had a Bailey bridge with which to span the flooding Omo River. The 3rd Nigerian Regiment had occupied the north bank of the Omo gorge since the 10th of April, waiting for reinforcements and the skill of the engineers. The demolished, convoluted road down the escarpment had been rebuilt almost to the river's edge in spite of small arms fire from the far sides and spasmodic shelling. Finally, on the 31st of May, sufficient material and manpower had been assembled for the task. The first casualties were three Nigerian sappers who attempted to swim the river, carrying a rope, as the first step to establishing a crossing. They lost their lives to the raging torrent. A new site for the crossing was then selected near the blown bridge some 1.5 kilometers downstream from the first planned crossing. On the night of the 4th of June, following two days with no rain, a crossing was attempted in darkness which successfully put the 3rd Nigerian Company across, along with one company of the KAR's, establishing an all important beachhead. In three days they successfully repelled four counterattacks, enabling the engineers to get on with the construction of their Bailey bridge.

In the meantime, the 1/1 King African Rifles managed a 15 kilometer flanking march to the south side of the escarpment, during the evening and the night without being noticed by the Italian forces. At dawn, to the amazement of the Italians at the top of the south side of the gorge embankment, they were faced with the KAR's who had assumed complete command of the road. They demanded the surrender of the enemy which was quickly agreed to. So rapid was the advance of the KAR's during the night that the Italian troops did not even know that the river had been crossed, much less demolish or mine the escarpment road. This entire operation, after the crossing of the river, had incurred one casualty — that of an Italian lorry driver. The KAR's, in taking over this lorry, turned it around and it helped transport them to the top of the escarpment for the surrender of the Italian forces who had bedded down for the night.

By 10:00 A.M. on the 6th of June, the Jima plateau was in the hands of the East African Brigade group. Hardly aware of what had happened, 2,800 surprised Italian prisoners were taken.

Threatened by a two pronged attack — one to the east from the Sciola crossing and one already across at the Jima crossing — the city surrendered without opposition. Not only was there a major civilian population in this regional capital of Sidamo, but there was a large military establishment and one of the best equipped Regia Aeronautica aerodromes outside of Addis Ababa. The operations of the Italian Air Force at Jima had been rendered null and void by repeated attacks from the South African Air Force based at Addis Ababa since the fall of the capital city on the 5th of May.

An element of competition between the two forces engaged in the crossing of the Omo River had developed. The 23rd Brigade had succeeded in crossing the Omo at Abelti on the 6th of June and were on the move to Jima city by the 9th of June. The 22nd Brigade group at Sciola did not complete their crossing until the 12th of June. At Sheshemane, it had been the 22nd Brigade which had crossed the Little Gibbe River first to receive the surrender of the town. Now, it was the 23rd which was able to receive the surrender of the city. So the 1st King's African Rifles sent a "gleeful" radio message to their 22nd KAR counterparts letting them know that it was now their turn. Two days later the 22nd and 23rd Brigade were together at the occupied city of Jima.

The take at Jima was tremendous. It included 8,000 prisoners, 500 vehicles, large supples of ammunition, medical supplies, food and military supplies and a number of drums of gold bullion which had been sent from Addis Ababa prior to the capitulation of the capital city. It also included 14 generals.

Those generals of major importance were the Corps Commander General Scala, the Regia Aeronautica Commander in Somaliland, General Sabatani, and the Vice-Governor General of the Italian East African Empire, General Daodace. There were two divisional commanders, General Tassi and Maynard, as well as General Bisson who was the Govenor of the city of Jima and who gave the official surrender of the city without resistance. In addition, there were several thousand civilians, the lives of whom were considered in danger as some 12,000 Patriots had flooded into the city, intent on looting and avenging the Italians. As a result, on the 21st of June, General Cunningham, who was the overall British commander, placed the city under military rule with a battalion strong force, supported by tanks and guns. Meanwhile, the 22nd and 23rd East African Brigade went on to occupy the surrounding territory.

A sidelight of the takeover of Jima city related to gold — gold bullion packed away in 200 litre barrels. It involved General Gazera on one hand and the Bishop headquartered at the Consulata Mission located on the eastern edge of the city on the other. When General Gazerra fled southwest across the Omo from Addis Ababa, as the South African Division approached the capital of Addis Ababa, he took a truckload of gold bullion from the Bank de Roma in Addis Ababa. The British were suspicious that this bullion was hidden away in Jima, and immediately after the city capitulated, the search was on. It was not found until one day, a week after the fall of the city, when the Staff Captain of the 23rd Brigade had a rather shabbily dressed priest arrive at this office, reporting that the Bishop wanted to see him. The Staff Captain's account of what took place is an interesting story of a non military episode:

> One day a measly little padre arrived at my office and said, "The Bishop wants to see you on an important matter." I went down to see the bishop and he said he'd got some barrels which were awfully heavy. He couldn't think what was left in them, but he wanted to be honest about everything, and he was a Godly man and had three barrels to disclose to me. I went and looked at the three

barrels, which were so heavy you couldn't shift the damn things at all, and I arranged for a lorry to collect them. Just then he said he'd got another eleven barrels but they were hidden somewhere else, not by him, of course. We went into a garage, chock full of tyres and spares, and unearthed a further eleven barrels, and took them all up to my office.

When we were taking them off the lorry, one barrel fell and burst, and a lot of half-dollar pieces fell out. We opened another barrel and another lot of half dollar pieces fell out. Some expert came along and said they were only nickel and were worth practically nothing, so in view of this, and the fact that a lot of spectators were trying to take souvenirs, I shut the barrels up and rather lost interest in them.

Next day the custodian of enemy property arrived and said he'd like to have a look at the barrels as they were really his concern. We opened some new ones up and found they were chock full of gold bars. We then opened another and found packets of rings, necklaces and the like. In fact, as the custodian said to me, "It is rather like a super sort of bran tub."

When I next went to the Mission, I said to the bishop, "You have been very stupid to produce these drums so late in the day. You really must realize you have been a little unwise. I don't want to search your Mission, but I have got to have an assurance from you there's nothing else, or I'll have to search the place." He immediately said, "There's nothing else. This is all I know about."

I was scared stiff at having all this gold about the place so I packed off the 14 barrels to Addis Ababa.

Sometime later the bishop admitted to the financial adviser that he had a few East African shillings and about half a million Maria Theresa dollars buried in the garden as well as some U.S. dollars and Egyptian pounds, but these, he explained, were for buying necessities for the Mission such as chickens and eggs. So, in the end, the bishop was a great help. It is obviously bad policy to kill a goose that lays golden eggs, but there is certainly no harm in giving it a bit of a squeeze occasionally.[2]

It was some four years later that the Department of Education carried on a more detailed search of the Consulata Mission property through Howard Thompson, a visiting Canadian Agriculturist under contract to the Ethiopian Government. While walking through a garden area, he felt the ground below him collapse, pitching him into an underground tunnel. On investigation, the tunnel was found out to be the connecting link between the Bishop's Church and the workshop area. The tunnel now had served, for these years, as a storage space for more barrels of coins and vast supplies of electrical wire, explosives, small arms, a Maria Theresa dollar die for a shop mint to make Maria Theresa dollars. There was other military equipment stored in this tunnel. It was also discovered that the altar housed a secret radio transmitter large enough to communicate directly with Rome and that the Bishop was actually an Intelligence Major in the camouflage of a Bishop's garb. He quickly received a delayed free flight back to Rome from whence he had come some years before. His Church and the property of the Mission became the site of a new Jima School of Practical Arts. The agriculturist who took charge was the brother of the author.

END NOTES

[1] Kenneth Gandar Dower, **The Abyssinian Patchwork** (London, Frederick Muller, 1949), pp. 170f.

[2] W.E. Crosskill, **The Two Thousand Mile War** (London, Robert Hale, 1980), p. 181.

THE FINAL CLEAN-UP

ANGLO-EGYPTIAN SUDAN

Dablak Islands

SOMALILAND (FRENCH)

SOMALILAND (BRITISH)

ETHIOPIA

ILLUBABOR

KEFA

GAMO GOFA

Strada Imperiale

Atbara

Kassala
Akordat
Keren
Massawa
⊙ Asmara
Gedaref
Tekeze
Adwa
Galabat
Wolkefit
Maychew
Aden ✪
Gonder ⊙
Blue Nile
L. Tana
Magdala
Bahir Dar
Dangla
Dese
Djibouti ⊙
Injabara
Kombolcha
Abay
Awash
Asosa
Fiche
Dire Dawa
Gimbi
Genet
Harer ⊙ Jijiga
Nekempte
⊛ Addis Ababa
Dembidollo
Gibe
Awash
Gore ⊙
Abelti
Asela
Agaro
L. Ziway
L.Abijata
Jima ⊙
L.Shala
L. Langeno
Adaba Kolito
Bonga
Shashemane
Shiala Sodo
L. Awasa
Shewa Gimira
Yirga Alem
Chencha
L. Abaya
Arba Minch
L. Chamo
Maji
Wabi -Shebele
Giabassire
Omo
Yabelo
Negele
Strada Imperiale
Chew Bahir
Genale (Juba)
Mega
L. Rudolf
Moyale
Juba

km   100   200   300

miles   100   200

N

Roads

El Wak

Mogadishu ✪

THE FINAL CLEANUP

With the fall of Jima, the remaining Italian armies retreated or consolidated yet farther south and west, into the mountain vastness of southwestern Ethiopia. They did this in spite of the stark reality that their cause was hopeless and that total defeat was inevitable.

At Bonga

General Bortello, the Italian Commander of an armoured column which had fled south from Mojo, was south of Jima with a large force at a point called Beletta on the road to Bonga. The 1st King's African Rifles Battalion, along with a section of the 1st South African Medium Brigade, was sent to intercept them. At the Didessa River, the Italians had established a defensive position from which they had no chance of escape, for a unit of the Sudan Defence force from Juba had already taken Maji further to the south and was now pressing in on their southern flank. General Bortello, along with a General Tosti, finally recognized their fate on the 28th of June and surrendered along with 2,850 troops to a Lt. Col. MacNab, who commanded the African troops.

At Nekempte

Immediately following the capture of Jima, General Cunningham ordered the transfer of the Nigerian Brigade to Nekempte via the well built road running west of Addis Ababa. This strategy closed the escape for the Italian remnants from Gambela and the general area towards Gore.

At Agaro

Thirty kilometers to the northwest of Jima, near where the

Patriots had taken the town of Agaro, the Italians again dug in, on the banks of the Didessa River, mining the road and destroying the bridge across the river. After a brief gun battle, the Italians capitulated. Before being removed to a prisoner of war camp, they were compelled to clean up the mines and rebuild the bridge, allowing the British troops to move on to Dembidollo where another force of Italians surrendered.

From Gore and Gambela

The road from Agaro to Dembi and then to Gore was a causeway of mud. Because of the impassable roads, Gore could not be reached. The alternative was for General Gazzera, the former Commander of the Italian forces in the East African Empire, to move southward to formally ask for surrender from General Gilliart, the commander of the Belgian contingent, who had moved from the Congo (now Zaire) through Juba, down the Nile and up the Dabus River.

From the Western Frontier

In the meantime, farther north along the Sudan-Ethiopian frontier was the Italian border post of Guba which was opposite to the Sudan post of Rosseires. The Italian garrison at Guba had been isolated since the advance of the British forces into the Gojam some ten months earlier. At this point, the Eastern Arab Corp of the Sudan Defence Force moved in to take Guba and the neighboring outposts of Geissan and Shehojele on the opposite side of the Blue Nile. The defending Italians were severely mauled in this attack. Shortly afterwards, on the 9th of March, the 2/6 King's African Rifles, based in the Sudan, moved to reoccupy the border outpost at Kurmuk. Two days later, the Belgians captured Asosa to completely destroy the Italian 10th Brigade, capturing 1500 troops. The remnants scattered or deserted.

Gambela, the former trading post of the British and the Portuguese some 400 years earlier, was taken by the 2/6 King's African Rifles on the 3rd of February.

Finally Gonder

General Wetherall's successful sweep through the Sidamo

region of south and southwestern Ethiopia brought to an end General Cunningham's campaign against the forces of Mussolini in East Africa. Now only Gonder in the northwest remained. A force of 170,000 Italian troops had been demolished in the Galla Sidamo area. The military might of Il Duce had been liquidated. Thirty Italian generals had been captured. Forty-two tanks, 403 artillery guns and a vast amount of military stores had been taken. An Air Force, the Regia Aeronautica and a naval fleet had been destroyed. What was now left was to be anti-climactic. Only Gonder and a small area surrounding the old Portuguese castles remained in the hands of the Italians. This last shred of Italian authority was now in the sole charge of General Nasi, small in stature, but an able and determined disciplinarian, who probably more than any other senior Italian general held some measure of Ethiopian respect. His wet and shivering Brigades were locked into the fortresses in the Gonder area, including Chelga, Wolkefit, Amba Giorgis and Gorgora as the full force of the rainy season pelted upon them. It almost seemed that five months after the fall of Addis Ababa and Ambalage that Nasi of Gonder had been all but forgotten. It had not been an oversight — rather it had been a sound strategy for as the Sidamo area had fallen from Italian hands, the remaining force in Italy's Amara had grown steadily weaker. The ultimate fate of Gonder had never been in doubt by the Italians, by the British or by the Ethiopians — it was just a matter of time and tragically, General Nasi chose to resist.

Plans had already been laid for the Gonder relief force to turn west in a direct route through Magdala and Debre Tabor just west from Dese. The heavy rains, however, had turned this route into a quagmire. General Fowkes, now in command of the 12th Division, instead moved round about through Adwa and Axum, across the Tekeze at Enda Selassie to the top of the magnificient Wolkefit Pass.

The approaches to Gonder had been narrowed down to four during the course of events in the liberation; the north, the west, the centre, the southeast and the south. To better understand what was now facing the 12th Division, it is well to briefly review the course of events that led to the start of the Gonder offensive in November 1941.

The first attack came from the Sudan in January before General Platt struck at Eritrea. The 9th Infantry Brigade had been based on the Sudan side of Galabat in January. The 52nd Commando unit moved up the Gandwa River valley on the Sudan approach to Gonder. This feint destroyed the Italian Garrison at Galabat on the 12th of January, forced the evacuation of General Nasi's forces based at Metema and ended in a crushing defeat at Wehni for the Italians. It was here that Lieut. Bhagat won the Victoria Cross for his sheer bravery in clearing fifteen mine fields, and forcing the Italians to dig in on the Chelga escarpment. As the 9th Brigade was needed at Keren, they discontinued the attack and only one Battalion was left, later to be supplemented by the 3rd Ethiopian Battalion. This effectively blocked the road to Gonder from the northwest.

The second attack on Gonder came from Adwa across the Tekaze River This approach also stalled at the Wolkefit Pass as the Ambalage route south was given priority. Following Ambalage, Dejazmatch Ayelu Birru deserted his Italian overlords to join a small British force to occupy Debark, south of Wolkefit. The rains stalled this action but, at least, the road to Gonder from the north was blocked.

Also, before the rains came, the third confining attack approached from the east out of Dese. At the same time a small British force, combined with a battalion of Ethiopian Scouts and Skinners Horse, moved to capture Magdala and Debra Zebit and Mota. Thus, on the 3rd of July, the eastern approach to Gonder was cut off, particularly when a mixed British force captured Debre Tabor taking more than 4,000 troops and a full complement of motor transport. Then, with the rains heavily upon them, this front also fell silent, cutting off the approach to Gonder from the east.

The fourth approach came from the south with the 101st Mission, and the effective Gideon Force under Colonel Wingate. The Italians had then withdrawn from all of the outposts south of Lake Tana in the Gojam except at Bahir Dar Giorgoris and Debre Markos. This combined with the desertion of most of their Ethiopian puppet chieftains who proclaimed their loyalties to the returning Emperor rather than their Italian overlords.

By April, Colonel Torelli, in command at Bahir Dar, and

Giorgoris, had been completely blockaded in his Fortress. At the same time, Colonel Natale was defeated at Bure and Colonel Maraventano was forced to withdraw from Debre Markos to face final defeat at Agibar on the 22nd of May. Thus, Gonder was completely cut off from any communication with the rest of Ethiopia when these south roads were successfully blocked. There was no real threat at this point on any large scale from any other direction until after the heavy rainy season because of the impossibility of mobility. To make matters worse for General Nasi and the few remaining outposts still in his command, the South African Air Force based in Addis Ababa and the Royal Air Force based in Asmara and Alamata maintained harrassment bombing and strafing, reminding the Italians that they faced inevitable defeat.

The first of the outposts to fall in the renewed campaign against Gonder was Wolkefit on the north, following the end of the heavy rains. Wolkefit, at the summit of the escarpment, was at an altitude of just over 3000 meters and more formidable in its location than had been Ambalage or Keren. The approach road from the north had 99 hairpin turns on the way up on its northern slope. On top, a small number of defensive gun emplacements should have been able to indefinitely prevent any attacking force from reaching the pass at the top. A Major Ringrose, with a strong well organized force of Patriots, was able to keep the mountain top fortress under continuing gun fire while the S.A.A.F. and the R.A.F. kept the fortress under daily bombardment. This nerve wrecking pressure on the impregnable fortress resulted in a formal surrender on the 27th of September, without major resistance.

The fall of Wolkefit opened the door for continuing attacks southward by the Patriots who were anxious for the final kill. General Nasi consolidated his defences at Gorgora, Chelga, Kulkaber, Ambazzo and Bahir Dar. The 2nd Ethiopian Battalion, under Lt. Colonel Benson, moved to capture Gorgora and Ambazzo. The Patriots and the remnants of the Sudanese Gideon Battalion isolated Chelga, another group of Patriots, under Major Douglas, isolated Kulkaber, and still another force of Patriots captured Amba Giorgis. It seemed that all General Fowkes had yet to do was to administer the "coup de grace". It was not that easy, as General Nasi did not surrender. During the first week of November, General Fowkes had set up Divisional Headquarters at Amba Giorgis which actually overlooked Gonder in the distance. Together with the Patriots, the 12th Division included the 25th and the 26th Brigade groups, a battery of 25 pounder artillery guns, and support from both Ethiopian Irregulars and newly formed Ethiopian regular army units. The gun emplacements were located on an unused but now cleared old trail which led into the city. This enabled a full scale assault, with artillery barrage, on the surrounding fortification of Kulkaber. It was captured on the 21st of November after a hard fought battle.

General Nasi was no quitter. He had the much larger military force of 34,000 seasoned troops with 60 artillery pieces and a still active Air Force. General Fowkes had 21,000 troops, plus 6,000 Patriots and 25 artillery pieces. The Italian defenses covered a wide area while the British were able to concentrate their assault at only a half a dozen points. The attack was launched at dawn on the 27th of November, supported by the S.A.A.F. and the R.A.F., all through the day. Both the Brigade groups had to contend with heavy mine fields and many counterattacks. It was a vicious battle. In the end, it was the Patriots who led the final offensive, seemingly coming from all directions regardless of heavy small arms fire and counterattacks. Nothing could stop their assault and the inevitable carnage which was to follow. By early afternoon, the defenders were blowing ammunition dumps signifying that they were about to quit. By late afternoon, the Patriots were inside Gonder, having covered 30 kilometers in ten hours, fighting all the way and under heavy firemost of the way.

General Nasi surrendered to General Fowkes late in the afternoon and by evening the Union Jack and the rainbow flag of the Ethiopia flew over the Governor's palace. Before nightfall, the Crown Prince Asfau Wossen was installed as Governor of Gonder.

Carnage and looting was inevitable, although in a remarkably short time, order was re-established. Looting was generally overlooked as souvenir hunting, celebrations of victory went on through the night. By morning, all was in order. The next day, on the 28th of November, prisoners were isolated from civilians and celebration organization took shape.

Perhaps the greatest souvenir of all was received by Major General Fowkes. It was a pair of congratulatory telegrams — the first from Prime Minister Winston Churchill and the second from Emperor Haile Selassie.

On the 1st and 2nd of December, at the immense Gonder Aerodrome, a huge victory celebration took place. It was more than a celebration for the victory of Gonder — it was to epitomize that "extradordinary concourse of men of diverse races."

"These parades did more than celebrate the taking of Gonder; they seemed to epitomise the East African campaign, for the extraordinary concourse of men of diverse races, which took part in them, was only typical of the international force which, welded together by superb leadership, had brought about the Italian collapse in East Africa. In addition to the Africans of Kenya, Tanganyika, Uganda and Nyasaland, there were other Africans from the Sudan and the Gold Coast. The South African Air Force was represented; so was the South African Light Armoured detachment with its Bren gun-carriers and tanks and South African engineers. The Kenya Armoured Car Regiment was there, so was half a battalion of that far-flung regiment, the Argyll and Sutherland Highlanders. There were Indian Mountain Batteries. There were East African, N. Rhodesian and Australian Medical Units. There were Cape Pioneers. There was a detachment of the new Ethiopian Regular Army, looking very sophisticated by the side of the various groups of Ethiopian Irregulars, who, under their leaders, newly shorn and shaved, were well represented at the parade. Amongst them there was the 79th Colonial Battalion, which was originally an enemy unit, but which, after its capture almost intact early in the campaign, had been reorganized to take its place in the field as the '79th Foot.'"[1]

Casualties on that memorable day of liberation were amazingly light — 116 killed and 380 wounded for the attacking British/Ethiopian forces. It was not so easy for General Nasi as casualties on his side were more than ten times as high — an unnecessary killing, for what was an inevitable defeat.

This great and final victory was truly the climax of the struggle to liberate a nation — the first to be freed. It was a different story in Europe and in Britain as they still faced the threat of invasion and the takeover by Nazi might which seemed, at that point, invincible.

Victory was not yet in sight for the country that had led in this victory but it was a source of encouragement to those in Great Britain whose vision and determination spelled "Liberation" for us as well!

General Wavell's objective had now been achieved. With a total force which never exceeded 100,000 and the vast majority of these from colonial Africa, in a country as large as all of western Europe, the Allies faced a well trained and well equipped army of nearly 300,000 men, and had come through victorious. Success was due to superb generalship, courageous officers and men of equal stamina and determination. The operation has well been described as a military masterpiece.

END NOTES
[1] British War Office, **The Abyssinian Campaigns** (London, His Majesty's Stationery Office, 1942), p. 143.

One of Gondar's castles, built between 1632 and 1637 by the Portuguese.

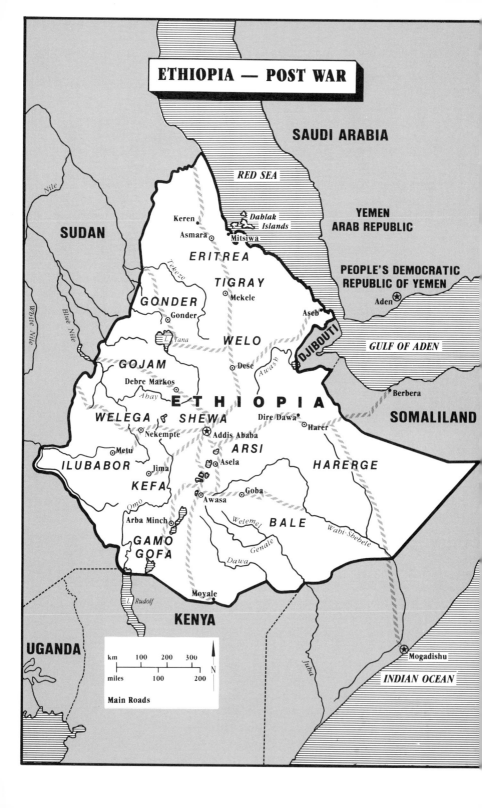

POST WAR REHABILITATION

The establishment of law and order in Ethiopia was an immense problem. The outside world did not grasp the vastness of the problem which faced the military administration and Emperor Haile Selassie in re-establishing a full civilian government. The struggle for survival from the first assault by the Fascist military machine in 1935, to the final battles of liberation in 1942, had involved every part of the country and practically all of its peoples.

Deliberately, the Italian Fascists had eliminated all of those who did not accept their dominating rule. This meant, for the most part, the elimination of the educated and trusted ruling elite, and there were few enough of these at the beginning of the new era for the country. It also meant that there was an entire generation lost, in those who had died in the struggle and the children who had no opportunity for education. The five years of Fascist occupation, as well as the war years before the takeover and after, had now resulted in chaos and confusion. It was a major challenge, first for the victorious military and later for the Emperor.

No part of the country had escaped the direct impact and horror of war. In the war of liberation, practically every bridge had been destroyed, demolitions had blown away much of the roadways, homes had been burned, buildings damaged, and transport abandoned everywhere. The country was full of rifles, guns and ammunition, grenades and land mines. Many of the 255,000 Italian soldiers had thrown their rifles away as they fled or had lost them to Patriots. Also, in the years of infiltration, the British had supplied thousands of rifles to the Patriots. The few hospitals and military medical personnel, including the Friends Ambulance Units, were kept busy caring for women and

Patriot Chiefs pay homage.

children whose bodies had been shattered by hidden land mines, grenades and shells. (One of the author's house boys came to work one morning bringing a grenade he found in his own backyard.) Tragically, not all of these tools of war had fallen into the hands of responsible people. Much of it was in the hands of disbanded Italian Banda soldiers or the more poorly organized Patriot guerillas who needed time to settle down or rejoin families. Before, liberation Brigands had been considered heroes, but afterwards, many became just plain villains and robbers. One of my first experiences of this was at Ambalage where, almost before the fighting had ended, the guerillas set up roadblocks demanding money, food and clothes. The pattern of civilian control by the previous Italian military rule was easier to duplicate than the strict disciplinary honesty of the liberating armies.

Ethiopia — The Military Administration
   The liberating military forces were confronted with the immediate problems of re-establishing order and simultaneously supplying the liberated villages and towns. This responsibility was always complicated by the masses of Prisoners of War and local Italian civilians who also had to be fed and confined. In the aftermath of ferocious battles, with wounded and dead from both sides, the front line soldier's first responsibility was for his own survival and the next action ahead. Follow up medical people and political officers were just not available in this campaign, unlike in the later European theatres of war. Yet, their ability to provide for their own needs and those of the masses of local people and Prisoners of War, was truly remarkable. Words cannot describe how effectively the African and Indian troops, commanded for the most part by British officers, were able to manage the situation.
   Unfortunately, as battles were won in East Africa, battles in other fronts were being lost or locked in struggle. The headlines of war paid little attention to events of the East African campaign. Instead, they found their stories at Dunkirk, Dieppe, North Africa or Leningrad. These battles not only monopolized the headlines, they also demanded soldiers and equipment,

particularly those proven in battle in the East African theatre. For example, after the hard fought victory at Keren, before the taking of Asmara and Massawa, the entire 4th Indian Division was hastily transferred to North Africa to block the counterattack in Cyrenaica, and later to take part in the advance into Syria. Most of the South African Division under the Command of Brigadier Pienaar was also transferred to North Africa after it participated in the taking of Addis Ababa, Dese and Ambalage. Rifles had no chance to cool.

Orde Wingate did not remain in Ethiopia to participate in the final cleanup or to see how his friend, Brigadier Sandford, assisted in the establishment of civilian government. Instead, he was rushed to Burma to take command there. Even some of the King's African Rifles were quickly moved on to the eastern theatre. The need for hardened fighting men was more urgent in every other part of the Allied cause in World War II.

Besides the feeding and handling of 60,000 Italian civilians and 225,000 Prisoners of War, the task of repatriation was immense. For the most part, the Fascist soldiers were shipped off to Prisoner of War camps in Kenya, in many cases taking the place of Ethiopian refugees who returned home at the first opportunity. Many trusted and some not so trustworthy people were used in the transfer to civilian government. One of my first assignments was to help screen Italian prisoners of war and I soon learned that everyone wanted to be recognized as "non Fascist." Some 50,000 of these Italian civilians remained in Ethiopia in gainful and free employment. Repatriatation to Kenya was the alternative for the majority of civilians before being returned to Italy. The first repatriatation ships to Mombassa left Berbera on May 6, 1942. Two more repatriatation ships left Massawa on December 7, 1942. Air flights had also begun, moving other repatriots to Kenya and even a few to the parts of Italy now free.

It is little wonder that the re-establishment of civilian government was left to the Ethiopians themselves with only a small corp of imported political officers. After the last British troops left Addis Ababa on August 6, 1942, there was only a skeleton military force in Ethiopia.

Eritrea and Somaliland

Two thorns in the new Government's feet were the outside territories of Eritrea and Italian Somaliland, both of which had been Italian colonies prior to 1936. Any permanent decisions regarding these two territories had to await the signing of a peace treaty with Italy, which did not take place until September 15, 1947. Therefore, given the financial requirements for maintaining these territories, and the attitude of the Allied victors towards Italy's continued control of colonies in Africa, British provisional governments were accepted in both regions.

In Eritrea, following the capitulation, large numbers of Italians became destitute, to the point of starvation. Thus, a system of relief had to be established immediately. This was complicated by the influx of local Eritrean people into the urban areas of Keren, Asmara and Massawa. Within a few months, most of the Italian population was transported via ship from Massawa Harbour to Mombassa, Kenya. General Platt moved as quickly as possible to establish a military administration in Eritrea. On February 5, 1941, the British Military Administration of Eritrea was formally announced. On July 20, 1941, final authority was invested in the position of Chief Political Officer. He, in turn, appointed a Military Administrator. Both of these offices were filled by senior staff generals responsible directly to the newly formed East African command in Nairobi. Ethiopia's new government would have much preferred to have Eritrea reunited with the Ethiopian motherland immediately. However, Britain was firm in insisting that Eritrea and Italian Somaliland were conquered territories and had to wait until after the war for final settlement. The reuniting of Eritrea to Ethiopia came to pass finally in 1950, and then only by the direct involvement of the United Nations.

Ras Seyoum of Tigray, grandson of Emperor John, had eventually submitted to Italian authority after sustaining a prolonged resistance. However, in April 1941, he gave his formal loyalty to the British military and assisted them in organizing the Tigray patriots. In July 1941, he was reunited with Emperor Haile Selassie in Addis Ababa. His youthful son, Mengasha Seyoum, was initially installed as Governor of Tigray. However, considerable restlessness, to the point of insurrection in Tigray, followed the setting up of the military administration in Eritrea. It was put down only after the intervention of the Royal Air Force and the establishment of a new provincial government.

It was here that the sheer popularity and prestige of Emperor Haile Selassie brought about rest and peace. His personal visits to every community in Tigray, Eritrea and every other part of the country brought to rest much of the post war emotionalism.

On April 15, 1941, Italian Somaliland was similarly placed under a formal Military Administration, later to be directly responsible to the East African Command located in Nairobi. The Somalian population was estimated at 1,200,000. Eight thousand Italian civilians had settled in the country during the years, most of them living in their own settlements. Some of these continued under the British Military Administration but most were gradually moved into camps in Kenya or transferred back to their homeland in Italy after the war. Following the war, Italian Somaliland and Eritrea both were placed under the United Nations.

British Somaliland was an entirely different situation from Italian Somaliland as it had been a protectorate of Great Britain under the League of Nations' arrangements prior to 1936. In 1940, after the takeover of British Somaliland by the Italian forces, Mussolini had made it an integral part of the East African Empire. When the establishment of the East African Command was set up in Nairobi, British Somaliland again came under the authority of the British Military establishment. One of the differences between the situation in British Somaliland and that in Eritrea and Italian Somaliland was that the local Somali population wholeheartedly welcomed the British back as liberators in 1940.

French Somaliland at Djibouti had been under the control of Vichy France following the capitulation of France and the establishment of Vichy France as an independent government. The direct Allied response at the time was to place Djibouti under a complete blockade. This was lifted in July 1942, when the Free French under de Gaulle took over the territories on behalf of the Free French Military.

While the situation in the Somalilands affected Ethiopia only indirectly, the policy of British control over the Ogaden, known as the Reserved Areas, was entirely different. Ethiopians insisted that this territory belonged to Ethiopia. These Reserved Areas actually were the strip of semi desert land between the foothills of the Ethiopian highlands and the veldt of British Somaliland which slopped out to the Indian Ocean. There was a similar area near Italian Somaliland as well. For centuries Somali livestock herdmen had moved into the highlands of Ethiopia for pasture at the onset of the dry season. Then as the rains returned, the nomadic tribespeople would return with their flocks to the plains. For years the Ogaden area had been plagued by tribal conflicts and unrest. The Ethiopians claimed it as their own territory and had done so since the abortive boundary negotiations with Italy began at the turn of the century. They had only reluctantly yielded to British insistance that this be left as a Reserved Area, the fate of which was to be decided at a later date. It became the one sore spot between Ethiopia and Britain, until it was finally handed back to the Ethiopians after the negotiations with Lord de la Warr from Britain. During these negotiations, Britain reluctantly gave in to the insistent demand by Haile Selassie that the territory was Ethiopian and must be returned to Ethiopia.

Internal Security and Recovery in Ethiopia

The return to stable civilian rule in Ethiopia was accomplished in an amazingly short time, although spotted unrest continued for several years. Credit must be given, by friend and critic alike, for the personal dominance of fair play and justice of Emperor Haile Selassie. While the country was weary and worn from seven years of war and bloodshed, military rule and Fascist imperialism, an attitude of peace and goodwill developed among the Ethiopians, Italians and military visitors. It was difficult for many of the Patriots, who during the Italian occupation were heroes, but who were considered criminals for performing the same acts after liberation. There was hardly anyone who had not witnessed bloodshed and who had not lost a father, brother, cousin or neighbour in prison or in armed struggle. Besides the emotional strife, there were tens of thousands of exiles returning to the country. All of these and more had to resettle and find work or farms to provide a livelihood. It may not have been chaos but, at the best, it was confusion.

In face of all of this, the safety of the people of the country had to be ensured. The first step was the formation of a Regular Army and a National Police Force. In January 1942, an agreement was signed with Great Britain establishing a British Military Mission composed of officers and non-commissioned officers. The first responsibility of this force was to form, train and administer the Regular Army. The Irregular army, composed of Patriot fighters under the direct control of the Ministry of War was given the task of maintaining internal security while the regular Army was trained. The Irregular forces were assimulated into the Regular Army in 1944. By that time, all but the senior officers of the British Military Mission had left the country.

The third responsibility for internal security as defined by the 1942 agreement with Britain was to recruit and train a National Police Force. This arrangement worked well. The model used in all cases was that of the Imperial Army and the Municipal Police establishment common in Britain. A Military Training College for officers was established at Genet just west of Addis Ababa and a Police College was established in the capital city. The Ethiopian Air Force was based first at Addis Ababa and later at Debre Zeit. An elite corp of the Imperial Body Guard was organized, with training by officers of the Swedish Army. The Imperial Body Guard maintained a strength of some 5,000 men and later became the source for much of the famous Kagnew Battalion of the U. N. Army in the Korean War.

The hard core of all of these forces came from the two divisions of Irregular troops which had been recruited from exiles trained in Kenya and in the Sudan. They were battle hardened and had performed well as a disciplined force in all of the campaigns except that from the northwest, usually alongside of the King's African Rifles, the Sudan Defence Force units and other colonial units. While many of these were given the opportunity to be demobilized and become part of the civilian administration, many re-enlisted in the new mobilization and became effective career soldiers.

Trade was dead in Ethiopia — villages had not yet been re-established. In fact, there was much hunger in a land where food had always been plentiful and available. Yet in spite of this, progress and peace had quickly been re-established. In his victory speech on the steps of the Menelik Palace, the Emperor had stated, "You are to collaborate with us in order to endeavor to develop the country, to enrich the people, to increase agriculture, commerce and education throughout the land, to protect the life and wealth of the nation and to complete those changes in administration to our new condition."

He further admonished his people, "Do not return evil for evil. Do not commit any act of cruelty like those the enemy committed against you."[1]

The 25,000 Italian civilians in Addis Ababa unnecessarily feared for their lives. They were not molested. Neither were the 5,000 in Jima or the similiar number in Harer, nor the 25,000 in Asmara or the hundreds in Mogadishu. In the course of 20 months, some 275,000 prisoners of war and civilians were repatriated to Kenya, and a few to Italy. Some also were integrated as immigrant civilians to Ethiopia. Some 50,000 became true civilians.

In a very short period of time, governors and judges were appointed. It was complicated by the fact that rank and merit could not be the only qualifications to office. There were patriot leaders and guerilla fighters who were justly awarded with positions of responsibility. However, a loyal soldier did not always qualify as the best administrator. The British military and political officers who did remain did a remarkable job of giving guidance and counsel. The Ethiopian Police Force rapidly became an excellent law and order organization under direct British command and tutelage. The British Medical Corp continued longer than any other British military department, simply because of the complete dearth of qualified medical and nursing staff. One Mission hospital was opened in Addis Ababa, supplemented by former Swedish, Canadian and American missionary volunteers. The British Friends ambulance unit and the American Mennonite Service Committee performed yeoman service in this regard.

Banking and commerce also had to reorganize from scratch. With the accidental death of the Emperor's Canadian financial advisor, C. H. Collier, an American, George Blowers, was brought in to establish the State Bank of Ethiopia. In the meantime, the Banco de Roma was allowed to re-open for an intermediate period of time and Barclays Bank opened a branch office. Italian currency was immediately replaced by East African shillings and pounds until new coinage and bills were introduced. The old silver Maria Theresa dollar (or thaler) which had been in common use since 1850 slowly disappeared from use.

One of my most interesting experiences with money in Ethiopia resulted from my one ton truck being commandeered by the local Governor at the southern town of Bonga. He loaded the one ton truck with three tons of Maria Theresa dollars under the guard of armed soldiers. We made some progress at first over difficult roads, but later had three tires blow out. We, therefore, had to spend several nights in the Beleta Forests waiting for my truck maintenance man to find replacement tires before we could get the heavy load of money to the Minister of Finance in Jima.

On the financial side, Britain, in spite of her hard pressed wartime economy, made annual assistance grants for the first three post war years to the new government. This was in addition to paying the cost of the British officials who stayed behind to assist the Emperor in the post war months. The American government gave a grant in equivalent Ethiopian dollars of $6,805,602.00 with subsequent grants aggregating to $21,250,000.00, later used for the construction of highways.

A personal and business tax was introduced in 1943. The first formal Budget was passed by the Ethiopian Government in 1944 with estimated revenues in the amount of $38,200,000.00 Ethiopian.

One of the economy related departments established soon after the first victory at Akordat and at Kismayu was the Custodian of Enemy Property. The value of this property was to become part of the war repatriatation schemes with Italy. This was headed by the trusted financial advisor, C. H. Collier, who was Governor of the National Bank of Ethiopia before 1936. He was able to set this organization up, but unfortunately was killed in a jeep accident at Dese.

The Emperor with his senior officials, the Crown Prince and Prince Makonnen, the Duke of Harer.

Education became a priority from the first days of the Emperor's return. The Italian government had already established many schools for the children of both civilian and military personnel. However, the great dearth of teachers limited the staffing of schools. Within a year, Makonnen Desta, the first Minister of Education, established a school in each provincial capital and some of the major towns. In 1943, the first Secondary School was opened with the first students being children of returning exiles who had had an opportunity for education while in exile. A Girl's Elementary School was established within months of the re-establishment of government. Within a year, a number of British, Canadian, American and French teachers were hired to staff the senior schools. A number of returning missionaries from the Sudan

Interior Mission were seconded to the Ethiopian Government. The British Council provided other professional educators. In the early months of 1944, the Emperor, himself, assumed the position of Minister of Education and Emmanuel Abraham, returning from his position with the Government in exile, became the Vice Minister of Education. Canadian Jesuits were brought in to develop a large comprehensive school in Addis Ababa, the Tafari Makonnen School. The author, in heading a team of American and Canadian teachers and school administrators, became the Director General of Provincial Education and General Advisor in Political Affairs.

Mention must include the role of the hundreds of Coptic churches as well as Protestant church congregations who defied the restrictions imposed by the Italians in the carrying on of traditional alphabet schools in connection with every church congregation. This had been the role of Christianity in Ethiopia for centuries and had served to keep literacy alive as well as the fundamentals of arithmetic for the Ethiopian culture. During the post war months, it was these schools which had kept the love of learning alive and which provided a base for a developing department of education.

Communications and transportation were urgent problems. The Djibouti/Addis Ababa Railway was in operation by July 3, 1941 and on full schedule by the beginning of September. By January 31, 1942, in a five month period, the railway had carried 228,900 passengers with a total ton kilometer record of 16,990,000. It was the first miracle of restored transportation as the major bridge across the Awash River was reconstructed. It is true that the Italians had left a legacy of a number of well engineered roads and highways. However, most bridges had been destroyed and many of the mountain roads had been blown away by demolitions. The great challenge was to restore and maintain these highways and it was for this purpose that American money was designated. There was a large supply of heavy trucks in the country with experienced drivers and mechanics available from repatriated Italian personnel, but without bridges and road repair, they were of little use.

One of my interesting experiences came one day when, in my Jeep, I was escorting a heavy lorry load of equipment, driven by a trusted Italian driver whose name was Pete. We came to a deep gorge where the bridge had been blown. The local people felled three huge trees across the gap and laid short logs and branches across the three tree girders. It became quite passable for animal traffic or jeeps and light vehicles. The discussion which followed our arrival was whether we should risk taking the loaded lorry across or whether it should be unloaded and then inched across to the other side. The load could be carried across by hand. Finally, I suggested to Pete that he take the loaded truck across while I would remain on the side and pray for safety. In his best English, he replied, "Sir, you drive, Pete will pray!" We unloaded the lorry and Pete took it across empty!

Ethiopia was often described as the African Switzerland. While the Italians left many roads both completed and uncompleted, the mountainous country made road building difficult. The job of repair and rebuilding was to be a long and continuous process. It was quickly realized that air transport was a very vital key and plans were made immediately to initiate a military pilot training program, coupled with the forming of the Imperial Flying Club of which Prince Makonnen became President and I, the Secretary Manager. Prince Makonnen was the first aviation student of the Flying Club! The US Air Transport Command made periodical flights into Addis Ababa from Cairo and became the forerunner of the soon to be formed Ethiopian Air Lines. The British Military Administration, now the government in Eritirea, used what aircraft could be spared for similar role in Eritrea.

Ethiopia had a long way to go in recovering from two major wars only four years apart. It could now pick up the momentum towards modernization which had first come into play at the beginning of the twentieth century through the rule of Menelik II and which Haile Selassie carried on during his years at Regent.

END NOTES
[1] Christine Sandford, **The Lion of Judah Hath Prevailed** (London, J.M. Dent and Sons, 1955), p. 105.

Refueling at an RAF base in the Indian Ocean. L. to R., Colonel Thompson, the RAF Base Commander, and Captain Daniel Rundstrom.

The first graduate pilots of the Ethiopian Air Force at Wings Parade, with Emperor Haile Selassie.

The author in 1945 at the Sudan-Ethiopian border as he begins to retrace the path of the "101 Mission."

Colonel Thompson on the Ogaden Reserved Territories.

13 REFLECTIONS

The campaign and the early years of "Liberation" were a great experience for a lone Canadian. During 1941 and on through the war years, Canada did not have a diplomatic mission in all of Africa. A few Canadian military units served in North Africa. R.C.A.F. personnel were to be found throughout North Africa and the Middle East but the Canadian identity of those individuals was all but lost as they served with the Royal Air Force. Apart from a few strays, such as myself, the only Canadians who really knew anything about the ancient land Ethiopia were the Missionaries. They, together with a few outstanding Ethiopian loyalists such as Sylvia Pankchurst in Britain, were also the only ones who really understood the takeover and the cruelty of the Fascists .

My initial encounter with Ethiopia came through the Royal Air Force. Serving with the Commonwealth Air Training Scheme, I was attached to an RAF Service Flying Training School base in my native Alberta. During this time, I came to know Wing Commander Gerald Gregson, the senior Chaplain of the RAF in the Commonwealth Air Training Programme in Canada. As the former Vicar of St. Paul's at Cambridge, Gregson had become a personal friend of Emperor Haile Selassie who had his home in Bath, just north of London and attended church at St. Paul's. In 1940, when the Emperor was at Khartoum, preparing for his re-entry into his own country, he cabled Gregson, now resident in Canada, to help find young men who might be willing to assist in the liberation and rehabilitation of the country. It was on this basis that Wing Commander Gregson approached me and finally convinced me of this challenge. It was also Gregson who persuaded the Department of Defence in Ottawa that I should be given reassignment for duty in Ethiopia. Although few Canadians knew very much about Ethiopia, there was a strong current of interest and support for Emperor Haile Selassie personally, which originated from his appeal to the League of Nations in 1935 and 1936. It was because of these events that I, as a High School student and later, as a school teacher in Alberta had any interest and knowledge of Ethiopia, meagre as it was at that time.

I began a search for contacts before leaving for Ethiopia, mostly among the missionaries who had served there before the Italian takeover. I learned that all such missionary personnel, whether clerical, educational or medical in their service had been expelled by the Fascists in the first year of the Fascist occupation. Mussolini, undeterred by the negative world opinion concerning the use of mustard gas and the bombing of Red Cross Hospitals in the early months of 1936, sent a message to Marshall de Bono giving the order, "I authorize you to drive away the Swedish Missionaries. . . . I authorize you to use gas, even on a large scale."[1]

Of the only two Canadians in any official capacity that I came to know personally during those critical years in Ethiopia, one was a Col. John Carberry, from Carberry, Manitoba who commanded the British forces in liberated British Somaliland. I met him in Hargeisa as the senior officer in the Imperial Ethiopian Air Force. Carberry, as a young man had gone to England several years before the beginning of World War II to enlist in the Imperial Army. Now as a Colonel, he was part of the liberation force headquartered at Hargeisa.

The second Canadian of any official status to come to Ethiopia, was a Major Fred Ney, D.S.O. MC who had been sent to Ethiopia by the Canadian Military and by the Department of External Affairs to report on the state of the rehabilitation and recovery in Ethiopia. As the senior Canadian in the country at that time, I was his point of contact.

I well recall the evening when the Emperor invited Major Ney, myself and my wife, Hazel, to a private dinner with the Emperor and Empress and their immediate family. We arrived at the palace gates in my Imperial Air Force vehicle which was a 1936 V-8 Ford which the Italians had crafted into a beautiful station wagon. I wore my Canadian Air Force uniform in honor of this very special Canadian evening. We were escorted into the palace entrance where we were received by the Emperor himself. Following a delightful dinner and a lengthy discussion of his days with the Gideon Force and his return to the throne, as well as the progress of rehabilitation since liberation, we took our leave. Expecting to be met by an Imperial Guard Officer at the door with my vehicle, we were instead informed that the battery was dead and that the engine could not be started. Taking charge of that embarrassing situation, I had several of the Guards push the car to the entrance of the palace, with further instructions that once we were inside the vehicle, they were to push us out towards the gate. Putting the car in gear, the engine quickly came to life and we made our exit in full dignity even having the presence of mind to salute the Emperor and Empress who were standing in the doorway in gales of laughter. The story of this event continued to be told for many years in Ethiopia as it related how three Canadians were forcibly pushed out of the palace grounds and survived with full honours.

In retrospect, I find myself most impressed by the memories of the individuals I came to know. First, the leadership ability and character qualities of the British officers from Platt and Cunningham down to those serving in the field was, almost without exception, remarkable and made me proud to be associated with them. The bravery, the morale, the loyalty, and the ability in combat or on partrol duty was always outstanding. The defeat of the Italian military was brought about in a major way by the Colonial troops who were commanded by these British officers from Africa and India, including the South Africans in the Army and the Air Force. One can but say that they were splendid characters willing to fight and if necessary to give their lives in the cause of freedom.

The Ethiopian Irregulars were also great soldiers, highly motivated, brave, able and disciplined in their commitment to restore freedom to their people and country. One cannot forget the Patriots, perhaps not so well disciplined and trained but courageous and committed to freeing their homeland. Without them, the Campaign could not have succeeded as it did. Many of them and their families became my very close friends in later years.

There are a few special personalities, who deserve mention in this narrative.

Emperor Haile Selassie

The first is the Emperor himself. Born in 1892, he became Regent under the aging Empress Zauditu in 1916. Prior to that, at the age of seventeen, he had become Governor of the Province of Sidamo. Less than two years later, he was appointed Governor of the prestigous province of Harer where his father had served as Governor before him. Even as a mere youth, this young man created for himself a reputation as quite an extraordinary person, energetic, a capable administrator, able to implement many of the principles of good government which he had learned from his father, Ras Makonnen. In 1911, he married Weizero Menen, who through her mother was granddaughter of King Mikail of Wello. As a Regent, with a common sense approach and an infinite amount of patience and perserverance, he initiated a number of changes, establishing the first national health services and educational system. He also abolished the slave trade which the Arab slave runner had managed in the country, and, in 1924, brought Ethiopia in as a full member into the League of Nations. Through incessant industry and unflinching resolve, he pressed continuously for steady advancement. Above all, his political sensitivity and his strong will of leadership was equal to each political crisis which confronted him. In March 1930, Empress Zauditu died. On April 3, 1930, Ras Tafari Makonnen was proclaimed Emperor as Haile Selassie I, King of Kings of Ethiopia. His Proclamation to the people of Ethiopia at that time was as follows:

"In accordance with the Proclamation which our Creator abiding in His people, and electing us, did cause to be made, we have lived without breach of our Covenant as mother and son. Now, in that by the law and commandment of God, none that is human may avoid return to earth, Her Majesty the Empress, after a few days of sickness, has departed this life.

The passing of Her Majesty the Empress is grievous for myself and for the whole of the empire. Since it is the long-standing custom that when a King, the Shepherd of his people, shall die, a King replaces him, I being upon the seat of David to which I was betrothed, will, by God's charity, watch over you. Trader, trade! Farmer, plough! I shall govern you by the law and ordinance that has come, handed down from my fathers."[2]

The Coronation was on November 2, 1930 in the presence of dignitaries from Europe, including the United Kingdom and Italy. In 1931, the first formal Constitution was proclaimed.

His programme of peaceful progress and development was shortlived when in December 1934, the Italians attacked the Ethiopian outpost of Wel Wel.

The noted Historian, Arnold Toynbee, in his second volume of "International Affairs 1935", commented on this development as follows:

"This episode is a tale of sins and nemesis. . . . If we try to marshal the several participants in the tragedy in their order of merit we shall find that the poorest figure was cut by those with the most specious claim to represent the fine flower of western culture. The 'beau role' was played by the Emperor Haile Selassie, the heir of a non-western tradition, who combined an antique virtue with an enlightened modernism."[3]

On October 3, 1935, Italian troops from Asmara crossed the border into Ethiopia north of Adwa in a full scale military invasion under the command of General de Bono. After the years of exile and the Emperor's diligent work which I have already referred to in Chapters 1 and 8, he returned as the mysterious Mr. Strong to his homeland.

When Haile Selassie reached Khartoum during the early days of July 1940, the British Command had not been informed of his imminent arrival. There was some resentment by many of the senior officers at his arrival, fearing that he would be in the way and his meddling would upset the strategy that was taking place. Through direct intervention by Anthony Eden, this feeling of resentment was cut short. His instructions were that all along the way Haile Selassie was to be kept informed of every development. Haile Selassie was part of the team and would be sharing in the development and drafting of strategy as they prepared to return the country to him. It was grudgingly admitted later by those who had objected to his presence that the western campaign could not have succeeded if it had not been for the presence and influence of the Emperor.

From the beginning of September, Haile Selassie watched, waited and worked. There was no question about his personal commitment and bravery. His personality was impressive to all who met and worked with him. He projected dignity and confidence as he overcame problems in a way that inspired loyalty and commitment.

The Emperor's appeal of mercy for all of the Italian enemy personnel was indicative of the character of the man. It was summed up in a simple statement:

"I reason with you to receive with love and to care for those Italians who fall into the hands of Ethiopian warriors, whether they come armed or unarmed. Do not mete to them according to the wrongs which they have committed against our people. Show that you are soldiers of honour with human hearts. Especially do I ask you to guard and respect the lives of children, women, and the aged."[4]

It is interesting also to note that Haile Selassie never spoke publicly without giving thanks to Almighty God and pleading for His guidance and wisdom. This personal faith, his concern for people, his determination, his fairness and judgement, his astute negotiating ability, and his loyalty to his family always impressed those of us who knew him best.

Orde Charles Wingate, Major General, D.S.O. and bar

The second most impressive person was Orde Wingate. Anyone who worked with him, whether it was in Palestine, in Ethiopia or in Burma, could not but be impressed with this man.

The record of Orde Wingate's checkered, but illustrious career is inseparably linked to Field Marshall Sir Archibald (Viscount) Wavell. The two men first met in Palestine in 1937 when Wavell was given command of the British Forces in Palestine and Wingate was an Intelligence Officer. Wavell, in his description of Wingate, said that he was

> "impressed by the young officer with piercing eyes; that he was no respector of persons because of their rank and that he had no hesitation in putting forward unorthodox views and in maintaining them. Yet, he had proved himself a most effective and impressive leader of men."[5]

Wingate went on to be the guerilla type fighter, receiving his D.S.O. for clearing Palestine of Arab terrorists. Enthralled by the prospect of the Jews returning to their homeland, he became fluent in the Hebrew language. He also mastered Arabic.

In 1940 when General Wavell, now as the Commander in Chief of the Middle East forces, looked for an officer to head the military penetration into western Ethiopia from the Sudan, he sent for Major Wingate (later Colonel and then, Brigadier).

After the completion of the Ethiopian Campaign and the collapse of the Italian East African Empire. Wingate returned to the Middle East for a medical rest. Field Marshall Wavell had been relieved of his Middle East command and placed in command of the India-Burma theatre of the war. He called again for Wingate to take charge of the inevitable guerilla type war which was planned to check the advance of the Japanese through Burma. Wingate was killed in the crash of a RAF plane before the final victory in Burma, but he is given credit for the stategy, planning and implementation of the successful campaign which led to the final defeat of the Japanese army.

Field Marshall Wavell gave full credit to Wingate as a genius in leadership who inspired his troops with his magnetic personality and gift of speech, who saw the blossom of the first fruit of his labours, but not the final harvest of victory. Wingate's biographer, Charles Rolo, in his book, "Wingate's Raiders" summed up Wingate's life as,

> "Wingate's peculiar brand of military genius was irreplaceable. A great rebel, he slashed through red tape, lashed out at the prejudices and complacency of 'the military ape,' and by dint of persistence and achievement saw his ideas endorsed by the highest-ranking strategists of the United Nations. An inspired planner with a bold but disciplined imagination, he was one of the few genuine tactical innovators on the Allied side. He conceived two campaigns unique in the annals of war — the first long-range penetration of enemy territory supplied exclusively from the air; the first large-scale airborne landing in enemy-held jungle and mountain terrain. To him goes much of the credit for putting into reverse the dismal story of Hong Kong, Singapore, and Rangoon.
>
> Daring in conception, patient in preparation, magnificently effective in execution, Wingate was at the same time a dreamer and a supreme realist. While dreaming of the reconquest of Burma, he could remember to equip his men with tourniquets in the form of spare bootlaces. He knew how to plan a whole campaign, or kill a mule silently with a deft stroke of the knife. He showed how to enlist the sympathies and co-operation of the Burmese, and established a pattern for dealing with the natives of South-east Asia which his successors would do well to follow. Above all, he was a great fighter, always ready to charge the enemy at the head of his men.
>
> His death was a hard and bitter blow to the troops he commanded. Officers and men felt for him a respect and affection that amounted to hero-worship in the best sense. They had supreme faith in his leadership and a lively admiration for his conduct in the field. He had always shared with

them, down to the humblest private, every hazard and hardship of jungle warfare, and, as one officer observed, 'He seemed to do everything better than anyone else in the force.'

Perhaps the most fitting tribute to Wingate, who achieved so much for the Jews of Palestine, the Ethiopians, and the conquered Burmese — certainly the tribute he would have liked best — is that of Mr. Michael Foot, who wrote in the 'Evening Standard' at the time of Wingate's death: 'He was a great man of God in the Old Testament sense, and a great Englishman. For the glory of England, the fact that has allied her name with that of freedom and humanity . . . is that such men as Wingate have gone forth to make their own the cause of some unhappy people, suppliant in its agony and looking to England as its champion.'

The sum of Wingate's qualities made him one of England's finest figures. The 'Lawrence' of Judea, Ethiopia, and Burma was not merely a military genius. He was something much rarer — a truly great human being.''[6]

Emperor Haile Selassie often spoke of his admiration of General Wingate, who astride a white charger, at the head of his troops, Ethiopian and Sudanese, led the Emperor at the takeover of Addis Ababa on May 5, 1942. A favorite quote of the Emperor about his friend, Orde Wingate was taken from the Orders of the Day, February 17, 1943 as his column crossed the Chindwin River in Burma,

"Finally, knowing the vanity of man's effort and the confusion of his purpose, let us pray that God may accept our services and direct our endeavors, so that when we have done all we shall see the fruits of our labours and be satisfied.''[7]

Orde Wingate came from a family of soldiers and ministers. The sword and the Bible were part of his heritage. He was a cousin of the Lawrence of Arabia and was known as the Lawrence of Judea, of Ethiopia, and of Burma. He had a Puritan upbringing, which left him with the habit of prayer and meditation of the Bible. He never failed to impart his faith to the men he led in his daring adventures. The Palestinians, the Ethiopians, and the Burmese loved him, followed him wherever he led. The Secondary School built in Addis Ababa, in post war Ethiopia, was named the General Wingate Secondary School in his honour.

Shialeka Mesfin Sleshi

This Patriot was an unforgettable character. As a guerilla, "Arabaynia" fighter, he was a thorn in the side in the occupying forces of Mussolini for six years. His field of activities were in Wollega, the Kaffa and Gojam provinces. He even harrassed the perimeters of the "walled" city of Addis Ababa. With a semi trained force of some 200 Patriots, he met the Emperor at Gedaref in the Sudan on September 1940, in company with Dejazmatch Negash and Dejazmatch Jembere. With the rank Shilaleka, a commander of a thousand, equivalent to Major, he went to the Gojam to join forces with Colonel Sandford and the 101 Mission.

Following the restoration of the Emperor to his throne, he participated in the crossing of the Omo River and the cleanup campaign in Kaffa Province. Raised to the rank of Dejazmatch, he was appointed Governor of Kaffa with the centre of his administration at Jima.

I came to know him best in this later office, when I became Director of Education in Kaffa. We worked together in the rehabilitation of the south west. He loved to show off his scars of battle, which included seven wounds incurred from rifle fire and shrapnel. As I so well remember, he would relate his many escapades of how Italian patrols repeatedly tried to get him in order to win the bounty which the generals had placed upon his head, dead or alive. They never quite made it, but his escapes were always breath taking, especially the raids which he made on the capital city itself.

Often I would engage in target practice with him. To his frustration, I could occasionally better him, particularly at 600 meters range with my trusty Lee Enfield, which I had effectively mastered in boot training at Sarcee near Calgary. Sleshi was a delightful person, although a harsh master who found it difficult at times to completely transform himself from brigand life as a daring Patriot, to that of efficient peace time senior government administrator.

His Patriot, and later, his official life was tempered by his wife, Weizero Yishimibeit, who was a gracious lady in every respect. She came from a noble family in Wollega and generously gave her time and energy in helping her neighbours who were in need or suffering from the results of war.

Pastor Mammo Chorka

Many Patriots in armed resistance and others in less violent ways ran the risk of death. Mussolini himself issued orders that all rebels were to be shot but Fascist officers often found torture a more profitable way of obtaining information or in controlling the populace. Included were those in leadership roles in the Church. One of these was a Presbyterian Pastor named Mammo Chorka. Together with his blind friend, Gidada, he was imprisoned in Jima. I knew him well, after his release from captivity. Fluent in Oromo, Amharic, as well as English and Italian, his own record of his brutal torture is better told by himself.

"For a month I was never left alone a minute of any time I was away from my home; when I went to market two men went with me; when I went to church two shadows followed me; each day I was watched all day and my house watched at night. Then I was taken to prison. My friend Gidada, who was blind, was called at the same time.

In Jima we were put in prison . . . five men started beating me from all sides at once. When they had forced me against the wall on one side, they beat me again, till I fell against the other side. When I actually fell on the floor, they used their heavy army boots and kicked me; then they took the wood of their guns and pounded me with them. One of them tried each time to hit my eyes and to knock them out. They used me as a football, knocking me from side to side, hitting and kicking me, as if they were playing some game. How my bones were not broken I know not. The flesh was bruised in so many places that I was in bed three months from the injuries.

After a little while they asked me, 'Why did you go to Mandi?' I answered that in Mandi there were many Christians, and they wanted their children baptized in the Christian way, and they wrote to me that the Ethiopian priest would not do it for them. Also, they wanted a minister to come to help them, and they had called me to come.

They began to say that I lied; that all I said was lies, and that I must now begin to tell the truth to them. I asked them if the Germans were not friends of the Italians. They said that it was so. Then I said that, if they wanted to see whether I were telling the truth, they might ask a German pastor who knew all about my trips, and their answer was, 'Why should we go to ask him when you are here and we can get the truth out of you?' My answer was, 'If you want the truth I have told it.' Again they began to beat me, with fists, with rulers, with gun stocks, and to kick with shoes, and I was soon bleeding from nose and mouth. As I fell one way, they knocked me back another way. Five men hitting as hard as they could with anything they could lay their hands on, and then kicking, too. The one man was still trying to blind me. This time it laster more than half an hour.
. . .

Again, they asked me what I had written to the English; what I had written to Haile Selassie. I said that copies of my letters were in my house, and they were welcome to them. That I had written neither to the English nor to Haile Selassie. . . . Then for the third time they began to beat me. This time I was too sick to know just what happened, or how long the torture went on, but I believe that it must have been well over an hour that the men beat and kicked me this time. My eyes were swollen shut, my lips, mouth, and nose were bleeding badly. Then the questioning began again. In each statement they accused me of lying, and demanded that I tell the truth.

For the fourth time they began their cruel beating and kicking, saying, 'Tell the truth, tell the truth,' with each beat of hand or kick of foot. This time I know not how long it was. I was too sick. It seemed endless....'Lies, lies, lies, all lies.' Now I could not even feel the hits. I was so sick that I was like a piece of wood. I tried to say that, if I were guilty, they must shoot me and not play with me. But they said that they intended to knock me about until I died, that killing with a gun was too good for me. Until the time when night fell, they treated me in this way, then told the guard to tie my hands and feet together till the blood ran from the cuts they made by the cords, and throw me into a tiny room, where I lay, alone, not able to move hand or foot. There are scars on my hands now, where the cords and the steel cut into my flesh. I begged that, as an Ethiopian Christian, the guard would loosen the cords and steel, but he said that his food was of more value to him than his being a Christian, and he left me that way. I lay there all night long. . . .

After many more questions, all along the same lines, the head of those who were questioning caught up a porcupine quill that was on the table and, taking the sharp end, thrust it again and again into the skin on my head, pushing it into the bone, tearing the skin in many places. I begged and begged that, if I had made a mistake, they would kill me and not torment me further. I said that Jesus Christ was my master and that I did not fear to die as He would care for me. . . .

When I was tied and thrown into the little room again, I broke down and cried to Jesus Christ, asking Him, if I had to suffer, to look down upon me and give me courage and strength, but, if it could be, that I might have a little rest from the torture; that I would be glad indeed to have the rest or to die if he wished. In less than five minutes I was released from bonds and sent back into the main prison where Gidado was."[8]

As well, many suffered death, as the cruelty of the Fascists became an efficient tool of repressive control. However, others like Mammo did survive, and became personal friends. Amongst them are heroes such as Abagoli, Shiguti, Danamaja and Hailu. Such individuals as these reminded me of the fact that the inborn desire for freedom runs deep within the human breast, more so than the need for food and shelter or physical security — even stronger than the innate demand for survival itself. Perhaps the exception is when the lust for power numbs or destroys the innermost desires of the human heart. If those who died at the hand of the Fascists could speak, they would tell us of their commitment to freedom and liberty even unto death that others might be free.

Four Missionary Soldiers

Two New Zealanders, one Australian and one Britisher who served in Ethiopia as Missionaries prior to being expelled by the Italians in 1937, returned as intelligence officers with the British military during the 1940-42 campaign. Each of these men knew Ethiopia well. They spoke the Amharic language and three of them spoke an additional tribal language. Each of them knew and understood Ethiopia's customs and culture. These qualifications made them a valuable asset to the liberating forces. In addition to their personal ability, they proved themselves excellent officers. As a group, they represented an important element in the overall victory. After the collapse of the Italian resistance, all four men withdrew from military service to return as civilian Missionaries, and assisted in the rehabilitation of the country.

In 1938, the Italian Regia Aeronautica bombed a mission station and hospital of the Sudan Interior Mission at Doro in the

Sudan, killing the Doctor in charge and his wife and severely wounding a second missionary couple. Doro was not far from the Ethiopian frontier and the Italians probably suspected the Missionaries of caring for Ethiopian refugees, many of whom had fled their country during the takeover of the Italians. The unwarranted bombing incident more than likely was a motivating factor in the decision of the four Missionaries to join the British military in the Sudan and in Kenya.

Major Glen Hall Cain from Australia served in Ethiopia with the Sudan Interior Mission. After being expelled from Ethiopia, he went to the Sudan where he continued as a Missionary in the Nile valley. Later, at a military outpost in the southeast Sudan near the Ethiopian border east of Juba, he served with the Pioneer Corps of the Sudan Defence Force. Early in 1940, he entered Ethiopia as an Intellignece Officer. Reaching Maji in May, after the decisive takeover of this Italian outpost, the Pioneers moved northward where they joined at Shewa Gimera with the clean up forces coming southward from Jima. Major Cain served as the senior political officer at Jima with the Occupied Enemy Territory Administration (O.E.T.A.) until the Ethiopian police and administration was established for Kaffa Province. He returned to the Sudan until his discharge in March 1946. He then returned to Ethiopia as a Missionary to head the Sudan Interior Mission.

Captain David Stokes was a Missionary with the Bible Churchmen Missionary Society from Britain. When the Italian armies invaded Ethiopia, Stokes served with the International Red Cross at a field hospital in the northern front and later at a hospital in Addis Ababa which ministered to the Ethiopian wounded. Caught behind the Italian lines, Stokes escaped Italian capture and finally reached the British Consulate in Harer just before the Italians took over the city. While there, the Italian General personally interviewed Stokes requesting that he testify that the Italians had not bombed Red Cross hospitals. This he refused to do as he himself had escaped a bombing raid on a Red Cross hospital at which he served. He had also been in an Ethiopian column of refugees which had been strafed from the air. After first being allowed to return to his mission base in Addis Ababa, he was later expelled from the Italian East Africa

Empire just after Easter in 1937. Going to the Sudan, he joined the British military at Khartoum serving as A.D.C. to the Governor General and later, as A.D.C. to Emperor Haile Selassie when the Emperor came to Khartoum in July 1940. He then served with Major Cheesman in the 101 Mission. After victory, he became an administrative officer with the O.E.T.A. in Addis Ababa. As the Ethiopian Administration assumed authority, Stokes was transferred to the British Legation in Addis Ababa as an Attache. He was later released from military service to resume his missionary career.

Lt. Col. Allen Smith, a New Zealander, served in Ethiopia with the Sudan Interior Mission in Sidamo in the early thirties. He escaped from Ethiopia as the Italians took over, fleeing with Swedish and Norwegian Missionaries and Red Cross workers to Kenya in the summer of 1936. He worked for the first several years in the Ethiopian refugee camps in Northern Kenya. In 1940, he enlisted with the British military and was attached to the 1st Ethiopian Irregular Division in their training as a first class fighting unit. In the fall of 1940 when the plans took shape for the invasion of Ethiopia from the Sudan, he was transferred with the 1st Ethiopian Irregular Battalion to the Sudan. His Battalion, along with a Brigade of the Sudan Defence Force made up the Gideon force under the command of Colonel Wingate. These troops rounded up and took charge of the 1,500 camels within the Camel transportation unit. The strength of the Gideon unit rarely exceeded 2,000 men apart from the support of the Patriots who joined to make it the master unit of guerilla warfare — a unit with which the defending Italian military were unable to cope. Smith was regarded by his military peers as one of the great field officers in the southern and western campaign.

After the victorious entrance into Addis Ababa by the Gideon force with Brigadiers Sandford and Wingate, Smith was transferred to Military Administration in Somaliland, where he became affectionately known as "Smith of the Ogaden." His last posting in the war was as Military Mayor of Mega. After discharge, he returned to study medicine at the Medical faculty in Dunedin, hoping to return to Ethiopia as a Medical Missionary. This goal was never attained as he died in Adelaide, Australia from the effects of his military service before completing his studies.

Lieutenant L. Alexander Davison, also a New Zealander, served in Ethiopia as a Missionary with the Sudan Interior Mission. He was expelled in 1937 and after home furlough, returned to the Sudan as a Missionary. When Italy declared war on the United Kingdom, Davison saw military service as the quickest way back to Ethiopia. Enlisting in 1941 in Khartoum with the rank of Lieutenant, he was immediately posted to Addis Ababa as a political officer travelling via the Kassala Keren route. In Addis Ababa, he also became part of the Occupied Enemy Territory Administration. As a result of his experience with both the Ethiopians and Italians, he was placed in charge of Italian prisoners of war and Italian civilians, including women and children. Most of the Italians were shipped by land and air to Camps in Kenya and Uganda. However, the "non-Fascists" and those considered trustworthy were allowed to remain in Ethiopia as tradesmen or professionals.

Included in the tens of thousands of Prisoners of War were the Ethiopian or Eritrean colonial troops. One of the very difficult tasks was in sorting out these troops because many of them were illiterate and did not know where their home areas were, but who somehow had to be returned to their own tribal villages.

One of my duties in reaching Addis Ababa city was to work with Davison in this relocation of Prisoners of War. Many of them, it was discovered, had been part of the Regia Aeronautica.

Davison finished his military service in Kenya continuing to work in the Prisoner of War Camps. On discharge, he returned to Ethiopia at the request of the Ethiopian Government to develop a School of Ethiopian Arts and Crafts.

In Conclusion

Following VE Day, I continued on directly with the Government of Ethiopia until 1951, first as Headmaster of the Haile Selassie I Secondary School, then for one year as Superintendant of schools in Kaffa Province and lastly, for five years as Associate Director General of Education. During these last years, I was also on call for a variety of foreign affairs assignments. These experiences allowed me the privilege of knowing Ethiopia as an insider, as well as from an international perspective. I became familiar with all parts of the country and was able to visit every major battlefield in the 1940-42 war of Liberation and to retrace the steps of the victors. Many of those who had been part of the Kenyan trained Ethiopian Irregulars became my buddies in uniform and some later became students and friends. Even some of the Italian civilians who had participated in the fighting related in great detail the stories of the various battles that took place. Likewise, many of the British officers and officials in the interim government became colleagues and friends. Most of all, to have worked directly with Emperor Haile Selassie was a great privilege. Rarely have I known a man of such indepth Christian faith, commitment and perserverance. His was a difficult task. Had his skin been of lighter hue and his domain in some European realm, he would have been ranked with the greatest names of the century's history. The last sixteen years of our relationship were at arm's length but they moved him from his greatest achievements to a time when age lessened his physical and mental stamina.

One of my unforgettable experiences in the first years after the hostilities ceased was to participate as a staff advisor to the Ethiopian delegation in the negotiation with the British representatives under Lord de la Warr for a final settlement regarding the Reserved Territories of the Ogaden, the area lying between the plains of Somaliland and the foothills of Ethiopia. The Ogaden was finally returned to Ethiopia to the chagrin of the British politicians and the delight of the Ethiopians. For the first and only time, my loyalty to the British Empire was questioned — after all, I was now in the employ of the Ethiopian Government.

However, the focus of this story is the liberation of Ethiopia — the first nation to be freed from the clutches of Fascism and Nazism in the years from 1936 to 1945. Some of which I have written, I have learned from history books. Some has come from others who were directly involved in this campaign. Much has come out of my own experience. Because of the vast territory that Ethiopia represents, it was impossible for any single person to be involved in all of the different campaigns. Thus, the few books that have been written about this liberation have been written by military historians or those who had been involved in parts of the war. Few have had my privilege in knowing the country, the language and the complete story of liberation, the first Allied victory of World War II.

It was a spectacular victory, first in the deserts of the Sudan and the Somalilands and then in the rugged mountain country of Ethiopia. The stories from these battles raised the spirits and the determination of the British troops for the annihilation of the Italian forces in Libya and the final defeat of Rommel's SS troops. These early victories led eventually, but very surely towards the total defeat of Mussolini's forces in Italy, and the final defeat of Nazi Germany. It is a story which deserves to be told and retold!

Peace returns to Ethiopia.

END NOTES

[1] Laura Fermi, **Mussolini** (Chicago, University of Chicago Press, 1961), p. 324.

[2] Christine Sandford, **The Lion of Judah Hath Prevailed** (London, J. M. Dent and Sons, 1955), p. 55.

[3] Arnold Toynbee, ed., **Survey of International Affairs 1935,** Vol. II (London, Oxford University Press, 1935), p. 1.

[4] Sandford, **The Lion of Judah Hath Prevailed,** p. 94.

[5] Charles Rolo, **Wingate's Raiders**

[6] Ibid.

[7] Ibid.

[8] Kenneth Gandar Dower, **The Abyssinia Patchwork** (London, Frederick Muller, 1949), pp. 213-19.

THE AUTHORS OF THE STEEL PACT:
At the signing of the "Pact of Steel" on May 22, 1939, Mussolini
declared "The two strongest powers in Europe have now bound
themselves to each other for peace and war."

APPENDIX I

THE ROME-BERLIN AXIS
CONFIRMED IN A SECRET PROTOCOL, ENTITLED

THE PACT OF STEEL
signed by Adolph Hitler on behalf of Germany and Benito Mussolini on behalf of Italy in Berlin on 22 May 1939

Preamble

The Following are the terms of the military pact between Germany and Italy signed in Berlin yesterday.

"The German Reich Chancellor and His Majesty the King of Italy and Albania, Emperor of Ethiopia, consider that the moment has come when the close relations of friendship and affinity which exist between National-Socialist Germany and Fascist Italy should be strengthened through a solemn pact.

Since a safe bridge for mutual help and support has been created by the common frontier between Germany and Italy, which has been fixed for all time, the two Governments acknowledge once again a policy which in its basis and objects has already previously been agreed upon by them and which has proved itself successful, both for the promoting of the interests of the two countries and also for the securing of peace in Europe.

Closely bound together through internal relationships of ideologies and through comprehensive solidarity of interest, the German and Italian peoples have decided in the future also side by side and with united strength to stand up for the the securing of their sphere of living and for the maintenance of peace.

In this way, which has been prescribed to them by histroy, Germany and Italy, in the midst of a world unrest and disintegration, desire to devote themselves to the task of securing the foundations of European culture."

The Pact

I

The high contracting parties will remain permanently in contact with one another in order to agree on all questions affecting their own interest or the European situation as a whole.

II

Should the common interests of the high contracting parties be endangered through international events of any sort they will immediately enter into consultations with one antoher in order to take measures to protect those interests.

III

Should the security or other vital interests of one of the contracting parties be threatened from outside the other contracting party will afford the threatened party its full political and diplomatic support in order to remove this threat. If it should happen, against the wishes and hopes of the contracting parties, that one of them becomes involved in warlike complications with another Power or with other Powers the other contracting party will come to its aid as an ally and will support it with all its military forces on land, on sea, and in the air.

IV

In order to secure in specific cases the rapid execution of the obligations undertaken in Article III, the Governments of the two contracting parties will further intensify their cooperation in the military sphere and in the sphere of war economics.

Similarly the two Governments will also keep each other permanently informed about the measures necessary for the practical execution of the provisions of this pact.

For the purposes laid down in paragraphs 1 and 2 of this article the two Governments will set up a Permanent Commission which will be subject to the direction of the two Foreign Ministers.

V

The high contracting parties bind themselves in the case of a jointly waged war to conclude an armistice and peace only in full concord with one another.

VI

The two contracting parties are conscious of the importance which must be attached to their joint relation with the Powers with which they are friends (Hungary, Japan, and Manchukuo). They are determined in the future to maintain and develop such relations in common and in accordance with the unanimous interests by which they are united with those Powers.

VII

The pact comes into force immediately upon being signed. The two contracting parties agree to fix the first period of its validity at ten years. They will come to an agreement about the prolongation of the validity of pact in good time before this period has elapsed.

The Secret Protocol[1]

On signing the friendship and alliance pact agreement has been established by both parties on the following points:

1. The two Foreign ministers will as quickly as possible

come to an agreement on the organization, the seat, and the methods of work on the pact of the commissions on military questions and questions of war economy as stipulated in Article IV of the pact.

2. For the execution of Article IV, par. 2, the two Foreign Ministers will as quickly as possible arrange the necessary measures, guaranteeing a constant co-operation, conforming to the spirit and aims of the pact, in matters of the press, the news service and the propaganda. For this purpose in particular, each of the two Foreign Ministers will assign to the embassy of his country in the respective capital one or several especially well experienced specialists, for constant discussion in direct close co-operation with the respective Ministry of Foreign Affairs, of the suitable steps to be taken in matters of the press, the news service and the propaganda for the promotion of the policy of the Axis, and as a counter measure against the policy of the enemy powers.

Comments in the address by Adolf Hitler, Chancellor of the Reich, at Berlin, September 28, 1937, following the signing of the Steel Pact.

"We have just witnessed an historic event, the significance of which has no parallel. More than a million people have gathered here, participating in a demonstration which is being closely followed by the national communities of two countries, numbering 115,000,000, besides hundreds of millions more in other parts of the world who are following the proceedings over the radio as more or less interested listeners.

What moves us the most at this moment is the deep-rooted joy to see in our midst a guest (Premier Benito Mussolini of Italy who is one of the lonely men in history, who are not put to trial by historic events but who determine the history of their country themselves.

Secondly, we realize that this demonstration is not one of those meetings which we can experience anywhere. It is the avowal of common ideals and common interests. It is the avowal pronounced by two men and it is heard by a million people assembled before us, an avowal which is expected and confirmed by 115,000,000 with a burning heart.

That is why the present demonstration is more than a public meeting. It is a manifestation of nations. The true meaning of this public gathering consists of the sincere desire to guarantee peace to our two countries which is not the reward for resigned cowardice but the result of a responsible policy safeguarding the racial, intellectual, and physical fitness of the nation as well as its cultural possessions. In doing this we hope to serve the interests of two nations and more than that, the interest of the European continent.

The fact that we are in a position today to hold this meeting reminds us of the changes that have taken place in the period which we have left behind us. There is no nation in the world which longs more for peace than Germany, and no country has suffered more from the terrible consequences of misplaced blind confidence than our nation. We recall a period of fifteen years before National Socialism came into power, a time which was marked by oppression, exploitation, the denial of equal rights with other nations, and an unutterable mental torture and material distress. The ideals of liberalism and democracy have not preserved the German nation from the worst depression histroy has ever seen. National Socialism was thus forced to create a new ideal and a more effective one, according all human rights to our people which had been denied the nation for fifteen long years.

During this time of bitter experience, Italy, and Fascist Italy, especially, has refused to take part in the humiliation Germany was subjected to. I must make it a point to say this tonight before the German people and the whole world. In the course of these years, Italy has shown understanding for the demands of a great nation claiming equal rights with other peoples in the endeavor to provide the means of subsistence, and, above all, to save its honor. We are only too glad that the hour has come, in which we are given the opportunity to recall the past and, as I believe, in which we have remembered our debt of gratitude.

The common trend of ideas expressed in the Fascist and National Socialist revolutions has developed today into a similar course of action. This will have a salutary influence on the world, in which destruction and deformation are trying to win the upper hand. Fascist Italy has been transformed into a new Imperium Romanum by the ingenious activities of a compelling personality.

You, Benito Mussolini, will have realized the fact that in these days, due to the National Socialist State, Germany has become a Great Power, thanks to her racial attitude and her military strength. The inherent strength of the two countries is the best guaranty for the preservation of Europe which is inspired by a sense of responsibility in the discharge of its cultural mission. It is not willing to allow destructive elements to cause its decline and dissolution.

You who are present at this very hour and those who are listening to us in other parts of the world must acknowledge that two sovereign national regimes have come into contact at a time in which the democractic and Marxist international revels in demonstrations of hatred which must result in dissension.

Every attempt to interfere with the understanding between the two nations or to play one up against the other, by casting suspicion and by obscuring the real aims in order to dissolve the ideal partnerhsip, will be of no avail because of the innermost desire of 115,000,000 people who are united at the manifestation of this very hour, and because of the determination of the two men who are standing here to address you.

Excerpts from a Speech made by Mussolini on 28 September 1937, on the occasion of the signing of the Steel Pact:

. . . I have come not merely as Head of the Italian Government but above all in my capacity as the head of a national revolution, which thereby wishes to give proof of its close connexion with your revolution. The course of both revolutions may have been different; but the goal they have wished to reach and have reached is the same: the unity and greatness of the nation.

Fascism and National-Socialism are both expressions of the similarity in historical events in the life of our nations, which have reached unity in the same century and by the same event.

There are no secret intentions hidden behind my visit to Germany. Nothing will be planned here to divide a Europe which is already divided enough. The solemn confirmation of the fact and stability of the Rome-Berlin axis is not directed against other States. We National-Socialists and Fascists want peace which does not silently ignore, but solves, the questions arising from the life of the peoples.

To the whole world, which is asking tensely what the result of this meeting will be, war or peace, the Fuhrer and I can answer with a loud voice: Peace...''

END NOTES
[1] Berlin 22 May 1939 XVIII.

APPENDIX II

AGREEMENT BETWEEN
THE UNITED KINGDOM AND ETHIOPIA

JANUARY 31, 1942

Whereas His Majesty the Emperor of Ethiopia, Conquering Lion of the Tribe of Judah, Elect of God (hereinafter referred to as His Majesty the Emperor), wishes to put on record His gratitude and that of His people for the overwhelming and generous aid He has received from the Forces of His Majesty The King of Great Britain, Ireland and the British Dominions beyond the Seas, Emperor of India (hereinafter referred to as His Majesty The King), which has enabled Him and His people to recover their national territory; and

Whereas His Majesty the Emperor, true to His coronation pledges not to surrender His sovereignty or the independence of His people, but conscious of the needs of His country, has intimated to the Government of the United Kingdom of Great Britain and Northern Ireland (hereinafter referred to as the Government of the United Kingdom) that He is eager to receive advice and financial assistance in the difficult task of reconstruction and reform; and

Whereas the Government of the United Kingdom recognise that Ethiopia is now a free and independent State and His Majesty the Emperor, Haile Selassie I, is its lawful Ruler, and, the reconquest of Ethiopia being now complete, wish to help His Majesty the Emperor to re-establish His Government and to assist in providing for the immediate needs of the country:

Now, therefore, His Majesty the Emperor of Ethiopia in person, and   Major-General Sir Philip Euen Mitchell, Knight Commander of the Most Distinguished Order of Saint Michael and Saint George, upon whom has been conferred the decoration of the Military Cross, Chief Political Officer, on the Staff of the General Officer Commanding-in-Chief, East

Africa, being duly authorised for this purpose by the Government of the United Kingdom,
Have agreed as follows:

ARTICLE I.

Diplomatic relations between the United Kingdom and Ethiopia shall be re-established and conducted through a British Minister Plenipotentiary accredited to His Majesty the Emperor and an Ethiopian Minister Plenipotentiary accredited to His Majesty the King, who shall be appointed as soon as possible after the entry into force of this Agreement. His Majesty the Emperor agrees that the Diplomatic Representative of His Majesty The King shall take precedence over any other foreign Representative accredited to His Imperial Majesty.

ARTICLE II.

(a) His Majesty the Emperor having requested the Government of the United Kingdom to assist him in obtaining the services of British subjects (i) as advisers to himself and his administration; (ii) as Commissioner of Police, Police officers and inspectors; and (iii) as judges and magistrates, the Government of the United Kingdom will use their best endeavours to assist His Majesty the Emperor in this matter. The number of such British subjects, their salaries, privileges, duties and powers, and the appointments they are to fill, shall be the subject of separate agreements between the Contracting Parties.

(b) His Majesty the Emperor agrees not to appoint advisers additional to those referred to in paragraph (a) above except after consultation with the Government of the United Kingdom.

ARTICLE III.

Subject to the provisions of the Military Convention concluded this day, and of Article VII of this Agreement, the jurisdiction and administration exercised by British military tribunals and authorities shall terminate as soon as they can be replaced by effective Ethiopian civilian administration and jurisdiction, which His Majesty the Emperor will set up as soon as possible. Nevertheless, British military tribunals shall finish any cases then pending before them. The Ethiopian authorities will recognise and, where necessary, enforce decisions previously given by British military tribunals.

ARTICLE IV.

(a) His Majesty the Emperor, having intimated to the Government of the United Kingdom that he will require financial aid in order to re-establish his administration, the Government of the United Kingdom will grant to His Majesty the sum of Pounds Sterling one million five hundred thousand during the first year and Pounds Sterling one million during the second year of the currency of this Agreement. If this Agreement remains in force for a third year, the Government of the United Kingdom agree to pay to His Majesty the Emperor the sum of Pounds Sterling five hundred thousand in respect of such third year, and if for a fourth year, then the sum of Pounds Sterling two hundred and fifty thousand shall be paid in respect of that year. Payments will be made in quarterly instalments in advance.

(b) His Majesty the Emperor agrees for his part that this grant shall absolve the Government of the United Kingdom from any payments in respect of the use of immovable property of the Ethiopian State which may be required by the British forces in Ethiopia during the war.

(c) His Majesty the Emperor agrees that there shall be the closest co-operation between the Ethiopian authorities and his British Advisers, to be appointed in accordance with Article II (a), regarding public expenditure.

(d) In order to facilitate the absorption into Ethiopian economy of the funds to be provided under paragraph (a) above, and to promote the early resumption of trade between Ethiopia and the surrounding territories, His Majesty the Emperor agrees that in all matters relating to currency in Ethiopia the Government of the United Kingdom shall be consulted and that arrangements concerning it shall be made only with the concurrence of that Government.

ARTICLE V.

(a) Jurisdiction over foreigners shall be exercised by the Ethiopian Courts constituted according to the draft Statute attached hereto as an Annex, which His Majesty the Emperor will promulgate forthwith and will maintain in force during the continuance of this Agreement, except in so far as it may require amendment in any manner agreed upon by the parties to this Agreement.

(b) Any foreigner who is a party to any proceedings, civil or criminal, within the jurisdiction of a Regional, Communal or Provincial court, may elect to have the case transferred without additional fee or charge to the High Court for trial. Provisions to this effect shall be included in the Rules of Court.

(c) In the hearing by the High Court of any matter to which a foreigner is a party at least one of the British Judges mentioned in Article II (a) shall sit as a member of the Court.

(d) His Majesty the Emperor agrees to direct that foreigners shall be incarcerated only in prisons approved for the purpose by the Commissioner of Police appointed in accordance with Article II (a).

ARTICLE VI.

(a) His Majesty the Emperor agrees to enact laws against trading with the enemy in terms proposed to him by the Government of the United Kingdom.

(b) His Majesty the Emperor accepts full responsibility for seeing that private enemy property is dealt with in accordance with international law. His Majesty agrees to consult with the British Diplomatic Representative as to the measures to be taken to this end.

ARTICLE VII.

His Majesty the Emperor agrees —
(a) That all prisoners of war shall be handed over to the

custody of the British Military Authorities, who will evacuate them from Ethiopia as soon as possible, and

(b) That he will enact such legislation as may be required to enable the General Officer Commanding-in-Chief the British forces in East Africa and officers acting under his authority to exercise such temporary local powers as may be necessary for the administration, control and evacuation of Italian civilians in Ethiopia.

ARTICLE VIII.

The Government of the United Kingdom will use their best endeavours —

(a) To secure the return of Ethiopians in Italian hands, and

(b) To secure the return of artistic works, religious property and the like removed to Italy and belonging to His Majesty the Emperor, the Ethiopian State, or local or religious bodies.

ARTICLE IX.

In areas in which the General Officer Commanding-in-Chief the British forces in East Africa may find it necessary to conduct military operations against the common enemy in future, His Majesty the Emperor will, at the request of the said General Officer Commanding-in-Chief, declare a state of emergency and will confer on the General Officer Commanding-in-Chief the powers resulting from such declaration. Any legislation necessary to secure these powers will be promulgated by His Majesty the Emperor. The Ethiopian Government and local authorities will give such aid and concurrence to the General Officer Commanding-in-Chief as may be needed.

ARTICLE X.

His Majesty the Emperor agrees not to conduct any external military operation which, in the opinion of the General Officer Commanding-in-Chief the British forces in East Africa is contrary to the joint interests of Ethiopia and the United Kingdom.

ARTICLE XI.

(a) His Majesty the Emperor will accord freedom of passage to, in and over Ethiopia to duly registered British civil aircraft, provided that such regulations governing air navigation as may be in force in Ethiopia are observed.

(b) His Majesty the Emperor will permit a British Air Transport organization or organizations, to be designated by the Government of the United Kingdom, to operate regular Air Services to, in and over Ethiopia for the carriage of passengers, mails and freight. For this purpose the said organisations shall be permitted to use such aerodromes, ground equipment and facilities as are available, and to provide such other aerodromes, ground equipment and facilities as may be necessary.

(c) His Majesty the Emperor will not permit foreign aircraft other than British to fly to, in or over Ethiopia without the concurrence of the Government of the United Kingdom.

ARTICLE XII.

The present Agreement shall enter in force as from this day's date. It shall remain in force until replaced by a Treaty for which His Majesty the Emperor may wish to make proposals. If it is not so replaced within two years from this date, it may thereafter be terminated at any time by either Party giving three months' notice to the other to this effect.

In witness whereof the undersigned have signed the present Agreement and affixed thereto their seals.

Done this thirty-first day of January 1942 in the English and Amharic languages, both of which shall be equally authoritative except in case of doubt, when the English text shall pevail.''

(L.S.) Haile Sellasie I. (L.S.) P.E. Mitchell

APPENDIX III

APPENDIX III

NOTES ON THE MILITARY GOVERNMENT OF OCCUPIED ENEMY TERRITORY — ERITREA AND SOMALILAND

SCOPE OF THE NOTES

1. These notes are intended for the guidance of officers of H.M. Forces belonging to an army occupying or about to occupy enemy territory. It should be clearly understood that the notes deal with conditions arising from a true occupation of enemy territory. In the course of a war, situations arise in which British forces are fighting or are stationed in non-British territories belonging to allied, or even neutral, powers. In these countries the part to be played by the British forces in the government of the country occupied, and the relations which are established between the British Army and the local government and population, will be peculiar, and may be prescribed by treaties and agreements or laid down **ad hoc** by H.M.G. or the army commander. Whether the task of administering the occupied country falls to the British commander on the spot will depend on the circumstances of the case, and, if it does, some of the material contained in these notes will provide useful guidance.

Military Government Defined

2. The administration of occupied enemy territory is technically called "military government", and is defined as "the government by military authority exercised by the C.-in-C. in the place of, or supplementary to, the civil government in occupied enemy territory." (See F.S.R., Vol. I, p. xvii).

Territory Occupied May be Metropolitan or Colonial

3. The territory occupied by an invading army may be a metropolitan country of the hostile State or a portion of its colonial empire. Though the general principles of international

law apply with equal force in both cases, the practical application of them must, from the nature of the case, vary considerably.

These notes are largely based on experience gained during the present war in the Middle East and East Africa Commands; the enemy territories occupied by the forces in these Commands up to date have been enemy colonies, as distinct from metropolitan territories, and in consequence the notes have particular reference to colonial conditions (especially in matters of detail) and should be read with this fact in mind.

Colonial Territory

4. In any enemy colonial dependency, the fundamental factor is that the enemy rule has at some time been imposed upon an indigenous alien populace and has probably been maintained by force in one form or another. When this element of force is overthrown, it is not possible to forecast the reactions of the local population which will normally comprise two main elements. Among the conquered population there will probably be a European community largely comprising the subjects of the enemy State, which, though small in numbers, may be influential and highly organised. Many will be State officials well trusted by their own government, and others will be trades, shopkeepers, technicians and colonists who are dependent on the territory for their livelihood. On the other hand, there will probably be a large native population of whom only a small portion are literate or politically minded, the majority being poor agriculturists or herdsmen of little education and limited outlook. The native population may harbour an intense hatred of their former European overlords, or equally well may have for them a strong loyalty and respect. In any event the local population may be hostile to the invading nation. In such circumstances the imposition of a military government by the invading army presents very grave difficulties, and relatively heavy demands on the personnel resources of the occupying army for administrative purposes may well result. To impose a military government in colonial territory it will probably be necessary for the occupying power to undertake the direct administration of the country with little assistance from the

government machine of the former administration or from the chiefs and notables of the indigenous population.

Metropolitan Territory

5. In metropolitan territory, the invading army will probably be faced by a uniformly hostile population, though the degree of active hostility may be reduced by the mental effect of a crushing military defeat. The machinery of government of the hostile State will largely remain intact, and beyond the maintenance of a substantial garrison and the establishment of Military Courts, it will probably only be necessary to superimpose a military government by the placing of a number of British officers in charge of each of the departments of State to ensure that they carry out their administrative duties satisfactorily and without danger to the safety of the occupying army.

Legal Sources

6. The rights and responsibilities of an army of occupation in enemy territory derived from the Laws and Usages of War contained in Section III of the Annex to the Hague Convention, 1907 (pages 382 to 385 of the Manual of Military Law). The terms of this Convention are explained and discussed in Sections VIII and IX of Chapter XIV of the Manual of Military Law (Amendment No. 12 issued in January, 1936).

Legal Position Summarised

7. The legal position arising from the Laws and Usages of War may briefly be summarised as follows:—

   (i) Occupation of enemy territory is not annexation. The sovereignty of the enemy is only temporarily latent and does not pass to the occupier. The occupier must not treat the occupied territory as part of his own territory or one of his dependencies, nor may he consider the inhabitants as his subjects.

   (ii) Since the occupier's rights are transitory he may only exercise such power in the occupied territory as is necessary for: —
       (a) The purposes of war;
       (b) The safety of the occupying army;

      (c) The maintenance of peace and good order;
      (d) The government of the occupied territory on a care and maintenance basis.

(iii) Subject to the exigencies of war, the occupier may not alter the existing form of government, upset the constitution, destroy the domestic laws of the inhabitants or ignore their legal rights.

(iv) In general, the pre-occupation laws of the occupied country remain in force, but it is competent to the occupying power to suspend, amend or supplement them for the following purposes: —

      (a) To ensure the safety and well being of its troops;
      (b) To maintain peace and good order;
      (c) To alleviate the lot of the civil inhabitants, and generally to adjust the administration to the peculiar circumstances of a hostile occupation.

Application to Civilised Nations Only

8. The "laws and usages" apply only to warfare between civilised nations, where both parties understand them and are prepared to carry them out. They do not apply in wars with uncivilised states and tribes, where their place is taken by the discretion of the commander, and "such rules of justice and humanity as recommend themselves in the particular circumstances of the case." While there can be no question of flouting rules to which H.M.G. have formally subscribed, the interpretation of these must often be left to the officers on the spot, who alone can decide how far the vital security or advantage of the forces is concerned; but it is desirable, wherever possible, that officers who consider it necessary to over-ride a provision of international law to gain an immediate advantage, should first seek authority of a superior officer.

SECTION II

THE NATURE OF MILITARY OCCUPATION

Relationship Between Occupant and Population

9. The occupation of enemy territory initiates a special relationship between the occupant and the population, involving on each side certain rights and duties. Such occupation is at once distinguishable from mere invansion, or from the temporary presence of reconnoitring or raiding parties; it must be actual and effective, and although it is usual and desirable for the victorious commander to make known by Proclamation the fact that occupation is established, this, in itself, does not constitute "occupation". Two conditions should be satisfied: firstly, that the legitimate government should be rendered incapable of exercising its authority, and secondly that the invader should be in a position to substitute his own. But this does not imply that the army has no control over the inhabitants in the zone of operations until the setting up of a military government is proclaimed, for the authority which any commander may exercise depends solely, in the last resort, upon the strength of the military force he has under his control.

International Restriction on Powers of Occupant

10. The commander of the occupying army derives all his power for the military government of the occupied territory from the fact of military conquest. The military government depends for its force and validity upon the will of the commander. Nevertheless, the comment by the Duke of Wellington that "in an occupied country the sole law is the will of the commander", is no longer strictly true, since most civilised nations have subscribed to the Hague Convention, which restricts in certain ways the unlimited powers which the military commander of an occupying power might otherwise wield.

Power of Commander Absolute

11. The power of the commander is absolute, and if in exercising his military government he trangresses the rules of

international law, the inhabitants of the territory are not relieved of their liability to comply with the commander's orders. The commander himself is, of course, answerable for all his acts to his own Government, who will normally expect him to observe the rules of international law to which that Government has adhered and if his conduct does not meet with their approval in this or any other respect, he may be removed from his office or have other disciplinary action taken against him. But so long as he remains in office, his power in the occupied territory is unlimited and the only remedy which lies open to those who deem themselves aggrieved by the commander's acts is the formulation of claims for monetary compensation which they, or their Government on their behalf, can lodge against the occupying power at the peace conference upon the conclusion of hostilities. Since the Government of the occupying power may be mulcted in damages after the war in this manner, it is in their interest that the commander of the occupying army shall generally conform to the principles of international law in carrying out his military government in the conquered territory.

Termination of Occupation

12. An occupation may be terminated by the withdrawal of the occupying forces (as in Cyrenaica in 1941 and 1942), or by the setting up of a local government empowered and competent to take over the administration (as in Iraq in 1920-1921), or by the act of handing over control to a third party, such as a former ruler of the territory (as in Ethiopia in 1942). Failing these or similar changes, the normal termination of an occupation is brought about by dispositions made the Treaty at the conclusion of the war, when the territory is assigned to some permanent Government.

SECTION III

AIMS OF MILITARY GOVERNMENT

Aims of Military Government

13. In general, the military government of an occupied enemy territory will endeavor to ensure:—

(i)   the security of the occupying forces;

(ii)   the preservation of peace and good order;

(iii) the exploitation of the economic resources of occupied territory;

(iv) the release of fighting troops for active operations;

(v)   good government in accordance with the rules of international law.

INDEX